T0329961

Technology and Innovation in the
International Economy

Technology and Innovation in the International Economy

Edited by

Charles Cooper

Director, United Nations University
Institute for New Technologies
Maastricht, The Netherlands

Edward Elgar
United Nations University Press

Published jointly by
Edward Elgar Publishing Limited
8 Lansdown Place
Cheltenham
Glos GL50 2HU
UK

Edward Elgar Publishing Company
Old Post Road
Brookfield
Vermont 05036
US

United Nations University Press
5-53-70 Jingumae
Shibuya-ku, Tokyo 150
Japan

Reprinted 1996

British Library Cataloguing in Publication Data
Technology and Innovation in the
International Economy
    I. Cooper, Charles
    338.91

Library of Congress Cataloguing in Publication Data
Technology and innovation in the international economy / edited by
    Charles Cooper.
            p.   cm.
        Includes bibliographical references.
        1. Technological innovations—Developing countries.
    2. Technological innovations—Economic aspects—Developing
    countries.   3. Technological innovations—Social aspects—Developing
    countries.   I. Cooper, Charles, 1936–
    T173.8. T4236   1994   93–39685
    338.9'27—dc20   CIP

ISBN 978 1 85898 027 0

Printed and bound by CPI Group (UK) Ltd, Croydon, CR0 4YY

Contents

Contributors

Charles Cooper is Director of the United Nations University Institute for New Technologies, The Netherlands.

Martin Fransman is Director of the Institute for Japanese–European Technology Studies at the University of Edinburgh, United Kingdom.

Jeffrey James is Professor of Development Economics at Tilburg University, The Netherlands.

Foreword

This book deals with some important aspects of the impacts of new technologies on economic and social development, especially in the Third World. It presents materials which played a significant part in the early evolution of a new policy research institute set up in the Netherlands by the United Nations University, and which have subsequently been revised and brought up to date.

The United Nations University Institute for New Technologies (UNU/INTECH) was established by the Council of UNU in October 1990 as a Research and Training centre devoted to the economic and social implications of new technologies. The Institute is funded through income from an endowment fund generously contributed by The Netherlands Ministries of Education and Science and of Development Co-operation, and by the Government of the Province of Limburg. The Institute is housed in an excellent building provided by the City of Maastricht. It has a small resident research faculty mainly from developing countries engaged in research projects which typically involve networks of Third World Institutes and individual scholars.

Since the 1960s, technological advances in microelectronics, biotechnology and other disciplines have had far-reaching impacts on a broad range of production and service sectors, and innovations have transformed many sectors of the global economy. For developing countries, these new technologies present both a threat and an opportunity. On the one hand, their adoption in industrialized economies can reduce or eliminate the already slim competitive advantage enjoyed by developing countries, which is based mainly on low-wage production. On the other hand, adoption of new technologies can offer the less-developed countries (LDCs) opportunities for rapid and flexible production, which can be the basis for expanding exports and growth of higher productivity high-waged, skilled employment opportunities. This latter pattern is exemplified well by the experience of some of the newly industrialized countries (NICs) in the 1980s.

The UNU/INTECH research will attempt to confront this duality. It will seek a better understanding of (1) the implications of new technologies for development strategy and industrialization policy; (2) the factors that influence diffusion of new technologies to developing countries; and (3) the impacts of new technologies on socioeconomic variables, such as output, trade, employment and distribution of welfare. Improved knowledge in these areas will provide the information that the LDCs need to develop sustainable economies, generate industrial capacity, improve their global competitiveness, and, ultimately, reduce poverty and improve people's welfare.

To address these issues, UNU/INTECH's programme comprises three principal components: (1) research; (2) advanced academic training; and (3) information dissemination. During its first biennium, the Institute's activities have centred around two main goals: development of its research and training programmes, and establishment of an institutional infrastructure in which those programmes could be carried through.

The focus of the UNU/INTECH research programme was worked out in the course of a feasibility study. It includes: work on the economics of technological change, innovation and diffusion, particularly in industry in the developing countries; studies on the politics of technology policy; and studies on how technological change influences the division of labour in society and in productive activities — especially related to womens employment.

The chapters of this book originate from work started in the feasibility study period, which has subsequently been updated and considerably developed. The first chapter, by Charles Cooper, deals with recent developments in the economics of innovation and diffusion of new technologies, and attempts to build a bridge between the study of Technology in the industrial sectors of developed countries — and the type of technology policy needed in the developing countries. Chapters 2 and 3 deal with particular fields of new technology. Chapter 2, by Martin Fransman, examines biotechnology; Chapter 3, by Jeffrey James, looks at microelectronic technology. Both are reviews of the literature on the diffusion and economic impacts of these technologies in the international economy.

Charles Cooper
Director, UNU/INTECH
Maastricht,
The Netherlands

1. Relevance of Innovation Studies to Developing Countries

Charles Cooper

1.1 INTRODUCTION

Studies of industrial innovations in industrialized countries, and similar studies in developing countries, tend to be done in isolation from one another. The isolation is not total, of course: there is a small number of authors for whom the relevance of studies of innovation in industrialized countries to the situation in developing countries is virtually taken for granted - see for example Katz (1987) or Pack and Westphal (1986). Nevertheless, the isolation is sufficiently noticeable in academic writing, to raise the question whether researchers concerned with technology policies in developing countries might not benefit from a more systematic exploration of what have been called 'innovation studies' (Dosi, 1988). The purpose of this chapter is to map out the territory of 'innovation studies' that could be useful in research on developing countries. This chapter attempts to relate studies on innovation and technological change in developed countries and those in developing countries. It also attempts to connect technology studies to the broader stream of development economics.

By their nature, maps are imperfect reflections of the scale and detail of underlying reality. That, as Joan Robinson once pointed out, is their whole point.[1] It is, nevertheless, quite possible to criticise some maps for being on a scale too small to be as useful as they might be or to be arbitrary in the detail they select. Perhaps the map drawn in this article is vulnerable to those criticisms, for it is the outcome of a preliminary reconnaissance, and not a comprehensive survey. If that

1

is so, we must hope that it at least reveals those parts of the terrain worthy of further exploration.

There have of course been good surveys of the issues of technology policy as they relate to developing countries. A particularly valuable, and quite recent, one by Martin Fransman (1986) covers part of the area of this chapter, but not all.

This chapter is set out as follows. The next section is a summary and discussion of recent literature on innovation in industrialized countries, which focuses on attempts to synthesize 'innovation studies' into a coherent theory. The theoretical structures that emerge from this effort go well beyond the explanation of industrial innovation phenomena *per se*: they raise rather fundamental questions about traditional theories of the firm and its behaviour. The emphasis is on innovation as a mode of competition, and as a source of sustained disequilibrium in the Schumpeterian style, an approach which is in contrast to the equilibrium stories which are at the foundation of received theory.

The subsequent section then deals with the possible relevance of this body of theory for developing countries. It addresses two questions. The first is how relevant are innovation studies to processes of technological learning in developing countries.[2] The second is how important is technological change in the trading relations of developing countries. The final section draws conclusions.

1.2 INNOVATION AND TECHNOLOGICAL CHANGE

The microeconomic processes involved in the adoption of innovations, which we are inclined to describe today as Schumpeterian, were, it seems, clearly recognized by Classical economists. In his chapter 'On Machinery' in the *Principles of Political Economy*, Ricardo (1830; edition 1971) remarks:

> He ... who made the discovery of the machine, or who first usefully applied it, would enjoy an additional advantage, by making great profits for a time.
>
> (Chapter XXXI, pp. 378-379)

Marx expanded considerably on this notion in Book One of *Capital* (Marx, 1858; edition 1961, p. 312) in the theoretical discussion of the origins of 'relative surplus value'. If an individual capitalist ('some *one* capitalist', ibid., p. 316), doubles the productivity of labour, whilst the value of the means of production remains the same, then

> The individual value (of the articles produced) ... is ... below their social value: in other words, they have cost less labour time than the great bulk of the same article produced under the average social conditions.
>
> (ibid., p. 317)

However,

> The real value of a commodity is ... not its individual value, but its social value; that is to say the real value is not measured by the labour time that the article in each individual case cost the producer, but by the labour time socially required for its production. ... If therefore the capitalist who applies the new method sells his commodity at its social value ... he sells it ... above its individual value (i.e., cost) ... and thus realises an extra surplus value.

In both of these accounts, adoption of the innovation which leads to the generation of extra profit or surplus value is implicitly assumed to happen against the background of some initial equilibrium position. The subsequent story (that is, after a period of extra surplus value) essentially concerns a return to this equilibrium situation. Thus in his discussion of the adoption of a new type of machine, Ricardo concludes:

> But, in proportion as the machine ... comes ... into general use, the price of the commodity produced, would, from the effects of competition, sink to its costs of production, when the capitalist would get the same money profits as before, and he would only participate in the general advantage as a consumer.
>
> (Ricardo, op. cit. p., 379)

Similarly, Marx observes:

> On the other hand, ... this extra surplus value vanishes, so soon as the new method of production has become general, and has consequently caused the difference between the individual value of the cheapened commodity and its social value to vanish. ... The law of the determination of value by labour-time,

a law which brings under its sway the individual capitalist who applies the new method of production ... this same law acting as a coercive law of competition, forces his competitors to adopt the new method. The general rate of surplus value, is therefore ultimately affected by the whole process, only when the increase in the productiveness of labour has seized upon those branches of production, that are connected with ... the necessary means of subsistence.

In short, technological change results in a *general increase* in surplus value, which for the present we may identify with profits, only when it increases productivity in the production of wage goods (or in the production of the means of production). The basis for this conclusion is that innovations in general ultimately leave the 'rate of surplus value' unaffected due to the reassertion of equilibrium; but innovations in the wage goods sector reduce the costs of labour time in all other sectors.

In its early form, Schumpeter's own analysis of innovation as a microeconomic process, especially in its early form, owes much to Marx (Schumpeter, 1912; edition 1961, Chapter IV on 'Entrepreneurial Profit'). In particular, in his early writing, which was much concerned to explain (even to justify) the additional profit generated for the innovating firm as a return to entrepreneurship, he placed considerable emphasis on the tendency of the industry to return to equilibrium. 'The second act of the drama' of innovation (op. cit., p. 131) comes when imitators enter production, thus driving prices down and leading to a 'complete reorganisation of the industry'. Consequently, after an innovation, 'that process of reorganisation occurs which must result in the annihilation of the surplus over costs' (p. 133). The idea that *reorganization* takes place in the reestablishment of an equilibrium might suggest that Schumpeter had in mind a more considerable process of adjustment than that described by Ricardo or Marx; but the return to equilibrium is still the keynote.

Subsequently, however, Schumpeter's thinking moved towards the notion of *continual* change as a result of a succession of innovations, leading to 'continual reorganisation of the economic system' (op. cit., p. 156), in which the reestablishment of equilibrium is preempted by further rounds of innovation. In his 1934 Preface to the English Edition of *Theorie der wirtschaftlichen Entwicklung,* he remarks:

The conclusion suggested itself that this body of theory might usefully be contrasted with the theory of equilibrium which explicitly or implicitly always has been and still is the centre of traditional theory.

(op. cit. p. xi)

Later in *Capitalism, Socialism and Democracy,* he wrote

the capitalist economy ... is incessantly being revolutionised from within ... existing structures and all the conditions of doing business are always in the process of change. ... *Every situation is being upset before it has time to work itself out.*

(Schumpeter, 1966; our italics)

It seems fair, then, to distinguish two distinct but closely related respects in which Schumpeter takes issue with the conventional Marshallian microeconomic theory of the firm. First there is a fundamentally different view of the nature of competition. In Marshall, the technology of production is given and available to all firms; the technology defines the parameters within which firms' minimum cost levels of production are to be determined by adjustment to competition. For Schumpeter, competitive behaviour, led by innovators, is primarily concerned with changing the parameters themselves: that is, with a search for new technologies, which, temporarily, are available to the innovative firm alone and confer the advantages of monopolistic rents. It is also concerned with the imitative process which then ensues. The search for the optimum level of output and minimum cost of production is largely overshadowed by the process of competition between technologies.

The second major difference between Schumpeterian and traditional views of the firm resides in Schumpeter's view that competition based on the search for new technologies generates a stream of innovations which preempt the attainment of microeconomic equilibrium altogether.

Christopher Freeman puts these points in the following terms:

In Schumpeter's framework it is disequilibrium, dynamic competition ... between entrepreneurs, primarily in terms of industrial innovation, which forms the basis of economic development.

(Freeman, 1989, pp. 209-210)

Intuitively, the Schumpeterian model of competition gives a plausible interpretation of competition in a range of important sectors — especially, of course, science-based sectors such as electronic capital goods, chemicals, pharmaceuticals, biotechnology, and the like. This explanation may seem less convincing in what development economists often call the 'traditional' sectors. Nevertheless, as I will argue later, even here innovative competition occurs, mainly in the form of adoption of innovative plant and equipment originating in the capital goods sector.[3] Later we shall discuss intersectoral differences in the sources of innovation and relate these to the apparently differing incidence of innovative competition between industrial sectors.

As well as intersectoral differences, there have been historical differences (i.e., changes within sectors over time) in the incidence of innovative competition. It is interesting to speculate whether Schumpeterian modes of competition are perhaps more characteristic of the modern (i.e., twentieth-century) industrial economy than they were, say, during and after the Industrial Revolution. The emergence of Schumpeterian thinking may reflect — with a considerable time-lag, of course — historic changes in the nature of competition itself.[4] Perhaps Marshall has been overtaken by events rather than shown to have got it wrong.

Recent theoretical approaches to innovation have been based importantly on empirical observation of firms' behaviour[5] and have been informed by the Schumpeterian concept of how competition takes place in the industrial sector. In particular, they draw on Schumpeter's notion that, at the level of the firm, competition is about creating a stream of disequilibrium situations, in which there are quasi-monopolistic rents.[6] The idea that firms continually search out innovations in this way has been shown in a seminal study by Nelson and Winter (1982) to generate a plausible explanation of economic growth processes.

There has, of course, been considerable development of these basic notions. At the risk of doing an injustice to the conceptual richness of the discussion of innovation, we will select three especially important and related developments for more in-depth discussion:[7] (1) the idea that technological change is *localized*; (2) the notion that innovation at the level of the firm is the outcome of a *cumulative* process; and (3) the different incidence of factors determining the *appropriability* of new technologies. After discussing these three elements, which primarily concern conditions within innovative firms, we will go on to look at two characteristics of the environment within which the firms operate. These are the *technological* and *institutional* contexts.

The idea that technological change may be *localized* was put forward in a theoretical article by Atkinson and Stiglitz (1969), who contended that a localized 'bulge' in the neoclassical industrial production function may represent technological change better than simply a uniform shift of the whole frontier. The location of the bulge depends essentially on the point at which firms were producing initially — in short, upon their prior technological choices.[8] At the same time as Atkinson and Stiglitz, Nathan Rosenberg (1969) put forward an economic historian's empirically founded notion of localization. These ideas were subsequently used by David (1975), who proposed an explanation of localization based on 'learning' processes in production:

> Because technological 'learning' depends on the accumulation of actual production experience, short-sighted choices about what to produce and especially about how to produce it using presently known methods, also in effect govern what subsequently comes to be learned.[9]
>
> (David, 1975, p. 4)

It is helpful, at this stage, to keep in mind that learning *cum* localization phenomena take place at the level of the firm. It is quite possible, therefore, that individual firms within an industrial sector have different 'vectors' of technological change; that is to say, firms have different patterns of localization within the particular technological fields relevant to the industry's production activities. There are many cases in which different patterns of localization coexist. An example is the simultaneous emergence of the Apple Macintosh computer system and the IBM PC system; another is the coexistence of several different methods of 'catalytic cracking' in various major chemical firms during the 1970s. Sometimes one or more of the competing variants on the basic technology will prove to be a dead-end, but this does not always happen. Implications of these differences between firms in their vectors of technological change, especially implications for market structures, are discussed later.

Second, there is the question of *cumulativeness*. David's account of the origins of localized technological change leads naturally to the concept of cumulation in the innovation process. Innovation processes are cumulative in the sense that David sketches out: technologies of production used today influence learning processes and the nature of accumulated experience. These, in turn, influence the uses to which innovative inputs [like research and development (R&D) at the level of the firm] are put, and so also the nature of tomorrow's production technologies. And so on.

The simplest examples of cumulative innovative processes at the level of the firm are the processes of 'learning by doing' (Arrow, 1962), and the other more empirically founded and realistic variants of those processes described in the literature.[10] These processes have the characteristic that the productivity changes they generate depend upon accumulated experience of actual production. They are aptly described as irreversible, dynamic economies of scale.

The cumulative processes in question in theories of innovation may include learning by doing in its traditional form, but they also refer to other learning processes which may not be so simply related to the experience of production *per se*: technological learning,[11] for example, or learning about effective resource allocation for innovation. By straightforward extension of the discussion of 'localization', the process of cumulation of 'problem solving capabilities' (Dosi, 1988), is likely to take firm-specific forms. The theory of innovation as it has developed in the recent past thus endows individual firms with histories, and these histories are of more than antiquarian interest: a firm's history determines what it is good at technologically, and that in turn has a direct influence on the rate and direction of innovation it pursues, and on the differences in performance between it and other firms in the same industry. Learning process of various kinds and the pattern of intrafirm accumulation of technological capability connect the firm's past with its present. The contrast between this and the ahistorical 'firm' of neoclassical microeconomics whose whole existence is supposedly described adequately by a set of cost curves identical to those of all other firms in the industry, is rather stark.

The third characteristic of innovation is that the knowledge incorporated in new technologies can, to varying degrees, be *appropriated* by the innovating enterprise. Appropriation of technological knowledge is essential to the innovative process, since it is appropriation which allows a temporary preemption of imitation and hence monopolistic rents (also temporary). It is the anticipation of these rents which induces enterprises to innovate in the first place.[12] Appropriation is achieved in a number of ways. In some sectors (drugs, for example, or fine chemicals) patents are especially important; in others, secrecy is enough. The lead times which imitators face can be important, as may learning curve effects in the innovator firm. Appropriability may also depend upon the extent of tacit knowledge associated with the innovation (for a discussion of tacitness, see Dosi, 1988). As implied above, appropriability differs between sectors.

The rate and direction of technological innovation are explicable up to a point by localization and the cumulative nature of the innovative process or by opportunities for appropriation. But these intrafirm factors are, as we indicated earlier, only part of the story. A more complete explanation depends also on 'technological trajectories' (the constraints imposed by the logic of technological development itself) and on institutional factors (which are usually nation specific). The institutional side is receiving much attention at present. Its parameters are set out with particular clarity by Nelson (1988a,b).

Intersectoral differences in innovation, and the flows of knowledge related to innovations between sectors, are important, especially in relation to developing countries (see below). That sectors differ both in the frequency and extent of innovation and in sources of innovation has long been recognized.[13] Initially, the literature of the 1960s and 1970s distinguished 'traditional' and supposedly non-innovative sectors from more 'science-based', innovative ones. More recently, ways of grouping industrial sectors in relation to the nature and sources of innovative activity have consciously or otherwise returned to a pattern very similar to that implicit in Marx's historical account of relations between 'science' and production (Marx, 1858, Book I, Chapters 13 to 15). Marx essentially differentiates the capital goods (machine-making) sectors as primary points of contact between science and production.[14] In the same spirit, Robson et al. (1988) distinguished 'user sectors' and 'producer sectors', whereby the latter are chiefly science-based sectors and the more traditional capital goods sectors. Pavitt (1984) and later Dosi et al. (1990; pp. 92-98) distinguished between three types of sectors: (1) supplier-dominated sectors, which in the main receive innovations embodied in producer goods and are essentially innovation-user sectors (they include traditional sectors of manufacturing); (2) production and scale-intensive sectors (largely machinery-making sectors, consumer durables, automobiles, steel, etc.), which are predominantly innovation producers; and (3) the science-based sectors, which are producers and a source of innovation for many other sectors (these include electrical and electronic sectors and chemicals). These sectoral distinctions will be useful in later discussion on developing countries.

Before discussing the relevance of these theoretical approaches to developing countries, we shall discuss two important implications: first, for market structure; and second, for international trade and competitiveness.

Innovation is seen as based on the cumulation of *firm-specific* technological skills, leading to *localized* technological changes. It is therefore preeminently a differentiating process, in which firms attempt to establish control over markets by developing new products and new processes. This, of course, is in contradiction to the conditions of 'perfect competition' and to firm behaviours, which are conventionally presumed to follow from those conditions. It suggests market structures closer at first glance to those of the Robinsonian model of imperfect competition.[15] There are, however, important differences. First, the Robinsonian model is commonly associated mainly with the explanation of trivial product differentiation, whereas the product differentiation associated with innovative activities is generally nontrivial and essentially depends for success on real technical advances. Second, imperfect competition models, Robinsonian or otherwise, are usually concerned with underlying trends to equilibrium — albeit equilibria different from those of perfect competition. Innovative competition, in Schumpeter's vision, is a process in which there is a continuing search for and attainment of new disequilibria in markets, from which rents flow.

Given this distinction, it would seem that innovation theory as it has evolved recently can be more convincingly related to concepts of market structure and competition which do not rely on tendencies to equilibrium. One obvious example is Kalecki's concept of the 'degree of monopoly' (Kalecki, 1971, Chapter 5, 'Costs and Prices', based on an earlier essay published in 1943). Alternatively, Sylos-Labini's analysis of oligopolistic market structures as a meta-stable configuration of competing firms might also provide a more convincing framework for describing and predicting innovative competition (Sylos-Labini, 1967).[16] A strength of the innovation theories discussed here is that they provide an explanation of market imperfection which derives from the competitive process itself — market imperfection is, as it were, explained by an endogenous process (Nelson and Winter, 1982).

The implications of these Schumpeterian approaches to innovation for *international trade* have been explored by Dosi et al. (1990). The theme, which is in direct confrontation with conventional trade theory, is sketched in their introduction (Dosi et al., 1990, p. 11):

> In so far as technology gaps and their changes are a fundamental force in shaping international competitiveness, their impact on domestic income, by inducing and/or allowing relatively high rates of growth via the foreign trade multiplier, will be significant. ... It is the relationship between technology, trade and growth which is at the centre of the analysis, rather than the question about the short-term gains from trade stemming from the open economy allocation of resources, so crucial in the conventional view.

Later (ibid., Chapter 6), Dosi et al. present a detailed econometric study of the member countries of the Organization for Economic Cooperation and Development (OECD). The study covers forty industrial subsectors and addresses the relationship between competitiveness (measured by each country's exports in each of the forty product groups as a proportion of total OECD exports in that industry) and an index of technological innovation (each country's U.S.-registered patents in each of the industry groups as a share of total OECD U.S.-registered patents in that industry group). The regression equations suggest that the technology variable is strongly associated with competitiveness in most of the science-based sectors, but the association is not significant in the so-called traditional sectors. These results support the idea that absolute trade advantages may be built upon superiority in innovation.

From the point of view of the discussion which follows, these results need to be handled with some care. In particular they must *not* be taken to show that innovation and the increases in factor productivities to which it gives rise are unimportant in determining competitiveness in the traditional sectors. In these sectors innovation does not show up in patenting, precisely because they are 'supplier dominated' sectors as far as innovation goes: they receive their innovation from suppliers of producer goods who do the R&D and hold the patents on the equipment used. Nevertheless, competitive position in these sectors depends importantly on the application of innovations developed in the supplier sectors. The traditional sectors may well be innovative despite the lack of patenting, but innovative in the sense of using new technology rather than producing it — a process which also requires a mastery of technology. This has special importance at the present time in view of the increasing *application* of innovations in microelectronics in such sectors.

1.3 IMPLICATIONS FOR DEVELOPING COUNTRIES

In principle the theoretical framework which has been developed from empirical studies of innovation and of the behaviour of innovative firms could provide useful guidelines for policy studies in developing countries from at least two points of view.

First, innovation theory contains insights into how and why technical capabilities are developed in the industrial sectors of advanced countries. In effect, they give some new dimensions of meaning to the concept of 'accumulation of local technological capabilities', which has come to play an important role in technology policy in developing countries. Second, innovation studies have much to tell us about the structure of international industrial markets. This kind of information is important in defining strategies for industrial export development.

This section in therefore presented in two parts: the first examines innovation studies and the accumulation of technological capabilities; the second focuses on trade and technological change.

1.3.1 Innovation Studies and the Accumulation of Technological Capabilities

An obvious problem in trying to relate innovation studies in industrialized countries to technology policy issues in developing countries is that comparatively little technological innovation is taking place in developing countries, especially if *innovation* is defined strictly as the first commercial introduction of a product or process in the international economy.

It is, however, a rather limited view of innovation theories that they are, or should only be, concerned with the *initial* introduction of products or processes. Clearly, the imitative phase is important too in any industry where innovation appears. There are two reasons for this. First, the behaviour of innovative firms is importantly influenced by expectations about the likely speed of imitation: innovators might seek to preempt imitation by strengthening their appropriation of the new technology. Thus, a convincing theory of the innovative firm, and particularly one which purports to explain intersectoral differences in innovative behaviour, must grasp the objective conditions determining imitation. Second, a theory of innovation must surely reach beyond explanations of the behaviour of individual firms, to consider the implications of innovation for industrial sectors, especially for market structures. Here too, the story will be incomplete without a reasoned consideration of imitation and of other processes that might be involved in the diffusion of innovations. At the level of industrial sectors, a theory of innovation must include a theory of imitation[17] if it is to be complete, though the relative scarcity of empirical work on imitation might lead one to believe otherwise.

It is probably sensible to assume that the skills commonly associated with innovative capability are to a large degree relevant as well to imitative activity — or, perhaps more precisely, that the skills needed for imitation are essentially a subset of those needed for innovation. To see this, recall the discussion of the main characteristics of innovative firms. The studies we have reviewed emphasize the localized, and cumulative, processes whereby firms build technological knowledge which ultimately becomes the source of new technologies. These capabilities, it is argued, are built around the methods of production in use [i.e., around 'previous choices of technique' as Paul David (1975) puts it]. But whilst this accumulation of partly explicit and partly tacit knowledge is argued to be a necessary condition for success in innovation, it does not follow that its existence in a firm is sufficient to ensure that the firm will innovate. More importantly, nor does it follow that firms pursue this accumulative (and costly) process solely for *innovative* success. For some firms at most times, and for all firms at some times, this capability may be as important for the purposes of effective imitation of technological leaders as for originating innovations.

As a corollary, it is possible that capabilities built through successful imitation become the base from which innovative capability finally emerges. It has been argued that there is a progression, in which skills initially applied to what might be termed 'sub-innovative' technological activities, like imitation or simply incremental improvement of productive efficiency, eventually become the foundation for true innovation. Such a progression is probably part of the historic experience of many firms.[18]

Chris Freeman (1989, pp. 169 ff.) helped to make this point in his analysis of firm strategies towards innovation. Freeman distinguished five types of strategy: offensive, defensive, imitative, dependent, and traditional.[19] The first two are concerned primarily with the early, if not always initial, introduction of new technologies and differ mainly in their timing tactics; imitative firms, in contrast, are 'content to follow way behind the leaders in established technologies' (p. 179). Imitative firms, Freeman argues, need compensating advantages to deal with this lag. These may vary from control over a captive market to decisive cost advantages. Firms following the 'dependent' strategy are mainly small sub-contracting enterprises, whose technology is usually determined (and often supplied) entirely by customer enterprises. Finally, the 'traditional' strategy is essentially non-innovative: firms do not change their products in technically significant ways because markets do not require them to do so.[20] The particularly interesting point here about Freeman's categories is his analysis of the technical functions (or types of technical skill) associated with each of them. He discusses a number of these technical functions, ranging from R&D functions, through design, quality control and technical services and on to patenting and scientific and technical information. These skills are expected to be needed to some degree in all strategies, though at different intensities (op. cit., Table 8.1, p. 171). It is not difficult to see how firms might progress from one strategy level to another through an historic learning process in which they strengthen particular learning functions. It is also clear that skills associated with imitation can reasonably be described as a subset of innovative skills.

The usefulness of these approaches to the understanding of circumstances in developing countries is suggested by three lines of analysis: (1) by extending Freeman's discussion of innovation strategies [and linking it to Pavitt's (1984) analysis of sectoral differences] and relating this conceptualization to the types of technology transfer used by enterprises in developing countries; (2) by considering how the account of localized, cumulative technology learning processes offered by 'innovation studies' relates to the knowledge we have of learning processes in firms in developing countries; and (3) by reexamining the concept of 'accumulation of technological capabilities', which has become so important in technology policy in developing countries, in the light of what we can learn from innovation studies.

First, then, we consider the question of innovation strategies used by firms in developing countries. An obvious point of departure is that for the most part even the most technologically advanced firms in developing countries are committed to be imitators in the Freeman sense. This is partly because of their limited technical resources, and partly because of their comparatively limited production experience. The terms under which imitation processes take place in developing countries are essentially mediated by the ways in which technology is 'transferred' from industrialized countries. Literature on developing countries customarily distinguishes two main 'mechanisms' of technology transfer: 'direct' transfers, which involve transactions with machine suppliers, engineering consultants, and other agents in industrial countries; and 'indirect' transfers, done by licensing agreements with innovative firms in industrialized countries that have successfully appropriated relevant segments of the production technology.[21] Indirect transfers may or may not involve foreign direct investments.

Whilst both groups of technology recipients are imitative, they are sharply differentiated in other ways. Recipients of direct transfers are 'supplier dominated' under Pavitt's categorization. They imitate earlier adopters in supplier-dominated industries in industrial countries. Recipients of indirect transfers on the other hand mainly operate in what Pavitt calls 'production-intensive or scale-intensive sectors', or even in science-intensive sectors, which are associated with relatively high R&D intensities in industrialized countries. Both of these latter types of sector in the industrialized countries themselves generate most of the technologies they use. In these sectors, therefore, new imitative entrants can generally access the technology they need only by contractual arrangement with the innovators.

This analysis suggests, interestingly, that there are *a priori* grounds to expect the imitative lag and associated competitive disadvantages faced by recipients of direct technology transfers to be less onerous than the circumstances facing recipients of indirect transfers. The reason is simple. Direct transfers centre mainly around the importation of innovative equipment from suppliers of capital goods, though they may require support from suppliers of other technological skills, such as engineering design and consultancy firms, or plant contractors. However, regardless of the complexity surrounding the process of transfer, none of the agents involved has a vested interest in delaying the imitative process. Suppliers of innovative machinery, in particular, are particularly interested in selling the machinery, regardless of the location of the customer. In partial contrast, indirect transfers involve supplying enterprises which agree to license the technology only when it is in their own strategic interests to do so. This often means, in effect, that they license only when a particular market is closed to other forms of exploitation, or when the firm's direct interest in exploiting that market directly is small. In particular, licensors will be concerned to avoid creating future competitors.[22] It follows that licensed technology transferred indirectly will, other things being equal, involve a greater imitative lag than technology transferred directly. This hypothesis is plausible, at least for policy research, and it may be particularly relevant to sectoral choices for export promotion in developing countries.

Following Freeman (1989), imitative firms in developing countries would be expected to have found other advantages to allow them to compensate for the competitive disadvantages arising from these imitative lags. Thus, if our hypotheses about the relative lags associated with indirect and direct transfers are correct, it must follow that, on average, the compensating advantages required are greater for firms receiving indirect transfers. The existence of these compensating advantages in import-substituting economies is all too obvious: they take the form of effectively captive markets. Extending this argument, whilst keeping in mind Marshall's warning on such matters,[23] a proportionately greater reliance on direct transfers would be expected in open economies with successful development of industrial exports — and this will have a significant effect on the sectoral pattern of exports.[24] These assertions await empirical research. They are researchable by relatively simple means and they have a significance for policy.

This discussion demonstrates that interesting points and suggestive hypotheses do emerge when we confront the established approaches to technology transfer in the Third World with the conceptualizations of innovation theory.

The second line of analysis is best formulated as a question: Are there similarities between the cumulative, localized learning processes described by innovation theory, and the learning processes which actually happen within enterprises in developing countries? As a first step, note that the types of imitative activity we associate with firms in developing countries — that is imitation in 'supplier-dominated' sectors and imitation via licence agreements in other sectors — are normally accompanied by cumulative learning processes *when they take place in industrialized countries themselves.* This is very clear in the case of licensee firms in industrialized countries. It is however, less clear in relation to supplier-dominated firms. On this question, Dosi et al. (1990) say that supplier-dominated firms (within industrialized countries)

> are generally small and their in-house R and D activities ... are weak. ... They appropriate less on the basis of a technological advantage than on the basis of professional skills, privileged access to a resource, ... trademarks and advertising.
>
> (op. cit., pp. 92-93)

At the same time, though, Dosi et al. stress the need for technological capability even in firms that obtain their new technology from outside equipment suppliers.

> The process of diffusion of an innovation (say a new machine) in a user sector is, in essence, a process of innovation for the user itself. ... An important consequence is that the process ... is also affected by the technological capabilities, ... and forms of production organisation of the users.
>
> (op. cit., p. 119)

Thus, in industrialized countries, even firms that acquire new technologies by buying machinery which embodies it need certain critical technological capabilities. The question we wish to address is whether such capabilities are also encountered in firms in developing countries.

The answer comes in two parts. The first part is a tentative 'yes'. Firm-level studies of learning processes in developing countries are unfortunately rather few. Honourable exceptions are the case materials referred to in Katz (1987), and related work such as (*inter alia*) Dahlmann (1978), Maxwell (1977), and Katz and Albin (1979). These, like the work of Lall referenced earlier (note (2) and see Lall, 1987), reported firm-level studies which confronted and substantially dismissed the negative predictions about learning and technological development advanced by theories of technological dependency. Subsequent studies on the newly industrialized countries (NICs), particularly South Korea,[25] have shown evidence of learning processes which could readily be described in terms similar to those used in 'innovation studies'. We are plainly dealing with very similar phenomena in developing countries *and* in industrialized countries as far as intrafirm learning processes are concerned.

The second part of the answer refers to the failure of learning to occur in certain cases (especially Dahlman and Westphal, 1982; Bell et al., 1982; and Dahlman et al., 1987). The authors referenced above all emphasized that learning is not 'automatic', as implied in the theoretical discussion by Arrow (1962). In fact, learning requires a conscious allocation of resources within the firm, and careful organization. In the absence of these, there may be no learning process at all. Furthermore, in the absence of appropriate external institutional conditions, learning processes may also fail to appear. An influential study on the failure of learning, based on case materials from Thailand, was done by Bell et al. (1982). Failure of learning processes in developing countries is in fact quite common. It is reflected in what is often called a 'black box' approach to production technology: firms in developing countries that receive technology via licence agreements are quite often unconcerned about how the technology works, provided only that they are able to produce with it. There are also reasons to expect that firms in developing countries may underinvest in learning processes (Cooper, 1980 amongst others). In short, whilst the cumulative learning processes associated with innovation and related activities in industrialized countries are reproduced in industries in developing countries, this is not automatic. Learning probably breaks down in developing countries more often than in industrialized countries. An interesting question is whether innovation studies can suggest ways in which this situation might be improved by policy.

The third line of analysis suggested above concerns the relationship between the processes described in the literature on innovation, and the 'accumulation of technological capability' as it is described in the development literature. Can innovation studies help to clarify the process of accumulation of technological capabilities? They probably can. One strength of innovation studies is that they are firmly based on clear ideas about *institutions*, whether these are the firms which do the innovation or the network of public and private agencies to which these firms relate. This perspective has often been lacking in the discussion of technological capabilities in developing countries, though the omission has been clearly recognized by some. For example, Bhalla remarks,

> In addition to macroeconomic policy instruments, both governmental and non-governmental institutions play a crucial role in the accumulation of technological capacity over time. ... Yet few institutional studies have been carried out.
> (Bhalla, 1991)

Enos (1991) in an important study, makes the following point (p. 2):

> There are three fundamental components of technological capability — the individual constituents, their organisation and their purpose. ... Technological capability resides in individuals ... operating singly in a technologically complex environment individuals can produce little. ... They need to be brought together within an institution ... which ... may be a capitalist firm, a family enterprise ... a state-owned company.

And then

> In identifying the sorts of institution within which technical skill reside the difficulty is not in enumeration but in making some sense of the list. ... Contributions to the absorption of technology can be expected from technical schools and professional faculties of universities, from producing firms, from their suppliers, customers and sub-contractors, from government departments, from consultants and laboratories, from specialised companies providing process and equipment design ... (etc).

One important contribution of the emphasis innovation studies place on both intrafirm skills and the institutional environment has been to distinguish the different roles these kinds of institution play in their relationships to industrial production and to 'make some sense of the list'. A valuable set of international comparative studies is given in Nelson (1993).

This brief consideration of institutional matters suggests another way that innovation studies may help us understand technology policy issues in developing countries. This involves analysis of *differences* in technological capabilities between firms. These are of two main types:

(1) differences in capabilities that are seen as *path dependent*, that is dependent on a firm's history, especially its technological history; and (2) differences in strategies employed to respond to technological competition, even in firms with similar technological histories.

These differences are likely to induce different firms to respond differently to policy interventions aimed in favour of technological change. To date, interfirm differences have not received much attention in empirical research or in policy design. However, they help to explain the emphasis on selective policies, such as selective infant industry protection, in some NICs.

1.3.2 Trade and Technology

This section discusses how the approach to trade issues associated with innovation studies relates to developing countries. It has three parts. The first deals with background. It recalls that development economics has always been concerned with relationships to the international economy as a central theme, and that many influential approaches to economic development have incorporated important assumptions about technological factors, albeit implicitly.

The second part argues that the shift from import-substituting industrialization to more open-economy models of development, has made innovation studies more relevant to industrialization policies in developing countries. The third part sets out a rough and ready typology of the technology policies which accompany industrialization in an open-economy context.

1.3.2.1 The background: technology factors in industrialization theories

Development economics is characterized by concern with changing the relationship of countries to the international economy. The transformations required have often been 'technological'. For example, learning curve arguments were implicit in List's espousal of the infant industry argument as a basis for protectionist policies (List, 1844). Preobrazhensky (1926) addressed this issue during the course of the Soviet Debate on Industrialization in the 1920s. In discussing the choice between importing the means of production or making them at home, he refers to the possibility of 'improving and cheapening our own products' (Preobrazhensky, 1926).

Similarly post-war writers on development frequently rationalized their underlying dissatisfaction with traditional trade patterns by appeal to 'technology' arguments. Rosenstein-Rodan's 'big push' (Rosenstein-Rodan, 1943) and the Nurkse formulation of 'balanced growth' (Nurkse, 1958, Chapter 1), were both in essence responses to problems of technological economies of scale. Prebisch (1950, *inter alia*) was less specifically concerned with infant industry arguments, but technological factors played a major role in his terms of trade analysis. Prebisch believed that the welfare gains from technological change in the world economy would mainly benefit the centre (i.e., the industrialized countries). Thus, increasing productivity in the oligopolistic industrial sectors at the centre would result mainly in increased profit margins and increased real wages in the centre's industries; whereas technological change in agriculture and primary production, where producers are inevitably price-takers, would benefit consumers and user industries mainly in the centre economies. Differential direct impacts of technological change also played a more direct role in the alleged tendency of the terms of trade to turn against the periphery, through product innovations (like the development of synthetic materials) which substituted for periphery exports.

The Prebisch inheritance passed to the Latin American *dependencia* school, which criticized Prebisch for failing to see that protected industrialization in the periphery would produce new patterns of technological dependency in the protected industries of Latin America. Technological dependency ensured that the biased distribution in gains from trade which had concerned Prebisch would simply be replaced by a biased distribution of gains from technological change, because of appropriation of technologies of production by industries in the centre. Furthermore, according to the technological dependency school, there were reasons to expect that these tendencies would be self-perpetuating (see for example, Cooper and Sercovich, 1971). There were different ways to account for this tendency. A purely descriptive approach, which had little to offer from the normative point of view, simply listed the different ways in which availability of centre technology would substitute for development of domestic technological capability. A more normative approach (surveyed in Cooper, 1980) focused on reasons why market forces and the institutional context in the periphery would likely result in sub-optimal investments in local technology. Both lines of argument were subsequently overshadowed by empirical research which showed the existence of considerable domestic technological capability in circumstances where *dependistas* had predicted that it would be absent (e.g., Katz,1987 and Lall,1984a).[26]

It is probably fair to say that the early post-war intellectual history of development economics was characterized by a series of swings from interventionist, 'delinking' ideas, to liberal open-economy proposals with occasional attempts at superordination and reconciliation of the need for growth and accumulation,[27] and the exigencies of short-run allocative efficiency. In these arguments, the technology factor came in repeatedly mainly on the side of intervention and infant industry. In fact, many of the arguments that appear today in the innovation studies literature have long been present in the writings of development economists.

1.3.2.2 The shift from import substitution to export promotion
Despite the repeated use of technological factors to justify various types of import-substitution policies, the approach to technology policy associated with import substitution was in many ways essentially defensive. The case of Indian technology policy in the 1960s and 1970s gives a reasonably representative picture of the way technology policy was approached under import-substituting, closed-economy conditions.[28] In particular it illustrates the relatively limited concern with technological change, which was common at the time.

From the late 1960s Indian technology policy-makers were increasingly seized with two main ideas: first, that innovative technologies licensed to Indian producers were often the source of monopolistic advantages to the licensors (a straightforward extension of the Schumpeterian innovative monopoly to international markets); and second, that ready availability of technology on licence would simply substitute for the development of technologies at home, and thus 'perpetuate technological dependence'. The response to the first issue was to set up a control system, which was largely bureaucratic, and involved the scrutiny of all proposals for technology licensing to see that the payments proposed under various headings (royalties, expatriated profit, input prices, and technical assistance) were within acceptable limits.

The second issue was less amenable to bureaucratic solutions. It was dealt with by requiring various Indian state industrial laboratories and other authorities to guarantee that no alternative Indian technology was available. Furthermore, there were checks to prevent 'repeated' technology imports, that is importation of the same or similar technologies by more than one Indian firm.

Whatever the conceptual background of Indian policy, it was unsatisfactory in important ways. There may have been some success in controlling various types of monopolistic pricing, but if so it came at the cost of long bureaucratic delays in processing technology agreements through the various Ministries. It is not clear whether the attempt to encourage the development of Indian technological capabilities worked at all. In any case, it is likely that it was wrongly directed: the key objective is to encourage development of technological capability within firms, so as to support their ability to compete in innovative sectors, and it is not clear that this would be facilitated by preventing importation of foreign technology in areas where Indian substitutes exist. On the contrary, there is growing empirical evidence of complementarities between importation of technology and development of local technological capabilities. Restrictive policies probably had the main effect of slowing importation of foreign technology just at the time when India was concerned to develop technologically intensive producer goods industries. It is curious that the objective of industrial self-sufficiency, which was dominant at the time, gave priority to producer goods industries, which were bound to depend importantly on imported technology, since they do so even in highly industrialized countries. It could be argued that there is an incipient contradiction between an industrial policy directed towards increasing autonomy and the simultaneous search for greater 'technological independence'.

The main point about the Indian case is that the approach to technology policy was very limited. It was concerned in the main with limiting the damage which might result from rent-taking by foreign enterprise, and only to a limited extent with the development of local capability. In practice the bureaucratic devices designed to protect domestic technological capability had very little effect. Much the same point could be made of many Latin American technology policies during this period.

As far as import-substituting economies were concerned, the shift towards open-economy industrialization and export orientation radically changed the terms of reference for technology policies, and added new relevance to the findings of innovation studies in the industrial economies. There were two key changes.

First, export orientation implies that industrialization policy must help firms in the home country to enter global markets, which in many sectors are oligopolistic. There is no need to underline in general what a radical change this is from the circumstances of import-substituting industrialization. A particular implication is that in the context of export-promoting policies monopolistic control of information by technology suppliers, whilst still often a reality, does not necessarily lead to the transfer-pricing practices which were so much a characteristic of the import-substituting case. At the least *licensees* — the recipients, or purchasers of technology — have much stronger incentives to avoid conditions which permit transfer pricing. Under import-substituting regimes, licensees in highly protected markets can afford to accept conditions that facilitate transfer pricing by suppliers, since all that is involved for them is a smaller share in the monopolistic rents accruing to an enterprise with unique advantages in a protected market. Provided they get some of the rents, they are likely to improve their profitability. But there is no such cushion of rents under the more competitive conditions of global markets. Consequently, one of the major concerns of policy under the import substitution regime is no longer relevant.

Second, when firms seek a place in a global industry they need to be concerned with more than just the problem of initial entry. They also have to find ways to sustain themselves in markets where, in varying degrees depending on the sector, there is innovative competition. This usually means that they must have access to relevant technological capabilities to cope with continuing innovation in the international market. Of course, this situation simply does not arise under import-substituting conditions, where the need for technological dynamism was generally much less pressing. From what we know of about situations in countries that have succeeded in manufacturing export markets — Japan in an earlier period, the Southeastern Asian NICs more recently — policies in each case have focused on using technology transfer arrangements with foreign enterprises in ways which help to cumulate relevant technological skills in the local firms. Not surprisingly, concerns with the costs of technology, in the forms of monopoly rent, have been of secondary importance.

1.3.2.3 Broader implications and a typology
In the open-economy context, issues of innovative competition and imitation have direct implications for industrial policy.

The starting point is the observation that the incidence of innovative competition varies between sectors — and also varies within sectors, since older products sometimes remain in competition to serve lower income segments of the market. These inter- and intrasectoral differences are of considerable importance. Entry into international markets where there is some degree of innovative competition requires that firms should be able to meet some fairly exacting conditions. They must have sufficient technological capability to obtain access to the technologies required; and they must be able to build on these capabilities sufficiently to keep up with subsequent process and product changes. The fact that conditions of innovative competition, are less present or less exacting in some sectors or parts of sectors than in others means that entry opportunities are not limited to firms, or countries with the best endowments of technological capacity, but that opportunities exist for less well-endowed firms. Tentatively we might distinguish three scenarios for countries attempting export-oriented industrialization.

1. Some countries have started industrialization in technologically undemanding sectors, and then, after accumulating a wider range of capabilities, have moved up to technologically more and more advanced sectors characterized by increasing intensity of innovative competition. The clearest example today is South Korea; Japan went through a similar cycle. China, or at least parts of China, may be starting such a pattern. Korea illustrates the potential of this stepwise process: over the 20 years from 1969, exports by volume grew at an annual rate of 15%. *Real wages* grew at 7% per annum, as did real value added per worker. Thus, profit's share in value added was more or less constant. The increase in labour productivity was facilitated by a shift from low to high value-added types of production, characterized by increasing degrees of innovative competition.
2. Other countries have entered manufacturing trade successfully, but have not achieved the step up to higher levels of innovative competition that Korea has managed. They have kept up with international technological change. Exports have grown but less rapidly and less sustainedly than in Korea. Hong Kong is a case in point. There has been a much less spectacular growth in productivity and also in real wages. Wage pressure on profits' share has been a problem from time to time. There have been periods when real wages in Hong Kong have fallen, probably in response to a slow down in productivity growth.
3. In yet other countries, the large majority of developing countries in all probability, where entry into manufacturing trade has been in sectors or subsectors with a low degree of innovative competition, competitiveness is based on low real wages and relatively low rates of productivity growth are required. Many countries have shifted into a pattern of this kind after adjusting out of the import-substitution policy. Chile seems a particularly clear example. Entry on these terms is evidently much less demanding

in terms of technological capability than in the preceding cases, but the economic and social outcomes are less favourable.

This differentiated pattern of entry is not stable. In a world of innovative competition matters do not stand still for long. There is a tendency for areas of production which were hitherto calm backwaters of steady technology and fairly predictable price competition to be caught up in new rounds of innovative competition. When that happens, success depends on whether existing producers possess the technological capabilities needed to imitate process and product innovations. If they do not, they may be forced out of international markets, or they may hang on by cutting costs through real wage reductions. This pattern seems to be present in a number of low-wage sectors in developing countries. Successful industrialization depends increasingly not only on efficient production at today's technology and relative price patterns but also a capacity to keep up with an often unpredictable pattern of technological change. The success with which countries do this affects importantly the welfare implications of export-oriented industrialization. High rates of technological change permit increases in real wages without adverse implications for profitability and the incentive to invest. Lower rates often imply that the only way to succeed internationally is by forcing the real wage down, and turning the functional distribution of income against labour.

Plainly what is in question is a specification of conditions for industrialization which go considerably beyond the relative factor availability conditions of Hecksher—Ohlin. There have indeed been attempts to expand that standard framework — for example by including 'human capital'. But the impacts of technology go much further than the human capital concept and cannot be contained in it without losing the essential point. What is needed is a wider framework that includes the standard Hecksher—Ohlin conditions at one end of the spectrum and the conditions of entry under innovative competition at the other. The Hecksher—Ohlin conditions would apply in sectors where technologies are more or less stable. Proposals along these lines have been made by Dosi et al. (1990).

1.4 CONCLUDING REMARKS

This chapter has been concerned with the relevance of 'innovation studies' in the industrialized economies for technology policies in the developing countries. Innovation studies usually take Schumpeterian hypotheses as their point of departure; they are characteristically strongly empirical; and they frequently (but not unfailingly) take the innovative firm within the innovative industry as the object of analysis. In this section we draw conclusions about their relevance for industries in the Third World. The section is in two parts. The first gives a listing of six main conclusions on the relevance of innovation studies; the second takes up three key issues which cut across the points of relevance.

1.4.1 The Relevance of Innovation Studies

This section gives six main conclusions on the relevance of innovation studies to developing countries. Issues that cut across these points are discussed in Section 1.4.2.

1.4.1.1 Strategies towards innovation

An obvious place to start is with the concept of the firm that emerges from innovation studies. This concept is quite sharply differentiated from the firm of standard Marshallian microeconomics. In innovative industries, firms compete primarily by introducing new products and processes, and not by simply adjusting to the optimum position on a given short-run cost curve. Firms may follow various strategies: they may seek to innovate; they may imitate products and processes brought in by innovating firms; or they may continue with older products and processes and seek other advantages (to compensate for their technological disadvantages), like lower material costs, or lower real wages.

Innovative and imitative strategies require that firms accumulate the appropriate technological capability. Firms' positions in this regard are (obviously) a function of their history: the capacity to innovate or imitate is 'path dependent'. Non-innovative firms try to compete on price — and since product markets are inherently imperfect (partly *because* of innovative competition), they may survive despite technological disadvantages. These ways of differentiating between firms (by history) might be the basis of a useful typology of industrial firms — somewhat similar to typologies of modes of production employed by agricultural economists. Such a typology would help industrial researchers in developing countries to distinguish the different responses there might be to particular policies — for example, to policies to encourage firms to import technologies from abroad, or to build up their technological capabilities. It would also help to specify which firms would follow technologically static, cost-reducing survival strategies.

1.4.1.2 Accumulation of technological capability

Innovation studies strongly emphasize firms' historic accumulation of technological capability as a basis for innovative competition (i.e., for attaining innovative leads *and* for successful imitation). There is a presumption that imitation usually calls on a subset of the technological capabilities needed for innovation. In industries in developing countries, imitative strategies, often based on licensing contracts or on deals with foreign machinery suppliers, will have priority. In more technologically advanced countries, there may well be some incremental adaptive innovations. Innovation studies point out the importance of policies to build up relevant capabilities for *imitation* in Third World industries. They also indicate that access to 'codified' (i.e., 'written') knowledge contained in licence agreements is not sufficient for a firm to imitate successfully, The transfer of 'tacit' knowledge about the new product and/or process is also needed, and this knowledge can usually be obtained from innovation firms. Although there is a consensus that accumulation of technological capability is an essential dynamic requirement for most strategies in innovative industries, knowledge of the underlying *learning* process is still imperfect, especially in developing countries. It is agreed that learning (including 'learning-by-doing') is not automatic but needs allocation of resources.

1.4.1.3 Changes in the global economy

As far as industries in developing countries are concerned, the need to confront innovative competition and the capabilities required to sustain it has become more pressing because of two important shifts in the international economy. First, there has been a shift away from import-substituting and other closed-economy approaches to industrialization, towards industrialization with a more open-economy emphasis, including, of course, export promotion. Second, new technological developments (in microelectronics, biotechnology, and other fields) have penetrated many sectors that were technologically stagnant during the 1970s and most of the 1980s.

The first of these shifts means that industrialization policies are increasingly concerned with the entry of domestic firms into industrially oligopolistic markets. The second means that innovative competition arises in an increasing number of sectors, including for example, textiles and garments. Third World industrialization policies need increasingly to take innovative competition into account.

1.4.1.4 Intersectoral variability

Despite the widening field of application of new technology and innovative competition, there are still considerable differences between sectors, in terms of the demands for technological capabilities for imitative strategies. Firms in developing countries naturally tend to enter international markets in technologically less demanding sectors. In countries where industrialization has been particularly successful (like some NICs for example), initial entry into technologically simple international sectors has been followed by subsequent entry into technologically more sophisticated industries with higher value added. This strategy (of climbing the technological ladder) has been associated — especially in South Korea — with highly successful learning processes and very rapid growth of exports, based on increasing value added per worker, and accompanied by rising real wages. Other countries, like Hong Kong, have been slower to diversify 'upwards'. Innovation studies, especially as they relate to imitative strategies, give a picture of the kind of learning processes involved in these alternative strategies.

There are, finally, other countries whose industries are initially able to export using relatively old product and process technologies, but whose ability to maintain their position in international markets comes to depend on other (i.e., nontechnological) means of cost reduction. In the longer run, the welfare implications of keeping firms in export markets despite static and backward technology can become unfavourable — for example, if real wages have to be forced down.

1.4.1.5 Intrasectoral variability
There are also intrasectoral differences in the incidence of innovative competition. In some sectors firms using older processes and products adopt strategies which allow them to survive despite rapid technological change in other parts of the sector. They are able to do this because a residual demand may remain for older, less sophisticated products in a part of the market. Firms in developing countries are sometimes able to exploit such 'niche' markets, which result from the high degree of market segmentation and imperfection which characterize innovative industries.

1.4.1.6 Nature of competition
The nature of competition in innovative industries — and the increasing range of industrial sectors experiencing innovation — raise special problems for firms in the least developed countries. It is widely presumed that firms are technologically backward, and, perhaps more important, technologically stagnant and therefore lacking experience in any kind of learning process. Very little research has been done on such firms. Thus, it is as yet not clear how far such strongly pessimistic assumptions are justified.

1.4.2 Some General Issues

Cutting across the conclusion discussed above are three main points, which are pertinent to industrial policies everywhere, and which are especially emphasized by innovation studies. At the risk of some repetition they are discussed below.

The first is that *technological capabilities*, and the way they are organized institutionally, are relevant to industrial policy in the Third World. Initial availability of such capabilities will determine the possibilities of entry into global industries. Furthermore success in building up these capabilities will influence the firm's abilities to survive in these industries in the longer run. This point applies across the board (i.e., to industries where technology at the time of entry is relatively stagnant and price competition may be the norm, as well as to sectors where innovative competition is dominant).

The second point is that the *learning processes* which underlie cumulation play an important role in determining points of entry. Understanding of these processes is improving through empirical research. The earliest approaches by Arrow (1962), Kaldor and others postulated learning-by-doing as automatic and related usually to the cumulative production of firms. This approach leads to analytically convenient formulations but it does not fit reality and is potentially seriously misleading. Many empirical researchers have pointed out that learning requires resources of various kinds, as well as skilful organization and management. It is not automatic, and the direction it takes depends on the decisions which firms make. It is perhaps fair to add that the 'doing' aspect — that is the link to production experience — remains as a necessary, but not sufficient, explanation of the cumulation process.

The third point is that the *imitative process* becomes a central concern. For the most part, firms in developing countries will be mainly imitators for the immediate future, although the Korean experience shows that this situation need not continue indefinitely. Imitation is mediated in various ways, depending on the sector, the extent of innovative competition, and no doubt on many other conditions. Common modes of imitation are licensing agreements, joint ventures, or other types of foreign direct investment. Other types of technology transfer, through producer goods suppliers or engineering bureaus, also promote the imitation process. Intuitively, there are likely to be relationships between these different types of technology transfer and the process of accumulating technological capability (i.e., learning), in firms. Some may be more favourable than others to local learning.

ACKNOWLEDGEMENTS

The author thanks his colleagues at UNU/INTECH for valuable comments — especially Larry Westphal — participants at the Development Economics Seminar at the Institute of Social Studies in the Hague, at seminars at Queen Elizabeth House, Oxford, and UNU/INTECH, Maastricht. A draft version of this chapter was previously circulated as UNU/INTECH Working Paper No. 3: *Are Innovation Studies on Industrialized Economies Relevant to Technology Policy in Developing Countries?*

NOTES

1. 'A model which took account of all the variegation of reality would be of no more use than a map at the scale of one to one' (Robinson, 1962, with a reference to Lewis Carroll, 'Sylvie and Bruno').
2. Sanjaya Lall has shown in a series of important papers that, from 1979 onwards Indian technological capabilities have accumulated to the point where India is an exporter of technologies. (See, for example, Lall, 1984a.)
3. Dosi, Pavitt and Soete (1990) suggest that Marshallian competition might be a limiting case appropriate to situations in which innovation has ceased.
4. Economic theory has often lagged behind changes in economic systems, or changes in policy. There are many examples, of which the Prebisch justification for import substitution is especially well known. For speculation along these lines about the Prebisch—Singer thesis, see Cooper and Fitzgerald (1989, p. 12). More appositely, it is worth noting that changes in perceptions of the innovative process are quite frequently ascribed to historical changes affecting industry structures. See, for example, Freeman (op cit., p. 10) on Schumpeter's change in view on sources of innovation, in particular his recognition of the role of intrafirm research and development.
5. There are useful surveys in Dosi (1988) and Dosi, Pavitt and Soete (1990).
6. The concept of 'quasi-monopoly' as applied to the temporary advantage of an innovating firm was first used by Vernon (1966).
7. The specifications which follow are drawn in part from the discussion in Dosi, Pavitt and Soete (1990, Chapter 4 on 'The Innovative Process'), which in turn draws on a large body of theoretical and empirical literature.
8. Frances Stewart and Jeffrey James (1982, pp. 9 ff.) apply the idea to the context of developing economies. Elsewhere Stewart (1979) used the localization of technological change in the Atkinson and Stiglitz style to explain why technology from industrialized countries is inappropriate for developing countries.

9. David makes much wider inferences, going well beyond the idea of localization: 'Choices of technique become the link through which prevailing economic conditions may influence the future dimensions of technological knowledge' (op. cit., p. 4). There is a useful discussion of these ideas in Rosenberg (1982, p. 166 *et seq.*).

10. Rosenberg (1982, pp. 120 ff.) broadens the concept to cover 'learning by using'. The automaticity of the learning process as formulated by Arrow (op. cit.) has been strongly criticized by a number of authors, including Bell et al. (1982, 1984).

11. Or what Dosi describes as 'cumulation ... in the acquisition of problem solving capacities' (Dosi, 1988, p. 1128).

12. In his first formulation of the economics of innovation, Schumpeter was much concerned to explain monopolistic rents from innovations as a return to entrepreneurship (Schumpeter, op. cit.). In a modern setting, the role of these rents is much simpler to understand: they are perceived by businessmen as the 'return' to the (often massive) allocation of resources (like R&D resources) to the production of innovations.

13. The history of industrialization (and of industrial technology) is in a sense an account of sectoral patterns of innovation which change over time: innovations in the United Kingdom during the Industrial Revolution were centred in the textiles sector itself. Later, as the capital goods sector emerged, innovations in textiles machinery and many other types of equipment came more and more from machine-making sectors. Further in response to bottlenecks in textile inputs (bleaching agents and dyestuffs in the first instance), the chemicals industry — the first 'science-based' sector — emerged. The story continues: it is hardly surprising that there should be intersectoral differences in innovation in modern industry which is a product of the historic process.

14. Discussions of these chapters of *Capital* can be found in Rosenberg (1982, Chapter 2, an essay reprinted from the *Monthly Review*, Vol. 28, July—August 1975). See also Cooper (1971). Marshall also reflects on the emergence of new forms of industrial organization and their relationship to the application of science to production (Marshall, 1899, Book IV, Chapters VIII and IX).

15. Freeman (1989) points to the relationship between innovation and product differentiation. He describes 'defensive' innovation (which is highly R&D intensive), as follows: 'Defensive R and D is probably typical of most oligopolistic markets and is closely linked to product differentiation' (p. 176).

16. Cooper et al. (1974) attempted to link the Sylos-Labini framework as developed by Modigliani (1958) to explain barriers to entry and intra-industry patterns of competition.

17. See Mansfield et al. (1981): 'It has long been recognised that the costs of imitating new products have an important effect on the incentives for innovation. ... If ... firms can imitate an innovation ... substantially below the cost to the innovator of developing the innovation, there may be little or no incentive for the innovator to carry out the innovation'.

18. On the importance of incremental improvements to production processes see Enos (1962).

19. In fact, Freeman distinguishes six types. His sixth category, 'Opportunist strategy', is not necessary for our discussion.

20. Freeman may understate the significance of innovation in the traditional sectors, or at least the technological pressure under which such firms have come, especially in recent times. Traditional firms are generally 'supplier dominated', and may from time to time be faced with a critical need to adopt new technologies as a matter of survival (or as an interim measure to drive costs down as far as possible by real wage reductions). This is evidently happening in a number of sectors because of the incidence of new microelectronic control systems, which widen the range for

mechanization (see Hoffman and Rush, 1988, for a discussion of the garments industry).

21. An early attempt to specify 'Channels and Mechanisms of Technology Transfer', which draws this distinction, is given by Cooper and Sercovich (1971). There is a survey of literature on this question in Stewart (1981).

22. There is some evidence that European technology-supplier firms to Indian industry are increasingly sensitive to the creation of potential competitors, especially in view of increasing competition in their home markets from the newly industrialized countries (see Cooper, 1988). But Bell and Scott-Kemmis (1988) express doubt whether this is true of British firms.

23. 'It is obvious that there is no room in economics for long chains of deductive reasoning' (Marshall, 1899, edition 1966, p. 644). It is a little unclear whether Marshall intended this as a statement of fact or as a normative judgement. As a statement of fact, it has not been borne out by recent developments in economics, many of which bear witness to a willingness to pursue long chains of deduction, to the almost total exclusion of embarrassing facts. Since Marshall was well aware of the methodological weaknesses of economists, it seems to me more reasonable to regard this as a normative statement — a stern warning in fact.

24. An important qualification to this is implicit in Freeman's further remarks that 'Unless imitators enjoy significant market protection or privilege they must rely on lower unit costs of production', and, in relation to innovative strategy in developing countries, 'even a successful imitative strategy, although it may lead to industrial development, will reach a point where export competitiveness in labour costs may increasingly conflict with the goal of higher per capita incomes' (op. cit., pp. 170 and 184). These arguments as they apply to trade patterns will be developed more fully below.

25. See, for example, Dahlmann and Westphal (1982), and Bell et al. (1982) for a review of some of these. See also Dahlmann et al. (1987), and Pack and Westphal (1986).

26. Subsequently, arguments about tendencies to sub-optimal investments as a justification for interventions by a social welfare state were largely brushed aside by the crude empiricism that 'bad markets are better than bad governments'. This of course is just as impossible of proof as was the crude delinking argument of the descriptive Dependency school.

27. The best known attempt at superordination is Chenery, 1961.

28. For a detailed history of Indian policy and experience see Nayar (1983). A critical account of Indian policy is in Desai (1988).

REFERENCES

Arrow, Kenneth (1962), 'The Economic Implications of Learning by Doing', *Review of Economic Studies*, Vol. 29.

Atkinson, A. and Stiglitz, J. (1969), 'A New View of Technological Change', *Economic Journal*, Vol. 79, No. 315, September.

Bell, R.M. and Scott-Kemmis, D. (1988), 'Technological Dynamism and Technological Content of Collaboration: Are Indian Firms missing Opportunities?', in Desai (1988).

Bell, R.M., Scott-Kemmis, O. and Satyarakwit, W. (1982), 'Limited Learning in Infant Industry', in Stewart and James (1982).

Bell, R.M., Ross-Larsen, B. and Westphal, L.E. (1984), 'Assessing the Performance of Infant Industries', *Journal of Development Economics*, Vol. 16, Nos 1/2, September.

Bhalla, Ajit (1991), 'Preface', to Zahlan (1991).

Chenery, Hollis B. (1961), 'Comparative Advantage and Development Policy', *American Economic Review*, March.

Cooper, C.M. (1971), 'Science and Production', *Economic and Social Review*, July.

Cooper, C.M. (1980), 'Policy Interventions for Technological Innovations in Developing Countries', *World Bank Staff Working Paper*, Nos 4—41, The World Bank, Washington, D.C.

Cooper, C.M. (1988), 'Supply and Demand Factors in Indian Technology Imports: A Case Study', in Desai (1988).

Cooper, C.M. and Fitzgerald, E.V.K. (1989), *Development Studies Revisited: Twenty Five Years of the Journal of Development Studies*, Frank Cass, London.

Cooper, C.M., Freeman, C. and Sercovich, F. (1974), 'The British Patent System and the International Patent System', Mimeograph Report, Science Policy Research Unit, University of Sussex, Sussex, U.K.

Cooper, C.M. and Sercovich, D. (1971), 'Channels and Mechanisms for the Transfer of Technology from Developed to Developing Countries', UNCTAD Report No. TD/B/AC.11.5, United Nations Conference on Trade and Development, Geneva.

Dahlmann, C.J. (1978), 'From Technological Dependence to Technological Development: the Case of USIMINAS Steel Plant in Brazil', IDB/ECLA Research Programme in Science and Technology, Working Paper No. 21, International Development Bank, Buenos Aires.

Dahlman, C.J., Ross-Larson, B. and Westphal, L.E. (1987), 'Managing Technological Development: Lessons from the Newly Industrialising Countries', *World Development*, Vol. 15, No. 6.

Dahlmann, C.J. and Westphal, L.E. (1982), 'Technological Effort in Industrial Development— an Interpretative Survey of Recent Evidence', in Stewart and James (1982).

David, Paul, (1975), *Technical Choice, Innovation and Economic Growth*, Cambridge University Press, Cambridge.

Desai, Ashok (ed.) (1988), *Technology Absorption in Indian Industry*, Wiley Eastern Limited, New Delhi.

Dosi, Giovanni, (1988), 'Sources, Procedures, and Microeconomic Effects of Innovation', *Journal of Economic Literature*, Vol. XXVI, September.

Dosi, G., Freeman, C., Nelson, R.R., Silverberg, G. and Soete, L. (eds) (1988), *Technical Change and Economic Theory*, Francis Pinter, London and New York.

Dosi, G., Pavitt, K. and Soete, L. (1990), *The Economics of Technical Change and International Trade*, Harvester Wheatsheaf, London.

Enos, J. (1962), 'Invention and Innovation in the Petroleum Refining Industry', in Nelson (1962).

Enos, John (1991), *The Creation of Technological Capability in Developing Countries*, Francis Pinter, London and New York.

Fransman, Martin (1986), *Technology and Economic Development*, Harvester Wheatsheaf, London.

Freeman, Christopher (1989), *The Economics of Industrial Innovation*, 2nd edn, Francis Pinter, London.

Hirsch, S. (1967), *Location of Industry and International Competitiveness*, Clarendon Press, Oxford.

Hoffman, K. and Rush, M. (1988), *Microelectronics and Clothing*, Praeger, London.

Jolly, Richard and Streeten, Paul (eds) (1981), *Recent Issues in World Development: A Collection of Survey Articles*, Pergamon Press, Oxford and New York.

Kalecki, Michal (ed.) (1971), *Selected Essays on the Dynamics of the Capitalist Economy*, Cambridge University Press, Cambridge.

Katz, Jorge (1987), *Technology Generation in Latin American Manufacturing Enterprises: Theory and Case Studies Concerning its Nature, Magnitude and Consequences*, Macmillan, London.

Katz, J. and Albin, E. (1979), 'From Infant Industry to Technology Exports: the Argentine Experience in the International Sale of Industrial Plants and Engineering Works', IDB/ECLA Research Programme in Science and Technology, Working Paper No. 14, International Development Bank, Buenos Aires.

Lall, Sanjaya (1984a), 'Exports of Technology by Newly-Industrializing Countries', *World Development*, Vol. 12.

Lall, Sanjaya (1984b), 'India's Technological Capacity: Effects of Trade, Industrial Science and Technology Policies', in Fransman and King (1984).

Lall, Sanjaya (1987), *Learning to Industrialize: the Acquisition of Technological Capability by India*, Macmillan, London.

List, F. (1844), *The National System of Political Economy*, English Translation from German, Longmans, London, 1904.

Mansfield, E., Schwartz, M. and Wagner, S. (1981), 'Imitation Costs and Patents', *Economic Journal*, December, pp. 907-918.

Marshall, A. (1899), 'Principles of Economics', Reprinted by Macmillan, London, 1966.

Marx, Karl (1858), *'Capital'*, English Translation from German, by Foreign Languages Publishing House, Moscow, 1961.

Maxwell, P. (1977), 'Learning and Technical Change in the Steel Plant of Acindar SA in Rosario, Argentina', IDB/ECLA Research Programme in Science and Technology, Working Paper No. 23, International Development Bank, Buenos Aires.

Modigliani, Franco (1958), 'New Developments on the Oligopoly Front', *Journal of Political Economy*, June, pp. 215-232.

Nayar, B.R. (1983), *India's Quest for Technological Independence: Policy Foundation and Policy Change*, Lancers Publishers, New Delhi, India.

Nelson, R.R. (1988a), 'National Systems of Innovation', in Dosi et al. (eds) (1988).

Nelson, R.R. (1988b), 'Institutions Supporting Technical Change in the United States', in Dosi et al. (eds) (1988).

Nelson, R.R. (ed.) (1993), *National Innovation Systems: A Comparative Analysis*. Oxford University Press, Oxford, New York.

Nelson, R.R. and Winter, S. (1982), *An Evolutionary Theory of Economic Change*, The Belknap Press of Harvard University Press, Cambridge, Massachusetts.

Nurkse, Ragnar (1958), *Problems of Capital Formation in Underdeveloped Countries*, Basil Blackwell, Oxford.

Pack, H. and Westphal, L. (1986), 'Industrial Strategy and Technological Change: Theory versus Reality', *Journal of Development Economics*, Vol. 22, No. 1, pp. 87-128.

Pavitt, K. (1984), 'Sectoral Patterns of Technical Change: Towards a Taxonomy and a Theory', *Research Policy*, Vol. 13, No. 6.

Prebisch, R. (1950), *The Economic Development of Latin America and its Principal Problems*, United Nations, New York.

Preobrazhensky, E. (1926), *The New Economics*, English Translation from Russian, Clarendon Press, Oxford, 1965.

Ricardo, David (1830), *Principles of Political Economy and Taxation*, Reprinted by Penguin Books, London, 1971.

Robinson, Joan (1962), *Essays in the Theory of Economic Growth*, Macmillan, London.

Robson, M., Townsend, J. and Pavitt, K. (1988), 'Sectoral Patterns of Production and Use of Innovations in the UK: 1945–1983', *Research Policy*, Vol. 17.

Rosenberg, Nathan (1969), 'The Direction of Technological Change', *Economic Development and Cultural Change*, October.

Rosenberg, Nathan (1982), *Inside the Black Box: Technology and Economics*, Cambridge University Press, Cambridge.

Rosenstein-Rodan, P.N. (1943), 'Problems of Industrialisation of Eastern and South Eastern Europe', *Economic Journal*, Vol. 53.

Schumpeter, Joseph (1912), *Theory of Economic Development*, English Translation of *Theorie der wirtschaftlichen Entwicklung* (Redvers Opie, Transl.), Oxford University Press, New York, 1961.

Schumpeter, Joseph (1966), *Capitalism, Socialism, and Democracy*, Allen and Unwin, London.

Stewart, Frances (1979), 'International Technology Transfer,' *World Bank Staff Working Paper*, No. 344, July.

Stewart, Frances (1981), 'International Transfer of Technology: Issues and Policy Options', in Jolly and Streeten (1981).

Stewart, Frances and James, Jeffrey (eds) (1982), *The Economics of New Technology in Developing Countries*, Pinter and Westview Press, London and Boulder, Colorado.

Sylos-Labini, Paolo (1967), *Oligopoly and Technical Progress*, English Translation of *Oligopolio e Progresso Tecnico* (original published by Giuffre, Milan), Harvard University Press, Cambridge, Massachusetts.

Vernon, R. (1966), 'International Investment and International Trade in the Product Cycle', *Quarterly Journal of Economics*, Vol. 80.

2. Biotechnology: Generation, Diffusion, and Policy

Martin Fransman

2.1 INTRODUCTION

Like new biotechnology itself, the study of biotechnology by social scientists is still in its infancy. While there is a wide consensus among governments, firms — both large and small, new and old — and scientists and technologists that biotechnology will have at least as broad an impact in the future as microelectronics and information technology, its potential has yet to be realized. This makes its study both interesting and dangerous. This follows from the great degree of uncertainty that is present in any new field of technology in the early stages of its development, and particularly a radical technology like biotechnology that will impact a broad range of products, processes, and industries.

Economists of different conceptual persuasions agree that changes in technology can have a major economic impact. As we have seen in Chapter 1, Schumpeter (e.g., 1966) in formulating his view on technological change and its economic effects, distinguished between invention, innovation, and diffusion. In the case of *invention* the ideas (sometimes embodied in material artifacts) that form the basis of the subsequent new technology are formulated. These ideas are used later to produce and sell new or improved products, processes, and services: that is, to innovate. In earlier work Schumpeter emphasized the role of the entrepreneur, who seizes the new body of knowledge made available by the invention process and transforms it into commercial output. Later, however, as corporations themselves grew in size and economic significance, Schumpeter increasingly stressed the importance of the formally organized search for new commercially exploitable knowledge embodied in the research and development (R&D) activities of these corporations. To analyse the economic impact of new inventions and innovations, however, Schumpeter pointed out that it is necessary to understand the diffusion process whereby new products, processes, and services are adopted and used by others in the economic system. The more widely diffused an innovation, all other things equal, the greater its effects.

Although writing from a perspective of neoclassical economics and emphasizing different secondary causal mechanisms, Hicks (1981) also sees invention/innovation as the 'mainspring' of economic growth. In his Nobel Prize address, Hicks analysed the process whereby invention/innovation provides an 'impulse' to the economy, raising output and thereby influencing wage rates and corresponding rates of profit. Subsequently, changes in relative factor prices induce factor substitution as well as secondary innovations, which he calls the 'children' of the initial impulse. These secondary effects also influence the ultimate equilibrium into which the economic system settles once the consequences of the initial impulse have been worked out.

The aim of this chapter is to examine critically the literature that analyses the socioeconomic implications of biotechnology. In doing so, the frameworks suggested by Schumpeter and Hicks will prove useful as a starting point. However, as we shall see, the framework will have to be modified and elaborated.

Biotechnology may be defined as 'the use of biological organisms for commercial ends'. According to this definition, biotechnology is almost as old as human civilization, as is clear from activities such as brewing of beer, fermentation of wine, and production of cheese. Since the early 1970s, however, biotechnology has received a significant boost from the introduction of a number of powerful new techniques known collectively as *genetic engineering*. These techniques (which will be considered in greater detail later) allow biotechnologists to alter the genetic structure of organisms by adding new genes that allow the organism to perform new functions. Genetic engineering together with other ways of manipulating and using biological organisms has provided a potent new set of possibilities with profound implications for a wide range of commercial activities, from agriculture to pharmaceuticals, chemicals, food and industrial to processing, and mining.

The potentially wide-ranging applicability of biotechnology invites comparison with microelectronics, and information technology, and this theme will be taken up in more detail later in this chapter. Certainly both sets of technologies share a number of important characteristics. Both consist of an interdependent cluster of technologies which jointly have a significant nonmarginal impact, modifying old products and processes and producing new ones in a large number of economic sectors. Both sets of technology are particularly worthy of examination as a result of the wide-ranging impulse, to use Hicks's terminology, that they provide for economic and social change. While biotechnology, strengthened relatively recently by the powerful new techniques mentioned above, lags behind microelectronics and information technology in terms of its current effects, there are some who believe that it will have at least as broad an impact as electronics in future years. Their arguments are discussed in more detail below.

In examining the relationship between biotechnology on the one hand and the economy and society on the other (with causal factors operating simultaneously in both directions), the first task is to identify the major questions that must be posed as a prelude to suggesting appropriate ways of analysing them. Here the frameworks put forward by Schumpeter and Hicks provide a useful starting point.

Since *invention* initiates the impulse and its effects, it is worth beginning by delving more deeply into the *inventive process* and its determinants. In the case of biotechnology, and particularly genetic engineering, this involves examining the scientific base which constitutes its backbone. To understand the contribution made by science to biotechnology it is necessary to examine the relationship between *science, technology, economy*, and *society*. Two opposing arguments serve to clarify the extreme positions. According to the first argument, *science* constitutes an autonomous subsystem within the broader socioeconomic system, operating according to its own internally generated determinants (for example, the objectives and relative degrees of influence of scientific institutions and scientists). Conversely, the second argument denies the autonomy of the science subsystem, holding that scientific activities are themselves shaped by technological, economic, and social determinants.

The importance of these arguments becomes clearer when they are translated into institutional terms and normative/policy questions are added. What is the nature of the relationships among (1) universities/scientific research institutions; (2) firms which draw on scientific knowledge in creating technologies used to transform inputs into commercial outputs; and (3) economic processes and variables such as competition and prices? Furthermore, what kinds of relationships should be fostered, to the extent that they are amenable to policy measures, if science is to make an effective contribution to biotechnology and desired economic change? As will be shown below, policy-oriented literature has begun to emerge around questions such as these. Returning to Schumpeter and Hicks, however, these questions make it clear that the process of invention, which results in an 'impulse' being delivered to the economy and society, is complex and its determinants need to be analysed carefully.

In addition to these questions about the creation of biotechnological knowledge are issues connected to the appropriation of financial returns from such knowledge. According to some views, one of the fundamental differences between *science* and *technology* is that the former deals with 'basic' knowledge with no immediate commercial applicability, while the latter is commercially exploitable and is therefore a commodity that can be bought and sold. This dichotomy has important implications for the different structure and function of science-based institutions such as universities and government scientific institutions on the one hand, and technology-based institutions like firms on the other. In science-based institutions, the flow of information is relatively free through publication and other forms of dissemination of results, notwithstanding factors, such as competitive rivalries between scientists, that retard the flow of information. On the other hand, the technological knowledge base of a firm can be (though not in all cases) a major determinant of profitability. Accordingly, firms often take steps either to ensure that their knowledge base remains secret or to obtain legal guarantees, as in the case of patents, that other firms will not be allowed to use their knowledge.

However, this sharp distinction between science-based institutions and technology-based firms is to an extent challenged by recent events in the biotechnology area. In 1973 the first gene was cloned, and in 1975 the first hybridoma (fused cell) was created. In 1976, the first so-called new biotechnology firm — Genentech, a spin-off from university-based research — was set up to exploit recombinant DNA technology. In 1980, in Diamond v Chakrabarty, the United States Supreme Court ruled that microorganisms could be patented under existing law. In the same year, the Cohen/Boyer patent was issued for the technique related to construction of recombinant DNA. By the end of 1981, more than eighty new biotechnology firms had been established in the United States. In the same year E.I. du Pont de Nemours allocated $US120 million for R&D in the life sciences; shortly thereafter, Monsanto committed a similar amount. Early attempts to exploit biotechnology commercially were based strongly on the fruits of university research. The resulting set of new interactions between the biological sciences on the one hand and firms, old and new, on the other influenced university research in ways that will be considered in more detail later in this chapter. At the same time, policy questions were posed about the extent to which international competitiveness depended on the appropriateness of national university functioning.

Firms also confronted difficult strategic problems as a result of the commercial potential of biotechnology. During the early stages, many of the large firms that made the strategic decision to move into biotechnology lacked in-house capabilities in fields that were becoming increasingly important, such as molecular biology, genetics, and biochemistry. Some firms, such as the large Japanese producers of pharmaceuticals, amino acids, and enzymes, compensated for such weaknesses by strength in complementary fields, such as bioprocessing, and by other complementary assets, such as strong marketing and distribution networks and links with financial institutions. Nevertheless, the longer-run strategic problems remained: how to develop a knowledge base in the new technology from which to appropriate adequate rates of financial return. A number of strategies formulated to address both this strategic problem, as well as their attendant social costs and benefits, will be assessed later in this chapter.

Small new biotechnology firms faced very different strategic problems. Although raising equity capital was facilitated in the early stages by the way in which biotechnology had caught the imagination of investors, more fundamental problems soon became apparent. (When Genentech shares were first sold on Wall Street in 1980 they set a record for fastest price increase, rising from $35 to $89 per share in 20 minutes. In 1981 the initial public sale of shares by Cetus established a new Wall Street record for the largest amount of money raised in an initial offering: $115 million.) The new biotechnology firms had a strong knowledge base in the disciplines underlying biotechnology, and soon began to to develop capabilities in bioprocessing (i.e., downstream processing). Nevertheless, it gradually became clear that the transformation of such knowledge into value required additional complementary assets. Most important of these were marketing and distribution networks. New vaccines, drugs, diagnostic kits, or seeds, for example, have to be sold to be profitable, and this requires the kind of distributional channels that new biotechnology firms lacked. In view of the constraints on developing such channels, most new biotechnology firms were forced to conclude marketing agreements with large companies in the relevant areas, thus giving up part of the financial returns from biotechnological innovations.

The structure of the biotechnology sector, which is determined by the configuration of large firms, new biotechnology firms, universities, and government research institutions, as well as by the pattern of state intervention, differed between countries. In Japan, for example, new biotechnology firms have not emerged as they did in the United States. This is a result of several characteristics of the Japanese economy: (1) the constraints on labour mobility, which made it difficult for employees of large firms to leave and set up their own enterprises; (2) the absence of a venture capital market in a predominantly credit-based system; and (3) contractual practices in the universities, which constrain university staff from either setting up, or being personally remunerated by, commercial enterprises. In addition, a very different pattern of interaction between universities and industry exists in these two countries, and their pattern of state intervention in biotechnology has differed. These differences raise a number of questions about the relative efficiency of the different structural configurations, including complex questions of market and organizational failure, which will be examined in more detail later in this chapter. The implications for analysing the determinants of international competitiveness are clear.

It is evident from the discussion above that developing scientific knowledge and transforming it to technological knowledge are intricate processes with a large number of complex determinants. In the case of biotechnology, the processes and their determinants need to be studied far more closely. Before embarking on a study of the effects of new technologies, however, it is worth understanding why the technology that has been generated assumes the form and moves in the direction that it does. Furthermore, the effects of technical change feed back to influence subsequent rounds of generation of new technology (and in some cases to influence science itself). For example, as technology is diffused, its use under a variety of different circumstances leads to the generation of further technological change as constraints are encountered and improved methods are devised. In some cases, the problems and puzzles that arise in the diffusion process result in the development of new research agendas to be tackled by scientists and technologists. In some cases of biotechnology, such as protein engineering, it may yet turn out that the technological practice will do more for the development of science than the other way around. On closer inspection, therefore, it often turns out that invention, innovation, and diffusion cannot be neatly separated into linear, sequential stages. For example, in biotechnology, downstream bioprocessing (which involves resolving problems related to purification, development of sensors to monitor fermentation processes, and the development of more general process control technology) will have a major impact on the efficiency of the technology. Indeed, as will be examined later, it may well be that process innovations such as these become more important in genetic engineering than basic scientific innovations in terms of improved efficiency and therefore competitiveness.

While it is important, for the reasons given above, to understand the determinants of the generation of new technologies, it is nevertheless legitimate to assume that the new technology is given and then to examine its effects. Economists have a good deal to offer in terms of analysing impacts on economic variables, such as output, price, and distribution, using partial and economy-wide approaches. Although biotechnology is still new with the great majority of potential products still in the experimental stage, a few important studies have been done which examine the economic effects of biotechnology in selected areas. These studies will be critically reviewed later in this chapter.

Numerous questions have been raised regarding the implications of biotechnology for Third World countries. As in the case of micro-electronics and information technology, the international diffusion of biotechnology is creating new opportunities in these countries and will do so increasingly in the future. This process is being assisted by the relatively low barriers to entry that currently exist in the development cycle in biotechnology. The relatively low barriers to entry are evident in the emergence of large numbers of new biotechnology firms in many industrialized countries, as well as in the biotechnology programmes being developed not only in larger Third World countries, such as India, Brazil, Mexico, and China, but also in smaller countries, such as Cuba, Venezuela, and Kuwait. The current low barriers to entry are, however, unlikely to remain a permanent feature of biotechnology. It is already becoming apparent, for example, that sophistication, scale, and therefore entry costs are increasing in the bioprocessing side of biotechnology. It is likely that larger size of enterprise will be an increasing advantage in the future. One reason for this is that economies of scale are beginning to be realized in bioprocessing. Another is the technological synergies that are increasingly becoming a major source of competitiveness. An example of such synergy is the convergence of microelectronics and information technology on the one hand and biotechnology on the other — the field of bioinformatics — in areas such as automated bioprocess control, automatic DNA synthesizers, protein modelling, and biosensors. Firms that either have in-house capabilities in the area of microelectronics, information technology, and scientific instrumentation, or like the large Japanese groups, are easily able to call on obligationally related enterprises for such expertise, are likely to develop considerable advantage in biotechnology. A third factor favouring larger size is synergy in distribution. For example, a firm with an extensive marketing network in conventional drugs will tend to *be able to distribute* new genetically engineered drugs at lower cost (by reaping the synergistic economies) than firms which lack this facility.

For all these reasons it is likely that the entry barriers will increase over time. However, this does not necessarily mean that Third World countries will be progressively excluded from participation as producers of biotechnology. Judicious control of the domestic market, particularly in the case of the larger Third World countries such as Brazil, India, and China, together with an appropriate set of science and technology policies which facilitate development of the necessary biocapabilities, may allow a country to participate actively as a biotechnology producer. The earlier example of microelectronics and information technology is instructive here. Despite similar economies of scale and attendant barriers to entry, countries like Brazil and Korea are managing to carve out areas that stand a reasonable chance of becoming internationally competitive. Second, Third World countries have the opportunity to opt for specialist niches in the international market. Finally, there are a number of areas in which their specific resources and problems will provide them with a decided competitive advantage. Examples include local plant varieties and diseases.

However, reference to opportunities in the field of biotechnology must not obscure the substantial difficulties that lie in the way of a successful entry into biotechnology, no matter how specialist the niche. Enough frustration has developed from post-war attempts to transfer science and technology to the Third World to require even the most optimistic person to remain cautious with regard to the prospects. For example, a Committee of Scientific Advisors from the United Nations Industrial Development Organization (UNIDO) evaluated Third World capabilities and facilities in search of a site for the new International Centre for Genetic Engineering and Biotechnology. The Committee noted serious weaknesses in key scientific disciplines, such as molecular biology, biochemistry, and genetics (UNIDO, 1986). The difficulties of developing such scientific capabilities in Third World countries, while simultaneously creating conditions necessary for successful operation and servicing of scientific laboratories and equipment, must not be underestimated. Scaling-up and development of efficient bioprocessing capabilities present additional difficulties. Even more problems arise in ensuring that the necessary links are established between the scientific base on the one hand and the productive using sector of the economy on the other. Despite these difficulties, the power and flexibility of biotechnology should allow many Third World countries to benefit from this technology.

As in the case of microelectronics and information technology, there is the potential to gain by *using* the fruits of biotechnology. In this connection, as will be seen in the literature survey below, a good deal of apprehension has been expressed regarding the increasingly proprietary nature of biotechnology. This is most evident in agriculture: many previous technological breakthroughs were made in public institutions, such as universities, government research centres, and international agricultural research institutes, and the resulting technological knowledge was disseminated relatively quickly and at relatively low cost. With the potential to patent microorganisms and new seed varieties, however, and in some cases to keep the knowledge underlying new agricultural products and processes secret, a good deal of agricultural research is moving into the private domain. In some cases, under circumstances that will be considered in more detail below, this may raise the cost of using new biotechnology-based products as the supplying firms set prices consistent with their attempts to maximize profits. This will have further consequences for diffusion rates, and thus output effects, as well as for distributional impacts.

Considering the effects of biotechnology in the Third World invites comparison with the Green Revolution, which refers to the development, using conventional techniques, of high-yielding plant varieties. As in the case of the Green Revolution, there is no inherent technological reason why biotechnology should not benefit the poor. In principle, genetically engineered saline-tolerance, pest and disease resistance, and nitrogen-fixation could have a significant effect on the incomes of the poor in Third World countries, even if, as in the case of the Green Revolution, they are slower to adopt the new technologies and their gain relative to richer farmers is reduced by longer-run decreases in commodity prices. In practice, however, as with the Green Revolution, the socioeconomic factors shaping the evolution of biotechnology are likely to favour the needs of those who constitute important sources of market demand and political influence. Despite such tendencies, the wide range and flexibility of biotechnology holds out at least the possibility of extending the agricultural revolution to geographical areas and agricultural products that have hitherto been largely unaffected while at the same time increasing the benefit derived by the poor.

This raises a large number of important policy questions for Third World countries. To the extent that they want to take advantage of biotechnology in productive activities, questions have to be asked and answered regarding the necessary preconditions, the constraints and the capabilities, that are required. For example, what is the best way for a country, given its particular circumstances, to go about developing general capabilities in genetic engineering and biotechnology? What factors should be considered in choosing areas of specialization? What sorts of science, technology, industrial, and trade policy should be adopted to facilitate the use of biotechnology in production? As will be shown in this chapter, while questions such as these have not yet begun to be examined, a fair amount can be learned from closely related issues in the literature on technology and development.

2.2 THE GENERATION OF BIOTECHNOLOGY: INVENTION AND INNOVATION

Social scientists have generally been reluctant to examine the causes of technical change, preferring instead to analyse its consequences. This is evident, for example, in the approach adopted by Hicks (1981) in his Nobel Prize address titled 'The Mainspring of Economic Growth', which was summarized in the introduction to this chapter. For Hicks, 'invention', which provides the major impulse for economic growth, remains exogenous to the economic system. Hicks's main concerns are the response of prices and profits to the impulse and the secondary innovations which they in turn induce. Similarly, until relatively recently (see Mackenzie and Wajcman, 1985), many sociologists of technology have been proponents of a technological determinism, whereby technology is seen to influence society unidirectionally.

The temptations underlying the bias to study the consequences of technical change are easy to understand. To begin with, technical change *is* a major force for economic and social change and social scientists are therefore correctly interested in the impact of changing technology. Furthermore, if the analysis were broadened to examine the *causes* of technical change, the task would be considerably complicated (and would present economists the additional problem raised by the need to consider determinants and processes that are not narrowly economic). For reasons such as these the causes of technical change, as Rosenberg (1982) noted, remain understudied.

Although understandable, this bias in the literature presents important difficulties. Since the analysis is partial, leaving out the determinants of technical change, technology is necessarily assumed to be static. This assumption more than any other has been the target of attack for students of technology, including economists interested in the process of technical change and related economic change.

However, far from being static, technology changes constantly, with important implications for studying the consequences of technical change. In short, understanding the consequences of technical change over time requires a more *general* conceptual framework which includes analysing the causes of technical change. Such a framework would acknowledge that the consequences of technical change also influence, through a variety of feedback mechanisms, the generation of further technical change with implications for later-round impacts of such change.

This section is devoted to an examination of the generation of biotechnology which at the same time will facilitate a critical review of the literature. The discussion is assisted by reference to Figure 2.1.

2.2.1 The Scientific Base

A distinct definition that draws a sharp boundary between *science* and *technology* is difficult, if not impossible, to produce. Science and technology frequently overlap. Nevertheless, it is possible to produce

Figure 2.1   Configuration of industries and institutions involved in biotechnology

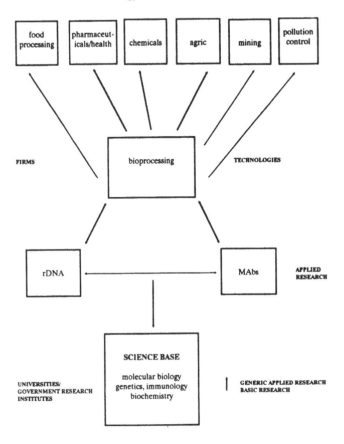

working definitions of *science* and *technology* that make a broad distinction. Accordingly, *science* may be defined as 'attempts to produce "basic" knowledge about natural phenomena which does not necessarily have any immediate commercial applicability'. *Technology* can be defined as knowledge related to transformation of inputs into commercial outputs, including production of new or different outputs.

Technological knowledge may be embodied in people, hardware (plant and equipment) and software, and forms of organization.

According to these definitions, biotechnology is related to science in the sense that the knowledge which underlies its three main technologies — recombinant DNA, cell fusion, and bioprocessing — clearly emerged from the science system. In a detailed account, for example, Cherfas (1982) traces the origins of biotechnology from the first recognition of DNA by Miescher in 1869, to Watson and Crick's model of the double helix in 1953, to the breakthrough of Boyer and Cohen on the recombinant DNA technique in 1973, and the work by Millstein and Kohler on cell fusion in 1975. A good deal of this work was influenced by research on the behaviour of bacteria and viruses and by the war on cancer. Despite the ultimately pragmatic objectives of such research, the research remained for the most part 'basic' in nature. Rosenberg (1982) points out that in many cases 'basic' knowledge has resulted from research undertaken with 'applied' motivations. This makes it difficult to sustain a distinction between basic and applied research in terms of the motivation for such research.

In this respect, biotechnologies contrast sharply with semiconductors, which developed largely, though not entirely, in response to the war and early post-war military demands of the U.S. Department of Defense (Borrus and Millstein, 1984). In contrast to biotechnology, whose major breakthroughs have occurred in universities, the transistor was invented in 1947 at Bell Labs, a part of AT&T which purchased its telecommunications equipment from Western Electric, its manufacturing arm. In 1959 the integrated circuit was invented at Texas Instruments and Fairchild, two small commercial companies which had spun off from Bell Labs. The milieu within which semiconductor technology was developed was therefore oriented more towards practical objectives than in the case of biotechnology, where 'basic' university scientific research, albeit health-related, played a more significant role. However, Borrus and Millstein (1984) can probably fairly be accused of being overly simplistic when they conclude that 'In the development of biotechnology, "science push", rather than the "market pull" that gave impetus to the US semiconductor industry, was particularly important' (p. 533).

Nevertheless, this dichotomy does raise the important question of what role the science base plays in science-oriented industries, such as microelectronics/information technology and biotechnology. Clearly, it is inadequate to see science as a subsystem, autonomous from the rest of the economy and society, or scientists as uninfluenced seekers of the truth attempting to understand the basic nature of the universe. The emergence of microelectronics/information technology and biotechnology has had a good deal to do with the twin social concerns — one may almost say neuroses — of military defence and health. Furthermore, scientific controversy and the progression of scientific ideas have often been greatly influenced by the interests of scientists themselves as some sociologists of science have documented (see Barnes and Edge, 1982, and references therein).

Neither can basic science that forms the core of biotechnology be assumed to be uninfluenced by commercial considerations or at least by the possibility of technological applications. Cohen and Boyer, for example, were aware of the commercial applicability of their recombinant DNA technique and this awareness led Stanford University to apply for a patent for the recombinant DNA (rDNA) process technique within the statutory one year after initial publication of results. In December 1980, Patent No. 4.237.224 was granted, providing for an initial nonexclusive licence fee of $10,000 and an equivalent annual amount for using the technique in research and development. In addition, the patent granted a royalty of 1 % on sales up to $5 million, falling to 0.5 % on sales over $10 million. Since this technique is fundamental to work in genetic engineering, the implications for Stanford University funding are enormous. Stanford University subsequently filed a second patent on the *products* produced by the rDNA technique. [The Cohen and Boyer patent is discussed, for example, in Yoxen (1983, pp. 95-97), and U.S. Congress, Office of Technology Assessment (1984, Chapter 16).]

Millstein, who together with Kohler developed the cell fusion technique in 1975, was also aware to some extent of the commercial implications of his research. Accordingly, he wrote to the Medical Research Council informing them of the possible implications, hoping the National Research and Development Corporation (NRDC), which was responsible for commercialization and protection of intellectual property rights of inventions coming out of public laboratories, might make the necessary arrangements for patents. However, the NRDC did not act and the key patents to work on monoclonal antibodies were eventually taken out by American researchers. In 1980, partly in response to this failure, Celltech was formed by the British Technology Group, which took over the role of the NRDC, and the National Enterprise Board. The company was partly publicly and partly privately funded and was given exclusive access to the research output of the Medical Research Council's laboratories (see Yoxen, 1983, pp. 128-132).

These examples and their implications make it clear that, while there is a functional, institutional, and organizational difference between scientific establishments on the one hand and commercially oriented establishments on the other, neither are entirely self-contained but rather exert a mutual influence on one another. This suggests that a more general approach, which will consider these and other inter-actions, is needed to understand and evaluate the function of these organizations. This has important implications for the study of factors like international competitiveness.

2.2.2 The Technologies

As is clear from Figure 2.1, the science base influences the development of biotechnologies. The influence is mutual, however, since problems and puzzles that arise in technological applications often feed back to determine scientific research agendas (see Rosenberg, 1982, on the notion of endogenous science).

In the case of biotechnology there are three closely related sets of technology (U.S. Congress, Office of Technology Assessment, 1984):

1. *Recombinant DNA technology* (rDNA) allows genes from different organisms to be combined within a single organism, enabling it to produce biological molecules which it does not normally create. In this way new products can be created or previously existing products, such as enzymes or other proteins, can be produced more efficiently. Applications for this technology include pharmaceuticals (for example, insulin, interferon, and interleukin);

chemicals; food-processing; and modification of microorganisms that can then perform commercially useful functions (such as degradation of toxic waste products, or mineral leaching to assist in minerals extraction).

2. *Cell fusion* technology allows different cells to be artificially combined into a fused cell or *hybridoma*, which allows their desirable properties to be combined. For example, fusing an antibody-producing cell with a cancer cell results in a hybridoma that can produce pure antibodies, and that is robust and able to multiply continuously. These pure antibodies, or *monoclonal antibodies* (MAbs), can be used for diagnostic purposes in divergent fields such as human or animal health or to diagnose viruses in crops.

3. *Bioprocess technology* allows biological processes to be used for large-scale industrial purposes. Such processes typically involve reproduction of cells and microorganisms in an appropriate environment, and subsequent extraction and purification of the desired biological substances. Although not in itself a new technology, the efficiency of bioprocess technology is an important determinant of the price and quality of biotechnologically produced products. Some have suggested that *protein engineering* should be thought of as a second-generation 'new biotechnology' (see Fransman et al., forthcoming, for more details on protein engineering).

These technologies are not static; they are constantly being modified and developed. Examples include automated DNA synthesizers or 'gene machines' and, in the field of bioprocessing, immobilization techniques, biosensors, and automated process control.

Since this chapter mainly addresses socioeconomic aspects of biotechnology, scientific and technical factors are not discussed in great detail. Nevertheless, it is worth mentioning a number of sources that give a good introductory account of the scientific and technical aspects of biotechnology. These include Cherfas (1982), who gives a detailed historical description of the development of the main techniques used in biotechnology; and two issues of *Scientific American*

(1981 and 1985), which provide details on the molecular and bio-process underpinnings of biotechnology. Two major reports on bio-technology by the U.S. Congress, Office of Technology Assessment (1984, 1986) provide readable and well-illustrated accounts of the technology; the first addresses biotechnology in general while the second considers agricultural applications. Yoxen (1983) situates his discussion of the scientific and technical aspects of biotechnology in a broader societal context by examining the social implications.

2.2.3 The Evolution of Biotechnological Knowledge

In analysing the evolution of biotechnological knowledge it is helpful to think in terms of a development cycle. During the earliest stages of this cycle individuals began to realize that the underlying scientific knowledge has possible commercial applications. Accordingly, steps were taken to appropriate financial returns from this knowledge. Examples are the patents taken out by scientists and universities and the founding of the first generation of relatively small new biotech-nology firms. This stage of the development cycle is typically charac-terized by a high degree of *uncertainty* — regarding markets, desirable product characteristics, production processes, forms of organization, sources of funding, and, particularly important in the case of biotech-nology, the features of state regulation. In the Schumpeterian sense these individuals were acting as 'entrepreneurs', seizing on the commercial potential of new scientific knowledge (see Kenney, 1986, for further details on the evolution of the new biotechnology firms). In view of the high degree of uncertainty, the prevailing macro-economic conditions may be particularly important during this early stage. For example, it is likely, and somewhat ironic, that the deepening world economic recession of the mid- and late-1970s, together with the relative, and in some cases absolute, decline of some of the older mature industries, created the climate of optimism which greeted the first stock market flotations of equity in the new biotechnology firms.

In some cases biotechnology offered new ways to produce either existing or similar products, or substitutes, for established markets. In these instances, uncertainty related less to the existence and size and more to the ability of biotechnologically produced products to compete efficiently.

An example of an identical or similar product is insulin, which is used to treat diabetics. The gene for insulin was first cloned and expressed in bacteria by Genentech in 1977. Previously, insulin was extracted from the pancreas of pigs and cattle, and about 80% of the world market was controlled by Eli Lilly of the United States and Novo Industri of Denmark.

Two examples of substitutes, one successful the second so far unsuccessful, are starch-based sweeteners and single-cell proteins. In the case of starch-based sweeteners, immobilized enzymes are used as catalysts to transform starch from sources such as corn, potatoes, wheat, or cassava into high-fructose syrup. In many areas, fructose-based sweeteners have competed successfully with sugar and sugar beets. In 1980, for example, Coca-Cola switched half of its sugar purchases to high-fructose corn syrup (HFCS) and 7-Up is now sweetened entirely by HFCS (Ruivenkamp, 1986). The story of single-cell protein (SCP), however, has been less successful. SCP was hailed in the 1970s as an important new industry and received large invest-ments from big firms in sectors such as chemicals and oil. SCP was produced by microorganisms, such as bacteria and yeast; from feed-stock, like North Sea gas, ammonia, and air; and from sugar cane derivatives, such as molasses and bagasse. Used for animal consumption, SCP was seen as a substitute for soya meal. However, despite low prices of oil and oil by-products, SCP has not yet proved to be clearly economically preferable and some of the large industrial SCP projects have been discontinued.

These examples illustrate the extent to which *competition between technologies* influences technological development. As Rosenberg (1976) has shown, this competition can also stimulate change in old technologies. For example, SCP may provide a replacement for soya as an animal feed. On the other hand, by introducing nitrogen fixation systems to nonleguminous plants, biotechnologies may also increase the productivity of soya plants, which is the old competing product.

In other cases biotechnology opened up the possibility of entirely new products and markets. For example, the production of monoclonal antibodies made possible the development of diagnostic techniques in humans, animals, and plants. One instance is *in vivo* diagnosis using injectable radiolabelled antibodies to facilitate tumour imaging. In addition, monoclonal antibodies have potential therapeutic uses (e.g., a way to target attack accurately on a particular kind of cancer).

In these cases the uncertainty relates more to potential markets and desired product characteristics. In the early stages of the development cycle, profitability and competition are often based on product characteristics rather than cost (although, as shown above in the case of soya, when there is competition with preexisting products relative cost can be important). Furthermore, there is a relatively high degree of flexibility and variation in process technology as scaling-up proceeds and the search takes place for new methods to overcome constraints and bottlenecks and to make improvements.

In this respect there are important similarities between biotechnology and other industries whose innovation process over time has been closely studied. The relationship between product innovation, including design and process innovation, has been examined for a number of industries (e.g., Abernathy and Utterback, 1975; Utterback, 1979; Abernathy et al., 1983; and Clark, 1985). These studies show that in the early stages of the development cycle, before the emergence of hierarchically structured dominant design concepts, process technology remains flexible, and competition is based largely on product innovation. Clark (1985) elaborates further on the relationship between the emerging dominant concepts that underlie market demand and the development of dominant design concepts.

During later stages of the development cycle, however, the dominant market concepts and dominant design concepts tend to converge. It is during these later stages that Nelson and Winter (1982) hypothesize that further technical change occurs only within the confines of the prevailing 'technological regime'. Such change may result from alterations in relative costs; from shifts in demand within the limits of the existing dominant market and design concepts; or from 'compulsive sequences' (Rosenberg, 1976), 'technological trajectories' (Nelson and Winter, 1977), or 'technological momenta' (Hughes, 1983), which are relatively impervious to shifts in economic variables. Abernathy and Utterback (1975) and Utterback (1979) argue that during these later stages, process technology becomes relatively rigid; process innovation becomes incremental rather than radical; and considerations of economies of scale tend to dominate as the basis of competition shifts increasingly to cost-competition. During these stages market structure also changes, with oligopolistic markets becoming increasingly prevalent.

The main difference between the industries studied by these authors and biotechnology lies in the relationship between the final product (including its dominant design concepts) and the production process. For products such as automobiles, the relationship is close: production is partly structured by the characteristics and stability of design. In bioprocessing, on the other hand, systems are employed in which complete living cells or their components (such as enzymes) are used to effect desired physical or chemical changes. The output of a bio-processing system (for example, a packed-bed or fluidized-bed reactor) can be used for any number of final products. Accordingly, the relationships among market demand, product design characteristics, and process technology differ from those in industries like automobiles or semiconductors. In this sense, biotechnology is more like process industries, such as chemicals, petrochemicals, or steel, in which the output can be incorporated into a wide range of final products.

Despite these differences, there are important similarities between biotechnology and the innovation cycle studied by the authors cited above. This can be seen clearly by the flexibility and variability of process technologies being employed during the current early stages of the cycle. One example of this flexibility is the current choice between the alternative techniques of *batch processing* and *continuous steady-state processing*. Both processes are used in the conventional chemical industry (this overlap also illustrates how knowledge in the 'new' biotechnology industry draws and elaborates on the inherited stock of knowledge). In batch processing the bioreactor is filled with the medium containing the substrate and the nutrients and the bio-catalyst are added. After the conversion is completed, the bioreactor is emptied and separation and purification take place. In continuous steady-state processing, raw materials are added and spent medium withdrawn continuously from the bioreactor.

Although most biotechnology production currently employs batch-processing methods, they do have a number of drawbacks. These include the costly turnover time between batches; the greater difficulty of product recovery due to the presence of contaminating biocatalyst; and the greater cost resulting from the difficulty of reusing the biocatalyst. In principle these difficulties can be overcome by using continuous processing methods, which have resulted from the development of techniques to immobilize biocatalysts. This allows the catalyst to be reused, which reduces cost and simplifies product recovery. However, continuous processing methods have their own drawbacks. These drawbacks include the difficulty of optimizing reaction conditions in a single-stage process; of maintaining the stability of biocatalysts over long time periods; and of maintaining sterile conditions over time.

Alternative techniques, and therefore flexibility, also exist at the product-recovery stage. The alternatives include ultrafiltration, which employs membranes and other filters to separate and purify the product; electrophoresis, in which separation is achieved using the different ionic charges of the products; and the use of immobilized monoclonal antibodies as purification agents (U.S. Congress, Office of Technology Assessment, 1984).

Careful analysis of the determinants of process innovation in biotechnology is an important area for future research. To what extent is the search (always an uncertain process) for new and improved biotechnology processes a response to economic conditions, such as cost, availability, and demand? And to what extent is it shaped by 'technological trajectories and momenta' that are relatively uninfluenced by economic considerations? Do competitive processes play a role in bringing about a convergence in processing techniques in areas where one or some techniques begin to establish their superiority to other alternatives? Questions such as these are not purely academic and answers to them would improve our understanding of the forces shaping biotechnological innovation.

One tendency noted in virtually all other industries and which has begun to assert itself in biotechnology is the attempt to realize *economies of scale* (i.e., reduction in unit costs as volume increases). Indeed Nelson and Winter (1977) go so far as to refer to the tendency towards increasing economies of scale as a 'natural trajectory'. One example in the field of biotechnology is the preparation of monoclonal antibodies (MAbs). The standard technique, pioneered by Millstein and Kohler, involves injecting a purified antigen into a mouse and then, after the mouse has produced the antibodies, removing its spleen and extracting the antibody-producing B lymphocytes. These cells are then fused with mouse myeloma (tumour cells). These tumour cells result in a fused cell, or hybridoma, with the ability to multiply continuously. The hybridomas are then cloned and screened for their ability to produce the desired antibodies (additional details are given in U.S. Congress, Office of Technology Assessment, 1984).

There are two ways to produce the antibody. When relatively small quantities are desired and purity is not at a premium, a hybridoma clone may be injected into mice where it will grow in the abdominal cavity fluid (ascites) from which the antibodies can be collected. When larger quantities are required, or when greater purity is desired (for example MAbs used for human therapeutic purposes must be free of mouse-derived contaminants), the hybridoma clones may be established in an *in vitro* culture system.

Large-scale cell culture systems may employ techniques of cell immobilization, which allow the MAbs secreted from the cells to be recovered. Damon Biotech Corporation of the United States has patented a microencapsulation technique. In this technique, the hybridoma is surrounded by a porous capsule, which allows nutrients and metabolic wastes to be circulated while retaining the antibodies. The company claims that this technique significantly reduces unit costs in comparison to the ascites method (U.S. Congress, Office of Technology Assessment, 1984).

The importance of economies of scale emerges from data released by Celltech (UK). As can be seen in Figure 2.2, as batch yield increases, the cost of labour per unit of output falls. The cost of materials per unit of output rises, but somewhat less than proportionally at batch yields greater than 100 g. The cost of depreciation per unit of output also rises, but begins to fall slightly after the same yield. Reduced unit costs with increased output thus appears to result primarily from a fall in unit labour costs. This leads the authors to comment that 'The development of small, highly productive fermenters

Figure 2.2   Effects of scale on components of unit cost

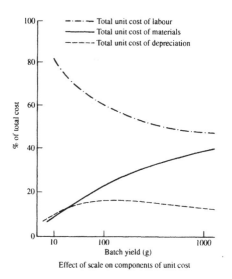

Effect of scale on components of unit cost

is therefore less critical in terms of production costs than has been supposed' (Birch et al., 1985). Conversely, however, larger reactors do not appear to offer significant capital savings.

Whatever cost components are responsible, to the extent that economies of scale are realized and become important, they imply (1) increasing barriers to entry and (2) increasing tendencies towards concentration of capital and oligopoly on the processing side of the biotechnology industry. These implications are important for the future of small firms and Third World countries in biotechnology, and they will be examined in more detail below.

These consequences of scale economies may be accentuated by other advantages that large firms or groups of firms might have in bringing together diverse technologies to improve bioprocessing. One example is the use of computers to analyse data from sensors and other monitoring instruments and to make optimal adjustments in nutrients and other variables during bioprocessing. Computer-aided design of proteins can facilitate the production of new enzymes. Another example is special instrumentation: liquid chromatography is used to identify chemical compounds and flow cytometry is used to measure factors, such as cell size, and to indicate the adequacy of nutrient flows.

Opportunities like these have induced many electronics firms to become increasingly interested in bioprocessing, as can be seen by the recent joint venture signed between Genentech and Hewlett—Packard (U.S. Congress, Office of Technology Assessment, 1984, p. 53). However, as we shall see in more detail later, potential contract problems, such as opportunistic behaviour on the part of a research partner, may be an obstacle in the way of joint research. For example, the electronics company might subsequently sell the equipment to other biotechnology firms, thus undermining its initial research partner's competitive advantage derived from the research. (See Williamson, 1975, for a discussion of the possible costs of transacting across markets.) As an alternative to subcontracting or jointly developing desired equipment, a firm has the option of in-house production. However, the viability of this option will be limited by the firm's existing technological capabilities and by the attendant risks and uncertainties.

When limitations such as these prevent in-house production through vertical integration (the 'hierarchy' approach), and when high transaction costs prohibit market-contracted joint research (the 'market' approach), then alternative forms of organizing the search for new biotechnologies become potentially important. One example of such an alternative is the Japanese group, or *Keiretsu*, in which noncompeting firms are loosely structured around the group's trading company and one or more financial institution. These firms are linked by obligational, rather than arm's-length, market relationships, and these relationships are reinforced by (1) regular meetings between the Presidents and Vice-Presidents of the most important firms in the group; (2) common dependence on credit from the group's financial institutions; and (3) a common relationship with the group's trading company (see Fransman, 1986d, for further details). The large Japanese groups, such as Mitsubishi, Mitsui, and Sumitomo, contain both biotechnology-using firms (in areas such as pharmaceuticals, chemicals, and brewing) as well as electronics and instrumentation firms. As a result of the obligational relations these large groups are well placed to reap the benefits of technological synergies.

Forms of cooperation also exist among firms belonging to different groups. The biotechnology project established by the Japanese Ministry of International Trade and Industry (MITI) will be examined in greater detail below. Other biotechnology projects have been established privately. For example, the Biotechnology Product Research Development Association was established in 1983 to develop chemical products biotechnologically. This association includes both chemical and electronics firms — Kao Soap, Mitsui Petrochemical, Dainippon, Sanyo Chemical, Ajinomoto, Hitachi Electric, and Mitsubishi Electric (Tanaka, 1985, p. 26).

These alternative forms of organization to 'markets' and 'hierarchies' tend to favour large firms. As is made clear in a report on Japanese biotechnological capabilities undertaken under contract from the U.S. Department of Commerce (1985a, b), and published in June 1985, it is from such firms that the United States 'sees the strongest future competition coming'.

> Japan will rapidly become more competitive with the US and Europe [in the field of biotechnology] because much of the commercialisation of biotechnology in Japan is being carried out by large established companies. These companies have extensive experience in necessary process control and the financial backing so necessary for bringing products to market.
>
> (U.S. Department of Commerce, 1985a, p. xviii)

In reporting on a recent visit to the United States, a team from the European Community (EC) pointed to a contradiction in the conventional wisdom there: on the one hand, a large part of the vitality and competitive strength of the U.S. biotechnology industry is argued to be derived from the efforts of relatively small biotechnology firms, while on the other hand the greatest fear of future competition arises not from small new biotechnology firms, but from the established Japanese giants.

Two points emerge from the present discussion. (1) As the development cycle evolves for biotechnology, large firms and concomitant oligopolistic market structures are likely to become more important for the reasons outlined above. This will imply a tendency towards increasing barriers to entry with important implications for small firms in industrialized countries and for the Third World. (2) Understanding the evolution of biotechnological knowledge requires analysis of forms of organization.

2.2.4 Appropriating the Rent from Biotechnological Knowledge

2.2.4.1 Conceptual framework

In capitalist societies, investment for knowledge-creation, like all investment in these societies, is motivated by the promise of expected returns. However, special problems arise under capitalism in the case of investment in knowledge-creation. These arise, as Arrow (1962) has shown, since knowledge has many characteristics of a public good. Once knowledge becomes available it can be used relatively easily (but usually not without cost) by others who did not originally create it. Such unauthorized use reduces the returns to the creator, and brings in question the incentive to create knowledge, for a potential creator may be deterred from making the effort and bearing the cost for fear of 'free-riders' who simply use the knowledge once it becomes available.

To resolve these problems of incentive, a system has evolved in all capitalist societies to protect intellectual property rights. However, state protection is not always necessary to safeguard for the innovator the appropriation of financial returns arising from the innovation. In some cases, the innovator may be able to prevent the knowledge from becoming publicly available by keeping it secret. In other cases the innovator may be able to take advantage of a 'first-mover strategy', which might facilitate development of brand loyalty before competitors move in, and give the firm a head start in 'moving down the learning curve', to the extent that one exists and is a significant determinant of output price and quality.

Despite these three possible ways to ensure that the creator of knowledge is able to appropriate the returns from such knowledge, and that an incentive exists to create knowledge, obstacles frequently remain to adequate appropriation of financial returns by the creator.

For example, competitors are often able to 'patent around' an innovation, using the information about the innovation disclosed as part of the legal requirements to obtain a patent, but ensuring that their own 'innovation' is sufficiently dissimilar to avoid prosecution. Similarly, in some cases it will be difficult to maintain secrecy. This is particularly true in the case of product innovation, since products must be sold and cannot therefore be prevented from being made available to a wider public, although restrictions of various kinds might be imposed. However, it might not always be possible, such as in the case of some chemicals, to 'work backwards' from the product to the underlying knowledge necessary to produce it. Reverse engineering and imitation often have their limitations, are not costless to undertake, and furthermore take time to complete successfully. These limitations may provide a measure of protection to the innovator. Finally, first-mover advantages may be outweighed by second-mover advantages: for example, lower entry costs that arise once a market for the product has been established, and learning from mistakes made by the pioneer.

For these reasons, appropriation of returns from the innovation by the innovator might remain problematic. Following Teece (1986), it is possible to capture these potential difficulties by distinguishing between relatively tight appropriability regimes, in which a firm, through one means or another, is able to limit leakage of its knowledge base or its use by competitors. The converse applies in the case of loose or weak appropriability regimes.

Incentive is only one problem relating to knowledge as a good in capitalist societies. Another problem relates to maximizing the net benefit to society from the use of that knowledge. As Arrow (1962) has shown, the dilemma is that granting incentives to innovators (such as the temporary monopoly conferred by patents) pushes the price of the knowledge above its marginal cost (the addition to total cost of producing one extra unit of that knowledge), and this in turn means that the knowledge will not be purchased and used in a socially optimal way. (Furthermore, the marginal cost of knowledge is usually very low, possibly zero, as a result of the public good nature of knowledge and this increases the problem — an 'idea' once created can be reproduced at little or no cost). To take an example from the field of biotechnology, the benefit to society would be maximized if a successful vaccine for acquired immune deficiency syndrome (AIDS), once developed, were distributed at its marginal cost. (The marginal cost would include not only the extra cost of the knowledge embodied in each additional unit of vaccine, which would probably be zero, but also the cost of materials, labour, depreciation, etc.) However, it is likely that when (and if) an AIDS vaccine is developed, its price will be substantially above the marginal cost as a result of the patents granted. We shall return later in this section to a discussion of the social cost of protecting intellectual property rights in connection with the patenting of new plant varieties.

However, the trade-off between the additional knowledge created on the one hand and the cost to society of the temporary monopoly that results on the other is not as absolute as is often suggested. The reason, as Nelson (1986) notes, is that a good deal of scientific and technical knowledge is created in the public sphere (e.g., in universities and government research institutions), where questions of incentive to invest in creation of knowledge do not arise (even though other problems of incentive do). For Nelson (1986) this is one important reason why the capitalist 'engine' works better than might appear from the trade-off argument. Later in this survey we shall return to the importance of the public sphere and to arguments that its relative significance is decreasing.

Before the returns from knowledge can be appropriated the knowledge itself must first be created. In principle, three alternative approaches, or a combination thereof, are available to firms to create knowledge. (1) Knowledge can be created in-house (the 'hierarchy' alternative). A firm may use existing facilities or extend its boundaries through acquisition or merger. (2) Knowledge may be bought from other firms or institutions (the 'market' alternative). A number of further alternatives are available. The knowledge may be purchased from (a) suppliers (e.g., process plant and equipment suppliers); (b) actual or potential competitors (e.g., through licensing agreements); or (c) universities or government research institutions. (3) Knowledge may be created jointly with other firms or institutions, for example in the case of joint research ventures (the 'mixed-mode' alternative). This third alternative, however, raises the problem of knowledge-leakage.

In general, the more important the knowledge is for the firm's profitability, and the easier it is for the firm to maintain a tight appropriability regime, the more likely it is that the firm will try to rely on in-house knowledge-creating activities. An important constraint, however, will be its existing resources and scientific/technological capabilities.

Possessing the 'core knowledge' underlying a product innovation for which there is adequate market demand is not a sufficient condition for reaping all the rent that accrues from the innovation.[1] This point, which has important implications for biotechnology, will be clarified by an example. For products produced by recombinant DNA techniques, *core knowledge* might involve the ability to clone a gene for a particular protein or enzyme and express it in a host microorganism (e.g., bacteria, yeast, fungi). However, this core knowledge is usually not sufficient to turn the output into a commercially viable product. *Complementary manufacturing knowledge* is required to transform the laboratory processes into a viable manufacturing operation. This transformation involves scale-up, and development of efficient techniques for processing, recovery, and purification, all of which are likely to differ significantly from the laboratory processes from which the core knowledge was initially derived.

Even possessing both the core knowledge and the complementary manufacturing knowledge will not be a sufficient condition for reaping all the rent that accrues from the innovation. Additional *complementary assets* will be required. These include a marketing and distribution network, and, in some cases, possession of brand names and access to the necessary financial resources. A firm that lacks these complementary assets might find that, although it possesses the core knowledge, and even perhaps the complementary manufacturing knowledge, it is forced to relinquish a large proportion of the total rent that accrues from the innovation in return for access to a marketing and distribution network (e.g., by concluding distribution agreements) and to financial resources (e.g., by paying above-average rates of interest). Evidently, the business of reaping rent from innovation involves far more than possessing the core knowledge.

The conceptual framework developed thus far in this section allows us to examine more rigorously (a) the fundamentally different problems confronted by the two main groups of private actors on the biotechnology stage: the large established firms and the new biotechnology firms; (b) the relationship between these two groups; and (c) the relationships of these groups with other institutions, such as universities and government research institutes. In examining these three areas examples will be drawn from the experiences of three firms: Monsanto, one of the largest American chemical companies, which has recently become heavily committed to biotechnology; and Celltech and Genentech, the two most important new biotechnology firms in the United Kingdom and United States, respectively.

2.2.4.2 The case of Monsanto

Monsanto is a large company (the fourth largest chemical company in the United States, behind Du Pont, Dow, and Union Carbide), which has been 'pushed' into biotechnology by declining profits in its traditional areas at least as much as it has been 'pulled' by the expected future prospects of biotechnology.[2] In this respect its entry into biotechnology has differed from that of other firms in areas such as pharmaceuticals, brewing, or other fermentation-based industries where pressure in existing product areas has not been as great. Monsanto's traditional concentration on petroleum-based products, such as bulk chemicals and plastics, led to difficulties when demand for these products began to mature in the early 1970s and when international competition in petrochemicals began to increase. Profitability was further hit by the increase in oil prices in 1979; in 1980 the company's earnings fell by 55% with over $300 million being lost in its traditional areas of activity (*Fortune*, 1984).

In the late 1970s, Monsanto developed a longer-term strategy that would enable it to reduce its dependence on low-return petroleum-based products. A central feature of the strategy involved an increase in activity in the areas of nutritional chemicals and agricultural products and a move into the new area of health care. Biotechnology, particularly genetic engineering, was attractive since it affected all three of these areas. In 1979 Monsanto hired Dr. Howard A. Schneiderman, a biochemist from the University of California, Irvine, who became a senior Vice-President and Chief Scientist in charge of the Corporate Research and Development Division. It was Schneiderman who spearheaded the company's drive into bio-technology and genetic engineering. To facilitate its move into new areas, the company's R&D budget was increased considerably, from 2.6% of sales in 1979 to 5% in 1983 and 7% in 1985 (Monsanto, 1985). In 1985, 57% of R&D expenditure was in the area of life sciences (ibid., p. 30). With 1985 sales of $6,747 million, the R&D budget for 1986 is around $470 million, implying a research budget of about $270 million in the life sciences.

In the area of nutritional chemicals the company moved into new kinds of nonsugar sweeteners. This is not a new product area for Monsanto since it began producing saccharin more than eighty-five years ago. However, in the early 1980s, a new low-calorie sweetener was introduced, and approved by the U.S. Food and Drug Administration in 1981. In 1985 sugar-free soft drinks accounted for about 25% of grocery store soft-drink sales in the United States, with sugar-free brands growing at 11% annually compared to 2% for sugar-based soft drinks.[3] Since then, Monsanto has achieved considerable success with its non-sugar sweeteners in this and other markets.

In the area of agricultural chemicals, Monsanto is using biotechnology to extend the application of existing products as well as introduce new ones. One example is herbicides, where two products dominate the sales and profits of the company's agricultural division. *Lasso* was introduced in 1969 and became very popular with farmers growing maize and soybeans. It selectively destroys weeds without harming the crop. In 1983 *Lasso* captured about 50% of the U.S. herbicide market among maize farmers and about 33% among soybean growers (*Fortune*, 1984). However, the *Lasso* patent expired in 1987 and the company is searching for ways to prevent market loss once competitors enter. The second product, *Roundup*, is a nonselective herbicide that kills both the leaves and roots of anything it is sprayed on. *Roundup* was introduced in 1974 and has captured a large part of the market; it is currently used in about 100 countries. *Roundup* has the environmental advantage that it breaks down without damaging soil. Despite the patent on *Roundup*, Monsanto has faced competitive challenges. Both ICI and BASF Wyandotte Corporation in 1983 began to market herbicides that use different chemicals but have similar effects as *Roundup*. In the same year, Stauffer Chemical applied to the courts for permission to introduce a herbicide with a chemistry similar to that of *Roundup*, but with different active ingredients. Monsanto not only denied the claim that the active ingredients were different 'but also claimed that the formula was leaked to outsiders by someone at the Environmental Protection Agency when the company was trying to get the product cleared in 1982' *(Fortune*, 1984). These examples provide a vivid account of the dangers companies face in their attempt to reap the rent from their knowledge base.

Biotechnology offers Monsanto the potential to develop an agricultural package that benefits from both marketing and technological synergies. For example, herbicide-resistant seeds could be developed from genetically engineered plants, and sold together with a herbicide, such as *Roundup*. Some progress has already been made in research on herbicide resistance. Calgene in California has developed *Roundup-resistant* tobacco (Monsanto Chemical Corporation, personal interview, July 1986). This resistance has not yet been achieved in other crops, such as maize, wheat, and soybeans. An agricultural package might also include seeds for plants engineered to have new characteristics. 'Longer term, the Monsanto goal is to use new technology in the seed industry. This might include plants that produce more protein, supply their own fertilizer, grow in dry or cold conditions or protect themselves against pests. Work also continues on developing microbes that produce natural pesticides for protecting plants' (Monsanto, *Annual Report*, 1985, p. 9).

To internalize the potential externalities to be derived from these synergies, chemical companies like Monsanto have extended their knowledge base and their distribution capabilities by purchasing seed companies. In 1982 Monsanto acquired the wheat research programme and research facilities of De Kalb Ag Research and used it to form Hybritech Seed International. In 1983, this subsidiary acquired the soybean research programme and facilities from Jacob Hartz Seed (*Chemical and Engineering News*, 1984, p. 8). These two divisions are involved primarily in the development of proprietary varieties of high-performing hybrids of wheat and soybeans. In the future, however, their activities and profitability may benefit from research on genetic engineering being undertaken in the company's research laboratories.

Biotechnology has also facilitated the introduction of entirely new products by Monsanto. One example is bovine somatotropin, a growth hormone that substantially increases milk production in cows. Commercial approval has not yet been granted by the authorities but Monsanto expects to begin marketing the hormone and anticipates a worldwide market of more than $1 billion (Monsanto, 1985, p. 20). We will examine below a number of pioneering studies that analyse the likely economic effects of the introduction of bovine growth hormones. Although in 1985 agricultural products accounted for 17% of Monsanto's sales, compared to 60% for chemicals, fibres, and plastics, the development of agricultural products using biotechnological methods is likely to increase its proportional contribution.

The third area that Monsanto intends to develop is pharmaceuticals. This is a new area for the company, and accounted for only 4% of sales in 1985. To expand its knowledge base in this area, Monsanto in 1984 acquired Continental Pharma, a privately owned research-oriented Belgian pharmaceutical firm, which produced a blood circulation enhancer being studied for the treatment of senility (*Chemical and Engineering News*, 1984, p. 8). Monsanto's biotechnology and distribution capabilities were further strengthened in 1985 with the acquisition of G.D. Searle & Co., a pharmaceutical company, for $2,754 million. In its 1985 *Annual Report*, Monsanto explained the latter acquisition:

> G.D. Searle and Co. significantly expands and complements Monsanto's research capabilities in biotechnology and human health care, adding both experienced professionals and facilities to Monsanto's existing research organization. In addition, Searle provides Monsanto with established organizations skilled at developing and marketing products that flow from the research program. The combination of [Monsanto's] strengths in basic and applied research in molecular biology and biotechnology, Washington University's powerful biomedical discovery capabilities and Searle's strengths

in product development and marketing will further Monsanto's goal of becoming a leading supplier in the pharmaceutical industry.

(Monsanto, 1985, p. 30)

Monsanto's university links The importance of biotechnology for Monsanto's long-run strategy is clear from the above. The company has followed a number of paths in its attempt to build its biotechnology-related capabilities. To begin with, Monsanto has established links with universities. Most important of these has been a link with the School of Medicine at Washington University in St. Louis. Monsanto provided the university with $23.5 million over five years in return for cooperative research projects in biotechnology (Daly, 1985, p. 27). One benefit the company has received from this relationship is Searle's development of atrial peptides, which control high blood pressure; these compounds were originally isolated and identified by Professor Philip Needleman, Head of the Pharmacology Department at the University. Monsanto has signed research agreements with a number of other universities, including Harvard, Oxford, and Rockefeller Universities. The company's university links were the subject of a congressional enquiry, headed by then congressman Al Gore, which concluded that the relationship was not detrimental to the university system.[4]

Unlike many other industry–university links, the Monsanto–Washington University link is intended to facilitate cooperative work between company and university scientists working collaboratively on research projects. An eight-member advisory committee divided equally between Monsanto researchers and Washington University faculty makes the final decision regarding research funding. The agreement stipulates that 30% of the research will be basic research, while 70% will be research directly applicable to human disease. The United States Congress, Office of Technology Assessment Report on Biotechnology (1984) summarized the provisions regarding intellectual property rights: 'Washington University faculty members will be at liberty to publish results of any research done under the Monsanto funding. Monsanto will exercise the right of prior review of draft materials, because they may contain potentially patentable technical developments. If they *do*, Monsanto can request a short delay of submission for publication or other public disclosure in order to begin the patent process' (p. 574). Patent rights will be retained by Washington University but Monsanto will have exclusive rights to licences. If Monsanto chooses not to license a patent then the university will be free to issue the licence to others. Royalties will go to Washington University and not to the individual researchers, but will normally go to their laboratory.

These details on Monsanto support some of the conclusions reached by Nelson (1986) in his discussion of the survey by Levin et al. (1984) on R&D appropriability and technological opportunity undertaken. The survey of U.S. Corporations yielded 650 replies from respondents in 130 different businesses. Summarizing the importance to different industries of a link with university research Nelson (1986) notes that

> those industries whose technologies rest on the basic and applied biological sciences seem to be closely tied to the universities for research as well as training. The same seems true for computer science.
>
> (p. 36)

Nelson argues that presently in these areas,

> The driving force is public new scientific knowledge, and the proprietary part of the system seems largely involved in exploiting this. The particular new applications are proprietary. The basic generic knowledge which is moving the system is public.
>
> (p. 37)

However,

> If the pace of advance of academic science slows down, or becomes less relevant to technical advance, the technology begins to stabilise, in broad form, and the particular special knowledge and R&D capabilities of corporate R&D becomes a longer and more independent part of the story. Technical change may still be rapid, but along routes where university research is not needed to clear the way. The industry may remain dependent on academia for training, but the industrial and university systems part.
>
> (p. 37)

Several comments may be made on the importance of industry-university links in biotechnology. First, to the extent that biotechnology remains driven by basic research, as it largely is now, universities will continue to play a significant role and it will be necessary for firms to retain a link with the science base in the universities. However, to the extent that biotechnology becomes increasingly driven by applied technology (particularly in technologies related to large-scale processing) — a tendency that is already emerging, as we saw above — universities are likely to become less important in terms of direct contact. Large firms are better adapted than universities to undertake large-scale processing and the attendant applied research. At present it is not possible to foresee which of these tendencies will dominate over the next fifteen to twenty years.

The second comment is that there is a danger that industry—university links, by their very nature, will have the effect of undermining, or at least diminishing, the basic science base which provides their *raison d'être*. This fear is expressed strongly in the main report commissioned by the Organization for Economic Cooperation and Development (OECD) on biotechnology (Bull et al., 1982), which was produced by a team of scientists working in this field. Regarding industry—university links they note that

Some people have been concerned by a number of recent events — excessive secrecy, withholding publication of findings, refusal to make available strains and vectors relating to published work and increased motivation towards financial gain have been noted amongst academics — and it is argued that fundamental values and important freedoms of the academic life are at risk.

(p. 60)

The report concludes by warning 'of the danger that excessive business orientation of university researchers could result in a reduction of fundamental research, or that certain types of industry—university links could lead to a loss of knowledge due to trade secrecy' (p. 12). Interestingly, this concern is not voiced strongly in the main American report on biotechnology (U.S. Congress, Office of Technology Assessment, 1984, Chapter 17, which deals with university—industry relationships) — a report which is concerned primarily with the international competitiveness of American firms in this area.

Monsanto's links with new biotechnology firms If one leg of the Monsanto strategy for structural transformation has been to develop links with the scientific base in universities, another, as we have already seen, has been to extend its boundaries through acquisition. The latter has enabled the company to internalize potential externalities and benefit from synergies in technology and marketing. A third leg of the strategy to build a knowledge base in biotechnology has been to create research ties with some new biotechnology firms. This has involved investment in emerging firms such as Genentech, Genex, Biogen, and Collagen (*Chemical and Engineering News*, 1984).

From Monsanto's point of view, although the new biotechnology firms are potential competitors, at least in some market segments, they are also possible sources of access to biotechnological knowledge. Failing access, Monsanto gains, by investing in the new biotechnology firms, the potential to share in profits that may result from the innovations these firms make.

From the point of view of the new biotechnology firms, the strategic problems appear in a very different light. This will be discussed in the following section with the aid of the conceptual framework developed earlier and with particular reference to two important new biotechnology firms: Genentech and Celltech.[5]

2.2.4.3 New biotechnology firms: Genentech and Celltech

Upon entering the field of biotechnology, the greatest strength of the new biotechnology firms lay in their core knowledge base. For example, Genentech, which was the most important new biotechnology firm in the United States, was founded in 1976 jointly by an industrialist, Robert Swanson, and a biologist, Herbert Boyer. Boyer, together with Cohen, had earlier developed the basic technique employed in recombinant DNA. Genentech may therefore be regarded as a direct spin-off from university-based research. Celltech was set up in 1980 by the British Technology Group, which was controlled by the British Government, with the expressed aim of commercializing knowledge generated within the public research domain. This followed the Millstein debacle, discussed above, in which the cell fusion technique, developed by Millstein and Kohler at the Medical Research

Council laboratories at Cambridge University, failed to be patented. As with Genentech, Celltech's core knowledge base derived directly from its links with the public research system and is one of its principal sources of strength.

With a strong core knowledge base, one of the first problems confronted by new biotechnology firms is development of complementary manufacturing knowledge. A further problem is obtaining access to complementary assets, particularly distribution and marketing networks, and in some cases access to brand-names. In principle, a new biotechnology firm can acquire the required knowledge and assets using one, or a combination, of the three alternatives discussed on page 69: (2) the 'market' alternative, whereby a contractual agreement is reached to provide the assets; (1) the 'hierarchy' alternative, that is to develop the assets and knowledge in-house, possibly by expanding employment and through acquisitions and mergers; and (3) the 'mixed-mode' alternative, where joint ventures are set up with other firms.

In practice the new biotechnology firms have pursued all three alternatives. For example, Genentech initially concluded marketing agreements with other large corporations. These included an agreement with Eli Lilly to market human insulin produced by recombinant DNA techniques. Similarly, the company established a marketing agreement with the Swedish company KabiVitrum, which gave the latter worldwide marketing rights (except in the United States) for Genentech's human growth hormone. Genentech also has marketing agreements with Kyowa Hakko and Mitsubishi Chemical to sell tissue plasminogen actinogen activator and human serum albumin in Japan and other East Asian countries. In similar fashion, Celltech formed a 50:50 joint venture with The Boots Company called Boots—Celltech Diagnostics. Celltech also had a marketing arrangement with Sumitomo Corporation and with Sankyo, the second largest Japanese pharmaceuticals group (Celltech, 1985). Agreements have been signed to give the new biotechnology firms access to the manufacturing facilities of the larger firms. For example, Genentech's agreement with Eli Lilly provides for the latter to manufacture human insulin and its agreement with Corning Glass Works allows that company to manufacture industrial enzymes.

In-house development of complementary manufacturing knowledge (the 'hierarchy' alternative) has also in some cases been important. Celltech has developed large-scale fermentation facilities (currently a 1,000-litre fermenter specially designed to produce monoclonal antibodies and other high-value proteins, with future plans for a fermenter with a 10,000-litre capacity). The company claims that this is 'the world's largest monoclonal antibody fermenter' (Celltech, 1985, p. 4).

There has also been resort to the 'mixed-mode' alternative. Examples are Genentech's joint ventures with Hewlett–Packard to develop instrumentation for biotechnology and with Travenol Laboratories to develop human clinical diagnostic products (Daly, 1985, pp. 70-75). [See also Pisano et al. (1989) for a detailed and illuminating discussion of cooperative ventures in biotechnology and Fransman et al. (forthcoming) for mixed mode agreements reached by Japanese Companies.]

Despite the options open to new biotechnology firms in their bid to survive and grow, and the current competitive strength of the core knowledge that underlies their product innovation, it is possible that their relative significance will decline over time. (It should also be recalled that the phenomenon of new biotechnology firms is largely American and to a lesser extent British; most European countries and Japan are dominated solely by large firms.) One possibility is that their competitive strength will be undermined if process technology becomes an increasingly important determinant of profitability. Large companies, and those which are members of broader groupings, are likely to be better adapted to the development of bioprocess technology, as was discussed earlier. If this does happen then the same forces which contribute to the divergence between firm and university biotechnology research may also lead to the demise of many new biotechnology firms. However, even if product innovations based on basic research continue to be important determinants of corporate profitability, the attraction of new biotechnology firms may result in increasing rates of take-over. Recent acquisitions, such as that of Hybritech by Eli Lilly and Genetic Systems by Bristol—Myers, may become more common in the future (see Chesnais, 1986, pp. 22-25). In this connection it is sobering to remember that Celltech's total 1985 sales of around £6 million compared with Monsanto's *research* budget of £313 million for the same year, a 52-fold difference.

Dramatic evidence has recently emerged to support the proposition developed here that new biotechnology firms are likely to decrease in significance in the future. In 1990, Genentech decided to cede 60% of its shares to the large Swiss company, Hoffman—La Roche, for a price of $2.1 billion. This signalled Genentech's failure to develop its own distribution and marketing 'complementary assets', and thus its failure to become a large, independent, biotechnology-based company. In 1988 Genentech was by far the largest of the top ten new biotechnology firms. In that year, Genentech had total revenues of $334 million, net income of $21 million, R&D expenditures of $133 million, and employment of 1,700. The second-largest firm was Biosystems, which had total revenues of $132 million, net income of $17 million, R&D expenditures of $16 million, and employment of 1,000.[6]

2.2.4.4 Social welfare effects: the case of patents

For the reasons mentioned earlier, it is widely accepted in capitalist societies that legal protection is necessary to safeguard incentives for invention and innovation. Recently a new slant has been given to the issue of the protection of intellectual property rights. This is evident in the conclusion by the Office of Technology Assessment of the U.S. Congress (1984) that

> The U.S. intellectual property system appears to offer the best protection for biotechnology of any system in the world, thus providing the United States with a competitive advantage with regard to this factor. This advantage results from the fact that the system provides the widest choice of options for protecting biotechnological inventions, the broadest scope of coverage, and some of the best procedural safeguards.

> (p. 17)

Together with university—industry relationships and health, safety, and environmental regulations intellectual property law was judged to be of 'moderate importance' as a determinant of U.S. international competitiveness in biotechnology. On the other hand, financing and tax incentives for firms, government funding of basic and applied research, and personnel availability and training were seen to be the 'most important' determinants (U.S. Congress, Office of Technology Assessment, 1984).

However, advances in the biological sciences have presented fundamental problems for the protection of intellectual property rights. As the main OECD publication on patent protection has put it (Beier et al., 1985),

> In the past the patent system rested safely on a semantically clear [and] objectively defensible separation between (patentable) 'invention' and (non-patentable) 'discovery'. The recent development of biotechnology where some scientific discoveries could be turned into commercial products almost immediately has blurred this separation. This may have far-reaching legal and practical consequences.
>
> (pp. 88-89)

The last sixteen years has seen some important changes in the area of intellectual property rights relating to the biological sciences. [For an excellent survey see Crespi (1985)]. For example, in the United States until 1970 the property rights to new varieties of open pollinated crops were not appropriable by those who developed the varieties. This changed in 1970 with the introduction of the Plant Variety Protection Act (PVPA), which provided patent-like protection for open pollinated crops. In 1972 an Indian scientist working for General Electric in the United States applied for a patent for a newly created *Pseudomonas* bacterium (not made with recombinant DNA) which had the ability to break down the major components of oil. The case [Diamond v. Chakrabarty (1980)] was referred to the Supreme Court by the U.S. Patent and Trademark Office and became seen as a test case of whether life forms could be patented (Yoxen, 1983, p. 98). In this celebrated case, the U.S. Supreme Court ruled to allow the patent. The Court held that 'The claim was not to a hitherto unknown natural phenomenon but to a non-naturally occurring manufacture or composition of matter, a product of human ingenuity having a distinctive known character and use' (Beier et al., 1985, p. 104). Despite the Chakrabarty case, the U.S. Patent and Trademark Office (PTO) continued to deny patent protection on seeds until September 1985 when an internal PTO appeal in *Ex parte Hibberd* ruled that it is permissible to patent any seed meeting the legal requirements (Lesser, 1986, p. 2).

Most studies on patents and biotechnology have been concerned primarily with (1) the extent to which patent legislation adequately safeguards incentives; (2) international differences in legislative provisions; and (3) the need for international harmonization of standards. In general, therefore, only the social benefit side of the equation has been examined, and that only insofar as the incentive to invent and innovate is concerned. Social costs have been largely ignored.

Two exceptions are work done by Butler and Marion (1985) and by Buttel, Cowan, Kenney, and Kloppenburg (Buttel, 1986a,b; Buttel and Kenney, 1985; Buttel et al., 1985a,b; Cowan, 1986; Kenney, 1986; Kloppenburg, 1988). After hearings on amendments to PVPA in 1980, the Agriculture Committee of the U.S. Senate requested the U.S. Department of Agriculture to analyse the economic impacts of PVPA. The study by Butler and Marion (1985) was a response to this request and their main conclusions will be reviewed briefly here.

With regard to incentives, Butler and Marion concluded that while 'PVPA has stimulated the development of new varieties of soybeans and wheat', there was 'little evidence that PVPA has affected R&D input or output for other open pollinated crops'. Although there was 'little evidence that ... PVPA has significantly impacted on public plant breeding' they went on to note that 'in recent years, large seed companies have encouraged Agricultural Experimentation Stations to reduce their involvement in cultivar development and concentrate on "germ plasm enhancement" and basic research'. The reason for this, according to Buttel et al. (1985a), is the desire of seed companies (most of which are controlled by large agrochemical companies) to (1) reduce competition from the public sector and (2) encourage development in the public sector of generic applied and basic research that will enhance the international competitiveness of these companies. Significantly, while Butler and Marion showed that by '1982 nearly 50% of the PVPA certificates issued were held by 14 conglomerates', they went on to argue that there 'is little evidence that current market shares of privately protected varieties or of leading companies seriously hamper competitive forces in the open pollinated seed markets'. The reason for this conclusion was that 'public varieties still dominate most seed species and are generally produced and sold by a large number of seed companies'. Furthermore, 'entry barriers into plant breeding are moderate for most seed species. Entry into the conditioning and distribution of seeds is still relatively easy because of access to non-protected and public varieties'.

With regard to the effect of PVPA on prices, Butler and Marion concluded that 'Prices for seed have risen in the past decade' and that 'PVPA contributed to this increase'. Nevertheless, they concluded that 'price increases have not been unreasonable or unjustifiable' since there are 'two important checks in many species on the pricing of privately protected varieties'. These 'checks' are, first, the existence of 'farmer saved seed' and secondly 'the availability of publicly developed varieties which tend to be competitively priced'. They went on to point out that the 'pricing discretion of seed companies is greatest for those species (e.g. alfalfa) in which neither of these constraints are [*sic*] important'.

PVPA has also influenced industry—university relations, particularly the exchange of both scientific information and plant breeding materials. 'PVPA has probably reduced the flow from companies to universities and has increased the flow in the opposite direction as private plant breeders have aggressively searched for information and germ plasm developed in the public sector'.

From their survey Butler and Marion conclude that the public plant breeders have a particularly important role to play. 'Public varieties contribute to genetic improvements and also provide an important check on the prices of privately protected varieties'. If public institutions discontinue their breeding activities in some species,

> Firms without plant breeding programs may be foreclosed from the market, the exchange of scientific information and breeding material is likely to be substantially reduced, genetic diversity would be expected to decline, the proportion of sales accounted for by the leading firms in each species would significantly increase, and entry barriers into the breeding and marketing of many seed species would likely increase.

In weighing up the social costs and benefits, the authors conclude that while there 'is no evidence that PVPA has triggered massive investments in R&D', the main intended social benefit, 'there is little evidence of substantial public costs from PVPA. Increases in prices, market concentration and advertising, and declines in information exchange and public plant breeding — the feared costs of PVPA — have either been nil or modest in nature'. Accordingly they conclude that 'at the present time' the Act 'has resulted in modest private and public benefits at modest public and private costs'. Nevertheless, while this conclusion is optimistic regarding the effects of PVPA, the authors stress that the 'impact of PVPA will depend on the long-run balance between public and private plant breeding' and note that 'currently this is shifting toward the private sector'. Furthermore, they point out that the 'growth of biotechnology — and particularly genetic engineering — will also influence the future organization of plant breeding, although it is not entirely clear in what ways' (pp. 1-3).

It is precisely the caveat contained in these conclusions that constitutes the point of departure for Buttel, Cowan, Kenney, and Kloppenburg (as cited above). They argue that

1. The shift in plant breeding towards the private sector, a tendency noted by Butler and Marion, is well under way and is significantly increasing the social cost side of the social cost–benefit equation.
2. In the future, biotechnology as applied to agriculture, together with the right to patent new plant varieties and associated microorganisms that might increase the productivity of plants, will accentuate the social costs.
3. Large private firms that will control an increasingly large proportion of applied research funds are likely to push technical change in this area in a direction that will enable them to maximize profits on their seed–chemical packages rather than maximize social benefits. For example, while biotechnology-related innovations like pest-resistance and nitrogen-fixation might have desirable social effects as well as increasing the sales and associated profits of seeds, they will reduce the sales of agrochemicals such as pesticides and fertilizers and are therefore likely to be resisted by the large agrochemical companies.

It remains to be seen how much control large companies will have over the trajectory of technical change in this area. Their control over biotechnologies combined with the regulatory regime for intellectual property rights will put them collectively in a strong position. Nevertheless, the public sector worldwide will continue to play an important role and potential competition from other international companies in areas like pest-resistance should not be underestimated. Clearly though there is a need for rigorous research which tracks and analyses events such as these as they unfold. As we shall see in Sections 2.3 and 2.4, the impacts of biotechnology on plant breeding will be significant in the future and it is important to anticipate, as much as possible, the likely consequences.

2.2.5 The Role of Government

There has been a good deal of interest in the role of public policy in biotechnology. In some cases, such as the report by the U.S. Congress, Office of Technology Assessment (1984), this has resulted from a concern with issues of international competitiveness.

There are a number of good descriptive accounts of biotechnology policy in the United States, Japan, and Western Europe (for example, see U.S. Congress, Office of Technology Assessment, 1984; Sharp, 1985a,b, 1986; Davies, 1986; U.S. Department of Commerce 1985a,b; Lewis, 1984; Anderson, 1984; Tanaka, 1985; Fransman et al., forthcoming).

One of the most interesting points to emerge from this literature is the substantially different pattern of government intervention that exists in the biotechnology field in the different countries studied. For example, in the United States there is strong support for basic research and relatively little for applied generic research and applied research. [It has been noted that 'The United States, both in absolute dollar amounts and in relative terms, has the largest commitment to basic research in the biological sciences. ... On the other hand, the U.S. Government's commitment to generic applied research (defined as research which bridges the gap between basic science done mostly in universities and applied, proprietary science done in industry) in biotechnology is relatively small' (U.S. Congress, Office of

Technology Assessment, 1984). The report goes on to observe that in 'fiscal year 1983, the Federal Government spent $511 million on basic biotechnology research compared to $6.4 million on generic applied research in biotechnology'. On the other hand, 'The governments of Japan, the Federal Republic of Germany, and the United Kingdom fund a significant amount of generic applied science in biotechnology' (p. 14)]. In the United States there is little attempt to direct government research funding into areas selected for their strategic and competitive value. Furthermore, little or no attempt is made by government to influence interfirm interactions in the area of biotechnology.

The pattern of government policy in biotechnology is fundamentally different in Japan, where the biotechnology system is characterized by a number of distinctive features, including (1) the relative absence of national new biotechnology firms; (2) the weakness of Japanese university research in frontier basic research in the life sciences relative to universities in other advanced Western countries; and (3) the evolution of government-initiated, innovative forms of organization for the acquisition, assimilation, generation, and diffusion of new generic biotechnologies. These organizational innovations include the biotechnology component of the Next Generation Basic Technologies Development Programme initiated by the Ministry of International Trade and Industry in 1981 and the Protein Engineering Research Institute (PERI) supported by the Japan Key Technologies Center, under the control of MITI and the Ministry of Post and Telecommunications (MPT). These features of the Japanese system are analysed in Fransman et al. (forthcoming).

The United Kingdom has displayed a pattern of government intervention somewhat intermediate between those of the United States and Japan. Although there is no 'grand strategy' for biotechnology in Britain, there are nonetheless some similarities with the Japanese case. In 1980, for example, a year before the MITI biotechnology programme was launched, the Spinks report (ACARD, 1980) proposed a strong government-led programme in biotechnology. Although the response was not as strong as might have been envisaged in the report, attempts were nonetheless made by various government agencies to encourage generic applied and applied research through interfirm collaboration and cooperation with universities. The Department of Trade and Industry, which set up a specialist biotechnology unit in the Department, has established a number of research 'clubs' which bring firms together for collaborative research. [In fact, it was after these clubs, first introduced into Britain at the end of the First World War, that MITI modelled its research associations — see Sigurdson (1986), p. 6]. Similarly, the Science and Engineering Research Council, which finances basic research, has identified a number of 'strategic' areas in which to concentrate research and has set up a number of collaborative research programmes involving firms and universities (Dunnill and Rudd, 1984). Like the United States, Great Britain has had an extremely strong base in basic research, at least until recently when the science budget has been adversely affected by reductions in government expenditures (see Sharp, 1985b).

It is one thing to *describe* different patterns of government intervention such as these, but quite another to *explain* them. All of the governments whose policies in biotechnology have been reviewed in the literature have confronted the same set of internationally evolving biotechnologies with different institutions, strengths, and weaknesses. Why have their policies and strategies in biotechnology differed to the extent that they have? Furthermore, how is the effectiveness of the different policies of different governments to be evaluated? Finally, how should governments go about the task of making policy in the biotechnology field? In posing fundamental questions like these, it becomes clear that existing studies of biotechnology policy have barely begun to scratch the surface.

Perhaps the major conclusion to emerge is that we do not yet adequately understand the determinants of the policies of different governments in the field of biotechnology. Accordingly, for example, we are not yet able to explain why the biotechnology policies of the United States, Japan, and the United Kingdom, discussed at the beginning of this section, differ in the ways that they do. In view of our current lack of understanding in this area it may be suggested that a priority for future research should be to examine why governments have intervened in the ways that they have in the biotechnology field. With an understanding of the political influences and constraints it will then be possible to ask how governments might attempt to construct better, more effective, biotechnology policies. Cross-country comparisons should be of great help in highlighting national differences and helping to identify determinants of policy.

2.3 ECONOMIC EFFECTS OF BIOTECHNOLOGY

2.3.1 Introduction

If, as is often done in the literature, a distinction is drawn between old and new biotechnology, the latter involving the application of genetic engineering techniques, then it is clear that the effects of new biotechnology to date are only just beginning to be realized. For example, many of the new biotechnology firms have not yet begun to make profits. If there is to be a biorevolution, then the equivalent of the storming of the Winter Palace remains some way off.

However, biotechnology has already begun to have some important effects. This is seen, for instance, in areas related to *medical sciences*. One example is diagnostic kits made with monoclonal antibodies, which are already being sold commercially. Bioscot is marketing a diagnostic kit that allows fish farmers to detect a dangerous fish virus that can rapidly kill the entire stock of fish, and is working on a similar kit, using the same technology, that will facilitate the identification of a potato virus. In the therapeutic area, where monoclonal antibodies can be used for tumour imaging and treatment, the potential has not yet begun to be realized.

Genetically engineered products are also beginning to have an impact in the area of animal and human vaccines. In July 1986, the U.S. Food and Drug Administration approved the first genetically engineered vaccine for human use: a hepatitis B vaccine. The conventionally produced vaccine for hepatitis B was introduced in 1982; it is made by harvesting the excess of a hepatitis B viral surface protein from the blood plasma of people infected by the virus. Although there is no evidence that the conventional vaccine may be contaminated by hepatitis itself or by AIDS, some are reluctant to use blood-derived products. This was one factor that motivated the pharmaceutical company Merck, Sharpe and Dohme (which also produces the conventional hepatitis B vaccine) to develop a genetically engineered version in search of an estimated market of $300 million. The genetically engineered vaccine is produced by inserting a gene from the hepatitis B virus into yeast cells, causing the latter to produce the viral surface protein, which triggers immunity to the virus when incorporated into a vaccine. This method avoids the use of human blood (*New York Times*, 24 July, 1986). Genetic engineering is also being used widely to produce certain proteins (for example, insulin, interferon, and some enzymes), with important industrial implications in some instances.

In the field of *agriculture and food processing*, where biotechnology will possibly have its greatest effects, the overall impact is still limited. For example, bovine growth hormones, to be examined in more detail below, have not yet been licensed for use in the United States, though approval is anticipated in the next two or three years. Moreover, they have been temporarily banned in Europe for environmental/health reasons. Porcine and chicken growth hormones are even further from commercial applications. The fruits of new biotechnology applied to plants remain distant, since plants are far more complex organisms than the bacteria, viruses, yeasts, and fungi on which most work to date in biotechnology has been done. For instance, nitrogen-fixation in nonleguminous crops, such as rice, wheat, and maize, remains a distant prospect, although genes from other plants and even from bacteria have been successfully introduced into various plants. Nevertheless, new biotechnology and related developments are already having a significant impact by improving efficiency and increasing the substitutability of various agricultural inputs. Examples include corn-based fructose sweeteners, which substitute for sugar cane and sugar beet (Ruivenkamp, 1986), and the cloning of palm plants in Malaysia to increase the efficiency of palm as a source of vegetable oil (Elkington, 1984; Bijman et al., 1986).

Old biotechnology is having an impact in *minerals* production. About 10% of the copper in the United States is being produced by bacterial mineral leaching; similar techniques are being used and developed further in the Andean Pact countries in Latin America. New biotechnology may be of use in improving the efficiency of the bacteria (Warhurst, 1985). Although bioprocessing is technically feasible as a substitute production method in the area of *bulk chemicals and energy*, it remains on the whole uneconomic under prevailing relative prices (particularly oil) and the existing state of bioprocess technology. *Single-cell proteins* are a further area where great potential was foreseen as a way of producing sustenance for both humans and animals, and where significant investment was undertaken by large corporations, such as ICI. But a combination of relative prices and technical factors has tended to rule out rapid expansion in this area as well in the near future. [For very useful surveys of recent developments in these and other areas see Sasson (1988) and Walgate (1990).]

In terms of actual achievement, as these examples illustrate, it is fair to conclude that at the present time the picture remains mixed. Not only are new biotechnologies being introduced in limited areas, but their rate of diffusion, upon which economic impact ultimately depends, is still very low. While there certainly are rumblings of change, by and large the forces of production of the old regime remain relatively firmly intact. The revolution may come. But most producers who are still, by choice or circumstance, locked into old technologies, or who refuse to be shaken by rumours of coming winds of technical change, are not yet seriously threatened.

In assessing the likely future impact of biotechnology, it is worth bearing two factors in mind, each having somewhat contradictory implications. The first is that there are many powerful groups in our society with a vested interest in highlighting, if not exaggerating, the potential future impact of biotechnology. Since for the most part the technologies and their associated products and processes have not yet been tested in the market place, the context is conducive to exaggeration. These groups include new biotechnology firms who must satisfy shareholders on the basis of their future prospects rather than their current financial performance; old companies that have moved into the biological area under pressure of declining profits in existing markets and who must similarly satisfy financial backers; consultants who have moved into biotechnology and are selling their wares; and university scientists who either were in, or have moved into, this field and who seek at least an increase in their research grants, or perhaps a share in the financial rewards that are to be made in an area of rising demand. All have invested their capital, financial or human, in biotechnology. Together these groups are capable of producing the same kind of 'hi-tech hype' in the field of biotechnology that has been a feature of other areas. An example of the latter is factory automation, where the much-heralded paperless factory of the future still performs much better on paper than on the ground [see, for example, Voss (1984) on the substantial problems of implementation that have been encountered in factory automation].

This is not to say, however, that the bio-optimists will be denied their revolution, but rather only to stress that they often have a vested interest in the predictions they make. This is where the second factor — uncertainty — enters. As with all nonincremental technical change, uncertainty is significant. In the face of such uncertainty, expectations will differ regarding what the future will bring, and therefore where investment chips should be placed. One way to assess future prospects of biotechnology is to attempt to measure these expectations, directly or indirectly. In doing this the firms, scientists, and consultants mentioned in the preceding paragraph may be viewed in a different light, as investors who could be placing their chips on alternative spots. Since they are placing their capital (financial or human) where their mouths are, it must be accepted that they are firm in their convictions that, like microelectronics and information technology, biotechnology will generate new products and processes, and with them opportunities for profit. For example, the expectations underlying Monsanto's investment of around $2.7 billion over the next ten years in *research* in the life sciences must be taken seriously. So must the decision of MITI in Japan to select biotechnology as one of the 'next generation basic technologies'.

Accordingly, it may be concluded that, while there are reasons to expect a degree of 'unwarranted hype', a number of important groups are strongly of the view that biotechnology — like microelectronics and information technology — will have a broad, nonincremental, impact. However, as with previous technological revolutions, it is also likely that the main effects will be some time in coming.

In view of the infancy of new biotechnologies it is hardly surprising that very few rigorous studies exist of the economic impact of biotechnology. When this survey was initially undertaken I was able to find only three that go beyond rather vague indications of the likely direction of economic effects, and attempt further quantification. These are considered, along with some critical comments, in the next section.

2.3.2 A Survey of Some Literature

2.3.2.1 *Technology, Public Policy, and the Changing Structure of American Agriculture*
(U.S. Congress, Office of Technology Assessment, 1986)
Aim This report examines the combined impact of biotechnology and information technology on U.S. agriculture.

Background This report was written within the context of a growing crisis in American agriculture. During the 1980s, the financial position of many U.S. farmers deteriorated seriously as a result of a long period of farm surpluses. According to the report, the 'decline in agricultural exports is largely responsible for this situation'. In turn the poor performance of U.S. agriculture is related causally to:

1. A weak world economy;
2. The strong value of the dollar (the report was published in March, 1986);
3. The enhanced competitiveness of other countries;
4. An increase in trade agreements; and
5. Price support levels that permit other countries to undersell U.S. agricultural products.

The 'lower costs of production in other countries' are seen by the report as 'the long-term primary factor in the decline of [U.S.] competitiveness'. In the case of wheat, maize, rice, soybeans, and cotton, at least one foreign country has been producing at or below the average U.S. cost since 1981. A major conclusion of the report is that 'Future exports will depend on the ability of American farmers to use new technology', hence the interest in the impact of biotechnology and information technology in U.S. agriculture.

A second background factor is the long-term structural change that has been taking place in U.S. agriculture, antedating biotechnology and information technology. For example, between 1969 and 1982 the number of small farms declined by 39% while the number of very large farms increased by 100%. The report expressed concern with the impact of new technologies on the concentration of land holdings.

Technologies examined The report examined the impact of both biotechnology and information technology. The following biotechnologies in the area of animal agriculture were analysed: production of protein (such as hormones, enzymes, activating factors, amino acids, and feed supplements); gene insertion (which allows genes for new traits to be inserted into the reproductive cells of animals); embryo transfer (which involves artificial insemination of super-ovulated donor animals, removing the resulting embryos nonsurgically, and implanting them nonsurgically in surrogate mothers). The technologies discussed in the field of plant agriculture include microbial inocula (used to increase the efficiency of, or introduce, a plant's ability to supply its own fertilizer, and to increase its resistance to pests), plant propagation (such as cell culture methods for asexual reproduction of plants from single cell or tissue explants), and genetic modification (which, though at present the least-developed area technically, makes it possible to move DNA from one plant, or even other species, into another plant).

Information technology will also impact both animal and plant agriculture. Uses of information technology in livestock include electronic animal identification (which assists in feed control, disease control, and genetic improvement), reproduction (for example estrus detection devices which enhance reproductive efficiency), and disease control and prevention. In plant agriculture, information technology is being used for pest management, and irrigation monitoring and control systems. In addition, radar, sensors, and computers are being used to ensure that the correct amount of fertilizer, pesticides, and plant growth regulators are applied by coordinating tractor slippage and chemical flow.

Research methods The research is based largely on the so-called Delphi method (see p. 75 of the report). This involves collection and coordination of expert opinion, and then feedback for reconsideration by the experts until a convergence is obtained. As the report notes, this makes the conclusions dependent on the experts chosen (and, it may be added, their interaction as a social group).

Conclusions The combined effect of biotechnology and information technology will reinforce the ongoing long-run tendencies in U.S. agriculture noted above. More specifically

1. These technologies will have a major effect in increasing productivity. The 'biotechnology and information technology area will bring technologies that can significantly increase agricultural yields. The immediate impact of these technologies will be felt first in animal production. ... Impacts on plant production will take longer, almost the remainder of the century'.
2. These technologies will be adopted more rapidly by large farmers partly because of their better access to information and financial resources: '70 percent or more of the largest farms are expected to adopt some of the biotechnologies and information technologies. This contrasts with only 40% for moderate-size farms and about 10% for the small farms. The economic advantage from the technologies are expected to accrue to early adopters'.
3. Biotechnology will encourage greater vertical coordination and control in agriculture which may 'induce a shift in control over production from the farmer to the integrator'. It will 'reduce market access [defined as 'the ability of sellers ... to gain access to buyers'] slightly for livestock producers in the long run', although its impact on market access for crop production is expected to be neutral. Finally, 'No significant impact on barriers to entry is expected ... for either crop or livestock production'.

4. The combined effects of biotechnology and information technology, together with preexisting trends, will significantly reduce the number of farms and increase the proportional contribution of the largest farmers to total output. 'If present trends continue to the end of this century, the total number of farms will continue to decline from 2.2 million in 1982 to 1.2 million in 2000'. Approximately '50,000 of [the] largest farms will account for 75% of the agricultural production by year 2000'.

2.3.2.2 'Biotechnology and the Dairy Industry: Production Costs, Commercial Potential, and the Economic Impact of Bovine Growth Hormone' (Kalter et al., Department of Agricultural Economics, Cornell University, December 1985)

Aim The study examines the likely future impact of bovine growth hormones (bGH) on the U.S. dairy industry.

Technology examined Milk productivity (output of milk per cow) has been rising since the 1960s as a result of traditional techniques. These include improved management and feeding practices, together with conventional methods of improving the quality of herds such as selection. These techniques have resulted in 'an average annual compounded increase in milk production of more than one% per cow since the 1960s' (p. 71). Biotechnology, however, promises to substantially raise the rate of increase of productivity.

> Daily injection of bGH beginning about the 90th day of lactation has been found to increase output by up to 40%. That level corresponds to a 25% increase over the entire lactation cycle. ... While the capacity ... to stimulate milk production was recognized in the 1930s, it has been only since the advent of biotechnology that the compound could be produced at a level and cost making it economical for farm use.
>
> (p. 71)

Research methods Using production and financial data the minimum cost of producing bGH was calculated. The minimum cost was $1.93 per gram of bGH at a plant capacity of 6.5 million cow doses per day (p. 29). This provided the basis to calculate the likely price of bGH to the farmer (which, accounting for distribution costs, producer and distributor profits, etc., would be above the minimum production cost). Allowance was also made for the fact that the cost to the farmer includes not only the cost of the hormone and its administration costs, but also the additional consumption of feed by cows receiving the hormone. On the other hand the benefit to the farmer was calculated by considering increases in productivity induced by bGH, together with assumptions about milk prices. Changes in the farmer's rate of return as a result of adopting the bGH were then computed. The resulting information was given to farmers in the form of a questionnaire survey to calculate diffusion rates.

Conclusions Results of the survey showed that

> Farmers expressed an acute awareness of the potential of increased milk output to further depress milk prices. Some farmers ... questioned the desirability of bGH being made available given market conditions, one farmer writing, 'It should be outlawed'. Others noted that if other farmers used bGH they would, practically, have no option but to adopt as well.
>
> (p. 81)

The report concluded:

1. That bGH will be widely adopted when introduced (with the diffusion path following the usual sigmoid pattern but with a high rate of early adoption);
2. That adoption will lead to a significant increase in milk output;
3. That in the absence of government price support, the price of milk will fall; and
4. That this will lead to a substantial reduction in both the number of dairy farms and dairy cattle (the precise numbers depending on the various assumptions made).

2.3.2.3 'The Impact of Biotechnology on Living and Working Conditions in Western Europe and the Third World' (Bijman et al., 1986)

The study by Kalter et al. (1985) is based on a partial equilibrium model. The effects of one kind of biotechnology product, bovine growth hormones, are examined within the confines of a single industry, namely the dairy industry. As we will discuss in more detail below, a partial equilibrium framework may produce misleading results by ignoring the causes and effects of more general interactions. For example, if one is concerned with the general effects of biotechnology on the dairy industry (and not only bovine growth hormones), it will be necessary to take into account:

1. The effects on this industry of biotechnology-induced events occurring elsewhere in the economy; and
2. The effects on the dairy industry of its own effects on other aspects of the economy.

An example of the first event is provided by Bijman et al. when they consider the implications of increased substitutability of vegetable products for dairy products induced by biotechnology. Their study will now be discussed in more detail.

Aim   The study examines the economic and political effects of biotechnology-induced increases in product substitutability (of both inputs and final products) in Western Europe and the Third World.

Technologies examined   The technologies examined include both old and new biotechnologies (for example, the use of enzymes and the use of cloning techniques to improve the quality of oil palm trees).

Research methods   The research involves collection of data, primarily from secondary sources, which are then used to calculate the effects of substitution, particularly on employment.

Conclusions   Conclusions were divided into two areas:

1. Substitution of sugar by other sweeteners. Biotechnology-induced substitution is most highly advanced in the case of sugar. This process has been encouraged by the high sugar prices resulting from protected sugar markets in industrialized countries. Sugar

may be substituted by high-fructose corn syrup, manufactured using immobilized enzymes, and by aspartame. A substantial increase in consumption of nonsugar sweeteners relative to sugar in the main industrialized countries has resulted in a major decrease in the world market price of sugar. Since 1982 this price has been below production cost. The decrease in the price of sugar has had a major negative impact in Third World sugar-exporting countries. For example, in the Philippines revenues from sugar exports decreased from $US624 million in 1980 to $US246 million in 1984, resulting in the relocation of some 500,000 field labourers. Furthermore, the potential for Third World countries to shift into alternative crops is also limited by new technology. In the Philippines, for instance, a substantial proportion of the sugar-producing land has been converted to rice. However, methods of improving rice yields have been introduced by institutions such as the International Rice Research Institute (ironically based in the Philippines) and this has resulted in productivity increases. Traditional rice importers such as Indonesia and India are becoming exporters with serious implications for the world market price of rice. Furthermore, as noted by the U.S. Congress, Office of Technology Assessment (1986), genetic engineering is likely to contribute further to increasing rice productivity in the future. [For a summary of the rice story see Yanchinsky (1986).]

2. Competing raw materials for oils and fats. The two most important sources of vegetable oils and fats are soya and oil palm. The productivity of the latter has been increased by 30% (oil yield per tree) by cloning oil palm plants. The greater profitability of oil palm production relative to rubber in Malaysia has meant that plantations previously producing rubber have switched to oil palm. Since rubber production is more labour-intensive, the jobs of Malaysian and migrant Indonesian workers on rubber plantations are threatened. Furthermore, future increases in the productivity of oil palm could lead to reduced world market prices of vegetable oils, which would reduce incomes of producers of other vegetable oils, such as coconut farmers, many of whom are small and lack

the resources to switch to oil palm production. In addition, less efficient oil palm producers, such as a number of African countries, may see their share of world markets dwindle.

2.3.3 The Need for a More General Approach

Ideally we would like to be able to trace the effects of biotechnology (including individual technologies and 'packages' of technologies) on economic variables, such as total output, employment, income distribution, trade flows, and regional impacts. In practice, however, the task is formidable due to the complexity of the socioeconomic system within which changes in biotechnology are occurring. For example, it is clear from two of the three studies just examined that the system is global. The report by the U.S. Congress, Office of Technology Assessment implies that in examining the effects of biotechnology on U.S. agriculture it is necessary to consider the impact on U.S. international competitiveness (although this is not adequately followed through in the study itself). To the extent that adoption of biotechnologies by American farmers increases U.S. international competitiveness, there will, through the export multiplier effect, be further consequences for U.S. output, employment, and possibly income distribution. Similarly, Bijman et al. (1986) note that one factor affecting the income of coconut farmers is the planting of improved oil palm trees, which resulted from successful cloning in other countries.

In view of the complexity of the pattern of interdependencies in the global system it is hardly surprising that analytical methods have been found wanting. Nevertheless, economists have attempted to capture more of these interdependencies, going beyond attempts to 'add up' the effects of technical change (which, because they ignore interdependence, often lead to erroneous results). A survey of some of these attempts is to be found in Lipton and Longhurst (1986) in the context of an examination of the effects on the poor in Third World countries of introducing modern seed varieties.

Lipton and Longhurst argue that 'because a national or village society or economy (we would add global economy) is a complete and interacting set of parts, the adding-up approach implicit in almost all the analyses of how modern varieties affect the poor ... is at best seriously incomplete and at worst dangerously wrong' (p. 88). They go on to examine three more general approaches that may be referred to as the general equilibrium approach, the Keynesian approach, and the Leontief approach.

The *general equilibrium approach*, based on the work by Walras and on subsequent development of this work by contemporary general equilibrium theorists, considers the effects of technical change on demand and supply and therefore on relative prices. Changes in relative prices lead in turn to a new set of price incentives for producers and consumers and hence to a new general equilibrium. The main strength of the general equilibrium approach is that it considers the effect on *prices,* and therefore resource allocation, of the interaction *between* markets. Its main weakness lies in the limiting assumptions which are made. It is assumed in general equilibrium theory that land, labour, and capital are fully employed; that prices are competitively determined; and that labour and other nonland inputs are perfectly mobile. Furthermore, unrealistic assumptions are made about technological knowledge and the nature of the production process (see Fransman, 1986b, pp. 10-11).

The *Keynesian approach,* as discussed by Lipton and Longhurst, considers the multiplier effect of expenditures (on items relating to the modern varieties) on incomes as the money is spent through successive rounds. For example, as large farmers purchase biotechnology packages (e.g., herbicide plus herbicide-resistant seeds) they generate income for the owners and employees of the producers and distributors of the packages who do the same when they spend their income, etc. To the extent that this creates a demand for increased production and therefore employment, small farmers may benefit, not from adopting the new biotechnology package, but from an increase in their off-farm income which is often an important source of total income for small farmers. This kind of interdependence is neglected by attempts to 'add up' the effects of technical change on different categories of farm, looking only at production while ignoring expenditures. Conversely, however, a major weakness of the 'Keynesian approach' is that it neglects a rigorous discussion of production.

The *Leontief approach*, on the other hand, examines the effects of successive rounds of production on incomes [for example, 'incomes from making extra grain via modern varieties; from providing the extra irrigation water, fertilizer, pesticides, etc. to grow the extra modern variety grain; from providing the extra feedstock to make the fertilizer, etc.; and so on' (p. 95)]. The Leontief approach assumes that all inputs increase in the same proportion as output rises. The main strength of this approach lies in its capture of intersectoral interdependencies.

Despite their drawbacks, these three approaches share an attempt to move beyond the partial analysis of the 'add-up' approach to capture more general effects. However, their progress is only relative, for the general effects are very general indeed. For example, in all three approaches, technical change remains exogenously determined. While this may be realistic in a Third World economy where at least in the initial stages, the new technologies are exogenously introduced, it does not deal adequately with the rich countries where, as we saw in Section 2.2, technical change is endogenous. Furthermore, as Lipton and Longhurst conclude,

> Even if we managed to combine neo-Walrasian, Keynesian and Leontief ... analyses of 'directional effects' of modern varieties on the poor, larger 'historical' interactions of modern varieties with the state, class structures, population change, and land distribution would be left out. And such interactions may be the main way that, in the long run, modern varieties affect the poor.
>
> (p. 102)

Despite the difficulties, a search for a more satisfactory way to analyse general effects is necessary if the total impact of technical change in general, and biotechnology in particular, is to be understood. The aim of the present section has been to point briefly to some of the ways being explored to move forward.

2.4 IMPLICATIONS FOR THE THIRD WORLD[7]

2.4.1 Introduction

Three key questions need to be examined in discussing the implications of biotechnology for Third World countries:

1. What are the effects of the global development of biotechnology on Third World countries?
2. What are the preconditions and constraints on Third World entry into the biotechnology field?
3. How may Third World countries go about selecting areas for specialization?

In this section we shall first briefly survey the literature that examines the implications of biotechnology for Third World countries. We shall then examine these three questions in more detail. Finally, the Cuban experience with biotechnology will be surveyed to examine the case of a small and relatively low-income country.

2.4.2 A Survey of Some Literature

It is clear from the present survey that relatively little literature examines the economic and social implications of biotechnology. Even less literature examines the implications of biotechnology for Third World countries. The latter literature falls into two categories. On the one hand are articles which deal with biotechnology in individual Third World countries, or the implications of biotechnology for Third World countries, from a mainly scientific/technical point of view. These articles are usually in the scientific/technical biotechnology journals (e.g., Bialy, 1986, on Cuban biotechnology, and Mang Ke-qiang and Lui Yong-Hui, 1986, on Chinese biotechnology, both in *Biotechnology*). On the other hand are a small number of articles (written by an even smaller number of individuals) which examine the socioeconomic implications of biotechnology for Third World countries. It is the latter literature that will be briefly surveyed in this section.

The authors of these articles agree on a number of central issues. First, they agree that, although there are potential dangers, biotechnology can be a beneficial force in Third World countries, improving the conditions of all sections of the population.

Secondly, they are concerned that, particularly in the area of agriculture, there is an increasing tendency for biotechnological knowledge to be privatized. As shown in Section 2.2.4, the ability to patent new plant varieties has induced a number of large agrochemical companies to acquire seed companies, with a view to marketing agricultural packages (e.g., fertilizer, herbicide, and herbicide-resistant seed package) and thus reaping synergistic economies. This situation, it is argued, contrasts strongly with the development of modern varieties during the so-called Green Revolution, where most of the generation and diffusion of varieties took place in and through public-sector institutions. Thus Buttel et al. (1985b) argue that 'the private and proprietary character of biotechnology research in the developed countries has become especially marked with regard to agricultural applications' (p. 41). They go on to state that

> The genesis of the Biorevolution ... introduces the problem of patents and proprietary information into the question of technology transfer. This was not a consideration of the Green Revolution: with public agricultural research agencies producing new varieties, there was no difficulty in arranging for the release and exchange of germ plasm in the public domain.
>
> (p. 43)

Similarly, Dembo et al. (1985) argue that

> There is concern among many groups that privatisation in biotechnology in industrialised countries will result in:
> - increased secrecy among scientists, for whom open communication of research results has historically been at the heart of maintaining the integrity of scientific research;
> - development of products based on profit motivation — rather than concern for public welfare;
> - hazards relating to the technology being overlooked because of monetary considerations or secrecy requirements;

- a narrowing of the genetic base due to the use of more profitable (for the seed companies and chemical TNCs) high yielding, often hybrid varieties; and
- increased concentration among industries affected by privatisation.

(p. 44)

Thirdly, it is agreed by these authors, following from the argument regarding increasing privatization, that public-sector institutions, and particularly international institutions, have an important role to play. In this connection it is argued that UNIDO's new International Centre for Genetic Engineering and Biotechnology, based in Trieste and Delhi, has an important role to play as a counter influence.

Fourthly, it is argued that Third World countries are likely to be increasingly buffeted, if not sunk, by the global winds of change being introduced by biotechnology. For example, some agricultural production is likely to move to rich countries as plants are made to tolerate temperate climatic conditions (e.g., by genetic engineering of 'ice-minus' microorganisms which reduce frost damage). Further disruption will result from increased substitutability between agricultural products (e.g., maize, cassava, or potatoes as sources of starch to produce sweeteners to replace sugar or sugar beets) and from the tendency for industrial processes to substitute for some agricultural products (e.g., single-cell proteins for animal or human consumption, reduced by microorganisms living off by-products from the oil industry, substituting for agricultural feeds and foods) [see, for example, Bijman et al. (1986); Ruivenkamp (1986); and Goodman et al. (1987)].

Since many of these issues have been discussed in detail earlier in this chapter (particularly in Sections 2.2.4 and 2.3), further comment will not be given here.

It is clear that the literature referred to here has been primarily concerned with the first of the three questions mentioned at the start of this section. However, Third World countries are not simply passive players in the biotechnology game. This more active role of Third World countries raises the second and third questions, which have not received much attention in the literature and which will now be considered in more detail.

2.4.3 Preconditions and Constraints on Third World Entry and Desirable Patterns of Specialization

It is important to stress that the current barriers to entry into the biotechnology field are relatively low. Evidence for this proposition comes from the proliferation, particularly in the United States and to a lesser extent Britain, of a large number of small biotechnology firms. Furthermore, some Third World countries have begun to enter the biotechnology area, and these are not only the large countries like India, Brazil, and China, but also smaller countries like Singapore, Cuba, Kuwait, and Venezuela. Buttel and Kenney (1985) note that

> Biotechnology is more knowledge-intensive than it is capital-intensive. For example, Nelson Schneider ... a vice-president of E.F. Hutton, has estimated that 'the critical mass of scientists needed to start a biotechnology firm would be at least 25 PhDs and approximately 10-12 million dollars would be needed in initial investment capital'.
>
> (pp. 77-78)

However, downstream processing, involving scale-up, is more expensive. Nevertheless, 'even Eli Lilly's rDNA insulin plants cost only 40 million dollars each' and a 'monoclonal antibody research endeavour would probably cost from 3.5 million dollars to 4 million over three years. If the objective was eventually to produce usable monoclonal antibody based products, the total cost would be from 20 to 40 million dollars over three years' (p. 78). Buttel and Kenney note that 'these costs, of course, may seem large, yet when compared to the outlays and subsidies committed to the building of luxury car assembly plants or importation of weapons, the costs ... are not unreasonable' (p. 78).

Accordingly, they conclude that 'biotechnology still provides a sufficiently open and fluid structure such that successful entry need not be limited to a mere handful of multinational corporations' (pp. 79-80). This contrasts strongly with microelectronics and information technology: few Third World countries, apart from the largest and most industrially sophisticated (such as South Korea), are able to produce products like semiconductors, computers, and digital telecommunications switches, although more are able to provide simpler peripheral equipment and still more are able to *use* these technologies imaginatively.

However, as noted in Section 2.2.3, it is likely that the barriers to entry will tend to rise over time. One reason for this is the increasing economies of scale being realized (as shown in Figure 2.2). Greater scale may not result in cost advantages in all cases. For example, the scaling-up of some kinds of fermentation processes might not lead to reduced unit costs. However, even in these instances, other factors may favour larger enterprises, or enterprises organized as part of large groups (like the Japanese *keiretsu*). For example, firms that are able to bring technological knowledge from different areas together successfully may reap a decided technical and competitive advantage, as in the case of bioinformatics which welds microelectronic and instrumentation technology with more conventional parts of biotechnology. Another example is distribution: larger firms with marketing networks and brand names may have an advantage in reaping rent from bioinnovations. To the extent that the evolution of biotechnology, for reasons such as these, tends to favour larger enterprises, the barriers to entry will become greater, with important implications for Third World countries.

In some cases this will mean that direct competition with firms and other institutions from rich countries will become even more difficult. Yet even here this does not mean that all Third World countries will be necessarily excluded from such competition. Some Third World countries, and particularly those with large domestic markets, will have the option of attempting to nurture infant bioindustries, while temporarily shielding them by one means or another from the harsh winds of international competition. Here the experience of Third World countries in other areas of technology is relevant. This includes the entry of South Korea into motor cars and semiconductors, the entry of Brazil into small aircraft production, and the Taiwanese entry into production of computer numerically controlled machine tools.

Even if it is assumed that eventual entry by Third World countries into export-competing markets will be difficult, or even impossible, other options will remain open. These include continued production for the protected domestic market despite a lack of international competitiveness in quality and/or price (which may not prove to be an attractive option for some countries) and production for speciality markets. The latter, based on Third World resources and problems, may prove particularly important and may facilitate additional 'South—South' trade. Examples might include genetic engineering of plants adapted to tropical climates, or vaccines against tropical diseases for use in humans or animals. These areas may not appear profitable to large multinational corporations. Furthermore, the ease of access to the basic biotechnologies will be a favourable factor and the economies of firm size discussed above will not be an obstacle if large firms from rich countries remain out of these markets (though such economies may favour larger Third World firms against smaller ones).

On the 'supply side', however, crucial questions are raised regarding the science and technology capabilities required for entry even into comparatively 'easy' protected and speciality markets. Here it is essential to understand that biotechnology is a *science-based* industry and probably more than any other industry in Third World countries it will require a firm foundation in the relevant sciences. In a publication on capability building in biotechnology and genetic engineering in developing countries McConnell, one of the scientists involved in the early stages of the development of the UNIDO-initiated International Centre for Genetic Engineering and Biotechnology (ICGEB), states that it is necessary 'to drive home the point that the basic ingredient of biotechnology is basic science in the relevant fields' (McConnell et al., 1986, p. 26). Genetic engineering, the heart of new biotechnology, 'is composed of many different experimental procedures ranging from organic chemistry through biochemistry to microbial genetics' (p. 26). However, unlike 'say applied micro-biology or applied botany which are parts of biotechnology for which the basic sciences exist in many developing countries, the basic science underlying genetic engineering is essentially absent' (p. 27). Accordingly, McConnell concluded,

> In general, the genetic engineering and biotechnology research base, particularly in molecular genetics, at institutes and universities in each developing country visited by the Select Committee (of UNIDO), was observed to be weak. In

effect none of these countries presented substantial evidence of genetic engineering and biotechnology research being conducted at a competitive international level.

(p. 15)

To increase the rigour of this discussion it is worth categorizing the different components of the stock of capabilities required for successful entry into biotechnology. This categorization is a variant of that developed in Section 2.2.4. (However, it must be realized that the greater the degree of international competition envisaged for a country's biotechnology industry, the greater the 'quality' of scientific and technical knowledge that will be required.) The following components of the 'biotechnology capability stock' may be distinguished:

1. Core scientific capabilities;
2. Complementary capabilities 1 (relating to scale-up and bioprocessing);
3. Complementary capabilities 2 (relating to infrastructure, transport and repair facilities, foreign exchange availability, etc.);
4. Complementary assets (such as marketing and distribution networks).

These components are part of an *interdependent knowledge system* on which the ultimate output and efficiency of the biotechnology industry depends.

Regarding core scientific capabilities and complementary capabilities 1, UNIDO has identified 'certain basic capabilities ... required to support all aspects of the scientific programmes to be undertaken at the International Centre for Genetic Engineering and Biotechnology' (UNIDO, 1986, p. 15). These include:

Molecular Biology
Studies with nucleic acids (genetic engineering, sequencing, synthesis), host-vector systems, cloning and expression in prokaryotes and eukaryotes.

Chemistry
Protein purification, enzymology, protein sequence determination, peptide synthesis, physical chemistry of biological molecules and natural product isolation, structure, and synthesis.

Biochemical Engineering
Bioreactor design, fermentation, product recovery and purification.

Microbiology
Studies of microorganisms, genetics, physiology, the development of novel
screening methods, and culture maintenance.

Cell Biology
Eukaryotic cell culture, immunology, including antibody production and
culture maintenance.

Informatics
Computing and programming as applied to the analysis of structure and
function of biological molecules, computerized control of instrumentation, data
base access and communication facilities.

(p. 15)

Several comments may be made. First, there may be some debate
about the areas included and excluded in this UNIDO list of 'basic
capabilities'. Second, while these may be the capabilities required for
UNIDO's programme of research, it does not follow that they are
necessary capabilities for Third World countries attempting to enter
the field of biotechnology. This, in turn, raises a number of important
further questions. For example, what meaning is to be given to
McConnell's statement, quoted above, that for Third World countries
to enter the biotechnology area it is necessary that they understand that
'the basic ingredient of biotechnology is basic science in the relevant
fields'. How basic must this 'basic science' be? It is presumably not
always necessary for Third World scientists, assuming that they and
their institutions are pursuing the pragmatic goals of using biotechnology to produce products judged to be of use to their country, to
master all of the fundamental knowledge pertaining to their field of
work. Although their work will be science-based, the 'depth' of their
scientific knowledge might not have to be as great as that of the most
advanced scientists in the field, given the practical goals that they may
be pursuing. Furthermore, it will be possible, to some extent, to 'free
ride' on the basic research being undertaken in the rich countries
without having to master the scientific capabilities underlying that
research. From the point of view of such Third World scientists the
open nature of the science system in rich countries, facilitated by

means such as publication and other modes of transmitting information, often makes the question of access relatively simple. An important policy question, therefore, revolves around the issue of deciding on the scientific capabilities, more specifically the 'depth' and the costs of acquiring them, that are required to make pragmatic use of biotechnology. (Incidentally, it is also worth noting that it is difficult to distinguish 'science' from 'technology' in discussing what we have termed the 'core scientific capabilities and complementary capabilities 1', the latter referring to scale-up and bioprocessing. Here the traditional disciplinary distinction between 'science' and 'engineering' tends to break down.)

Third, quite apart from the question of the knowledge itself, is the issue of the appropriate institutional and organizational forms that are required (a) to develop the knowledge and (b) to give it effect. This opens up a further range of policy questions that will, however, not be pursued here.

However, what we have referred to as 'complementary capabilities 2' are also necessary for an effective use of biotechnology, and are therefore included here in the interdependent system of capabilities. For example, Riazuddin, in the UNIDO publication on capability building in biotechnology (McConnell et al., 1986), notes that although 'new biotechnology does not necessarily require sophisticated and expensive working', the 'heart of the technology is the regular and reliable supply of rare biochemicals'. However, acquiring these materials in developing countries presents the following difficulties:

1. Hard currency. Since all of these materials have to be imported, payment is required in hard currency. If extra funds are available to scientists in developing countries, they are in local currency. Conversion into hard currency, if possible, consumes considerable time and effort.
2. Transportation: Most enzymes and related materials are unstable at ordinary temperatures and are generally shipped in dry ice. Standard-sized cartons cannot take more than a few kilogrammes of dry ice that normally lasts for 24-48 hours. However, the journey time to many cities in Asia and Latin America usually exceeds 48 hours. Increasing the quantity of dry ice makes air transportation charges prohibitively expensive. Moreover, there are usually no facilities for cold storage at the receiving airports in developing countries. Therefore, goods collection by the customer has to be extremely efficient, which is not always the case.

(pp. 52-53)

This gives a flavour of some of the problems that scientists and biotechnologists in developing countries will have to grapple with, problems that their colleagues in rich countries can assume away. The final part of the capability package relates to complementary assets, such as marketing and distribution networks. As shown in Section 2.2.4, these are essential for appropriating rent from biotechnological knowledge. Once again there are many special problems that confront Third World countries, including those attempting to engage in 'South—South' trade.

A further issue of critical importance is the nature of the relationship between the 'science base' and the country's production system. For a science-based technology like biotechnology to play a productive role, strong two-way links are required between science and production, with science and its expanding potentials 'pushing' production at the same time as being 'led' by the needs of the production system. This raises a number of complex issues which are highlighted by the literature on Third World countries. This literature has pointed to the frequent alienation of the science base from the requirements of domestic production in these countries [see references to Cooper in Fransman (1986a)].

Additional questions relate to the most appropriate mode of entry into biotechnology for Third World countries. This acknowledges that alternative ways of entering the biotechnology field exist, and raises the policy question of deciding on the most suitable. For example, Cuba, which was judged by the UNIDO team of experts setting up the International Centre for Genetic Engineering and Biotechnology to have one of the best biotechnology programmes in the Third World, used interferon as a 'model' for entering the area of genetic engineering. This programme utilized the well-developed health infrastructure that Cuba built up as a result of its national emphasis on the health sector since the revolution, as analysed in greater detail below.

By contrast, the Brazilian mode of entry has been largely through the ethanol-from-sugar programme [see Rothman et al. (1983) for details on the programme]. Genetic engineering has become important as a result of the ability to alter the genetic composition of microorganisms that transform sugar into ethanol, thus improving their efficiency. The existence of alternative modes of entry raises further questions, with important policy implications, regarding social costs and benefits of different ways of entering and establishing basic capabilities in genetic engineering in particular, and biotechnology in general.

The choice of specialization in biotechnology raises further issues. Since it will often be possible to import biotechnology-related products, the question arises 'When is it advantageous to establish local production capability?'. This question has crucial policy implications (e.g., Is it worth producing interferon in Third World countries?), although it is analytically complex. Fortunately, however, literature exists that addresses closely related areas, such as the policy question of when to import capital goods into developing countries, and when to produce them locally (i.e., the make–import decision) (see Fransman, 1986c, Chapter 1 for a detailed discussion). The conceptual approach in this literature can be applied to biotechnology and further developed for policy purposes.

Finally, it must be recognized that the Third World is a heterogeneous collection of countries. What is relevant for Brazil will often not be appropriate for Bolivia or Botswana. Clearly, despite the barriers to entry to biotechnology that are low relative to microelectronics and information technology, many Third World countries will not, and perhaps should not, develop biocapabilities as a result of the high opportunity costs. This raises further questions of how these countries may benefit as *users* of biotechnology-related products. Here too, many issues remain to be identified and researched.

2.4.4 An Illustrative Case Study: Cuba's Entry into New Biotechnology

The Cuban case illustrates dramatically what can be achieved when a firm commitment is made to develop biotechnology capabilities and apply them to a wide range of areas in accordance with the country's economic priorities. In this section the Cuban case is examined in greater detail, paying particular attention to the way this country entered the field of new biotechnology, the areas in which new biotechnology has been applied, and the institutional changes brought about to facilitate the development of biotechnology. Finally, based on this case study, conclusions will be drawn regarding lessons for other developing countries.

2.4.4.1 General approach

The crucial watershed in Cuba's scientific and technological development occurred after the Cuban Revolution in 1959. Until then, Cuba depended primarily on agricultural activities, which lacked sophisticated processing and R&D capabilities, and on tourism. In this way foreign exchange was earned, which financed imports of manufactured products, largely from the United States. After the Revolution, a new set of priorities was established. Most important for development of the biological sciences in general, and biotechnology in particular, was the emphasis given to the role of science and to the development of the national health service. Frequent reference is made by Cuban scientists to the conviction prevailing at that time that the future development of Cuba was inextricably bound up with the future development of science in the country. It was this conviction that inspired rapid growth in the school and higher education system. At the same time, an important result of the Revolution was the expansion and extended delivery of medical services to all sections of the population. This meant that within a short time, Cuba was able to develop a relatively sophisticated medical system, which included training and research facilities in universities and other national institutions. It was this medical system that was later responsible for Cuba's rapid and successful entry into new biotechnology.

However, new areas of science and research do not emerge automatically; their emergence depends on new groups of scientists and researchers, committed to the new fields of study and devoted to the institutional changes required to realize new scientific research. From this point of view it is significant to observe that the new institutions which evolved in Cuba to develop the biological sciences and biotechnology emerged in a pluralistic rather than a linear way.

At the apex of Cuba's scientific planning establishment is the Cuban Academy of Sciences, which was originally established in 1861 but substantially restructured after the Revolution. The Academy contains the Superior Scientific Council, which consists of about 77 distinguished scientists elected from the Academy's various institutes, from the Ministry of Higher Education, and from industry. The Academy also contains a number of other smaller but influential advisory groups. However, it is significant that the Academy does not totally dominate or control the scientific establishment. For example, only about 10% of the total number of Cuban scientists and engineers work in Academy institutes.

The Ministry of Higher Education, with some degree of autonomy from the Academy, has also played an important role in the establishment of scientific institutions. From the point of view of the development of Cuban biotechnology, an important example is the establishment of the National Centre for Scientific Research (CENIC), which was the major biomedical and chemical research centre and was set up in 1965 to stimulate research in new areas. CENIC has a staff of approximately 1,000 and is divided into four main divisions: biomedicine, chemistry, bioengineering, and electronics. CENIC has played a significant role in research and in training scientists who subsequently have become involved in other spin-off institutes.

An important example is the Centre for Biological Research (CIB), which was established in January 1982. The establishment of CIB is of particular interest as a result of its innovative and unbureaucratic origins. In 1981 a 'Biological Front' was established essentially outside the existing bureaucratic framework. The Front consists of scientists and policy-makers with an interest in extending and developing biological research in various directions. It served to coordinate and articulate the interests of those in different Ministries and institutes who wished to strengthen Cuban involvement in biotechnology. While the leaders of the existing scientific establishment were closely involved with the activities of the Biological Front, the Front was set up as a high-level policy-making body, relatively autonomous from the Academy and the various

Ministries involved in biological sciences and their areas of application.

From this position the Front supervised the establishment of CIB and later the Centre for Genetic Engineering and Biotechnology (CIGB). By helping to give birth to CIB and CIGB, the Biological Front served to increase pluralism in the Cuban scientific system. While biotechnology could be developed in existing institutions, such as those under the control of the Academy of Sciences and CENIC, this new set of technologies could also be advanced through new institutions such as CIB and CIGB.

CIB began with a staff of six researchers in a small laboratory. Its major initial mission was the production of interferon for use as an antiviral agent. The interest in interferon resulted in part from the outbreak in late 1980 of dengue haemorrhagic fever, which affected approximately 300,000 people and resulted in 158 deaths. In addition to this pragmatic goal, CIB also aimed to use interferon as a 'model' for development of the wider range of capabilities and assets analysed in Section 2.4.3. In other words, interferon would be used as a springboard for developing a Biotechnology-Creating System with expertise in the areas of genetic engineering and bioprocessing. CIB grew rapidly and by 1986 was divided into four laboratories: genetic engineering, immunology, chemistry, and fermentation. In addition to interferon, CIB also produces its own restriction enzymes. Its research also involves synthesis of oligonucleotides; cloning and expression of a number of other genes; and production of monoclonal antibodies for diagnostic purposes. Although recombinant DNA research was also done in a number of other institutes, notably CENIC and to a lesser extent the Cuban Institute for Research on Sugarcane Derivatives (ICIDCA), which was established in 1963, by the early 1980s CIB became the major location in Cuba for the development of capabilities in new biotechnology.

When CIB opened in January 1982, it began to produce human leukocyte alpha-interferon using a method (which did not involve genetic engineering) developed by Kari Cantell of the Central Public Health Laboratory in Helsinki. Cantell gave assistance by transferring his method to CIB and was surprised at the speed with which the

Cubans mastered the method. Having mastered this conventional method for producing interferon, CIB embarked on rDNA-based techniques to produce various kinds of interferon.

In this latter task a central role was played by scientists such as Dr. Luis Herrera, who was Vice-Director of CIB. Herrera's background is particularly interesting because it illustrates personally the way Cuba was able to enter the field of new biotechnology. In 1969 Herrera studied molecular genetics (working on yeast) at Orsy University in Paris. The following year he took a post as researcher at CENIC, where he started a laboratory dealing with the genetics of yeast.

Yeast was of interest in Cuba because it was used to convert sugarcane derivatives into single-cell proteins. These were used as animal feed to substitute for imported soya feeds, since the Cuban climate is not suitable to grow soya. Research on yeast partly aimed to improve yeast strains to increase the nutritional value of the single-cell proteins by eliminating some of the undesirable nucleic acids. Under the auspices of ICIDCA there were in total 10 plants each producing 12,000 tons per annum of single-cell protein for animal consumption. In developing their work, researchers in this laboratory became interested in new biotechnology.

In 1979 Herrera returned to France to study molecular biology and genetic engineering. With the formation of the Biological Front and the establishment of CIB in 1982, he joined the Institute as its Vice-Director. In 1983 he once again went to France where he spent time at the Pasteur Institute. Representing a new breed of young, post-revolution scientists who were quickly able to master the latest international research techniques, he has since established an international reputation for his research in new biotechnology.

Although in the case of Dr. Herrera entry into new biotechnology involved access to European institutes, Cuban biotechnology and CIB in particular have also benefited from Soviet science. A notable example is the group of chemists working in CIB and mostly trained in the former USSR. With a strong background in organic chemistry some of these scientists moved on to synthesis of oligonucleotides and DNA. Other groups in CIB are involved in immunology, including immunochemistry and protein purification and fermentation.

There is widespread agreement that the Cuban mastery of new biotechnology has been impressive. One example is the conclusion by a team of UNIDO experts appointed to find a Third World location for the new International Centre for Genetic Engineering and Biotechnology. This team visited the major Third World countries involved in biotechnology and concluded that the Cuban biotechnology programme was one of the best they had seen. Another example is assessments made by distinguished foreign visitors to Cuba. While acknowledging that the Cubans are not attempting to do world frontier basic research, many of these visitors have been impressed with the level of achievement of Cuban biotechnologists.

2.4.4.2 Interferon as a 'model'

Some further comments are in order on CIB's use of interferon as a 'model' for the development of new biotechnology capabilities.

The first point is that the development of core scientific capabilities in new biotechnology at CIB drew on the *already well-developed science base* that existed in Cuba by the time the CIB was set up in 1982. Mention was made in the last section, for example, of the earlier research done at CENIC on the molecular genetics of yeast. In entering new biotechnology, therefore, Cuba was not starting *ab initio*. Thus, Cuban entry into new biotechnology was facilitated by a preexisting stock of substantial scientific capabilities. Clearly, many developing countries are not in as fortunate a position.

The second point is that interferon was an appropriate choice for Cuba largely as a result of the country's well-developed health sector. This meant that development of interferon using genetic engineering techniques was not simply a 'pure' research activity. Rather, it was an example of scientific work being linked closely to the production of useful output, namely the delivery of medical services, a high priority in post-revolutionary Cuba. This link established a unity between 'science push' and 'demand pull' determinants of technical change, which in turn ensured that this part of the science system was not 'alienated' from the needs of the rest of the socio-economy. Interestingly, interferon has also been used as a 'model' by many Japanese companies entering the field of new biotechnology. In their case, however, the need determined from the corporation's point of view was for a way to acquire new biotechnology capabilities while simultaneously producing a commercializable product. Interferon, it was believed, was one of the first new commercial products based on biotechnology. For other developing countries, however, a different product may represent a more appropriate 'road' to the development of new biotechnology, depending on the circumstances and priorities of the country. For Brazil, for example, the ethanol from sugar project may have provided an appropriate road. In other Latin American countries the development of mineral-leaching bacteria for mineral extraction may provide an appropriate way of entering new biotechnology.

Third, the possibility of using interferon as a 'model' for the development of other applications and products illustrates the pervasiveness of new biotechnology. This point is further supported in the Cuban case by the history of the Centre for Genetic Engineering and Biotechnology.

2.4.4.3 Realizing economies of scope: CIGB and the pervasive applicability of new biotechnology

Encouraged by the success of CIB in developing new biotechnology capabilities and impressed with the potential of this set of technologies, the Biological Front recommended the establishment of a new and larger institute which would carry on and extend the work of CIB. Accordingly, on 1 June, 1986, the Centre for Genetic Engineering and Biotechnology was established on a new site near CIB.

CIGB was structured in terms of the following five groups, each dealing with a specific problem area:

1. Proteins and hormones. The aim of this group is to use recombinant DNA techniques to produce proteins for applications in human medicine and veterinary science. This group continues the work done in CIB on the chemical synthesis of oligonucleotides and DNA.
2. Vaccines and medical diagnosis. The aim of this group is to develop vaccines against diseases prevalent in Cuba and other

tropical and subtropical areas by cloning the surface proteins of viruses, parasites, or bacteria. The group is also working to develop monoclonal and polyclonal antibodies and DNA probes for detection and diagnosis of various illnesses.

3. Energy and biomass. The research of this group involves the transformation of various kinds of biomass via chemical methods and enzymes. For example, research is done on yeasts and fungi that transform the sugar by-products of molasses and bagasse into proteins for animal consumption. This group has produced a new strain of the yeast *Candida*, which increases the production of an amino acid important for both human and animal nutrition. CIGB will extend research in this area done at ICIDCA and CENIC.

4. Plant breeding and engineering. This group does research on improved plant varieties using genetic engineering and other biotechnologies, such as cell culture. Nitrogen fixation is one area singled out for study.

5. The genetics of mammalian eukaryotic cells. This group uses the cells of higher organisms to clone genes for protein production.

By using interferon as a 'model', first CIB and then CIGB have been able to develop core scientific capabilities in the area of new biotechnology and apply these capabilities to a wide range of areas consistent with Cuban development priorities. However, the research of CIGB has also been defined to include an emphasis on 'complementary capabilities 1', namely downstream bioprocessing. This has been done by making provision for a pilot bioprocessing plant at CIGB.

2.4.4.4 The importance of downstream bioprocessing

As noted earlier in this chapter, development of an effective biotechnology-creating system involves more than mastery of the core scientific capabilities. One necessary feature of such a system is downstream bioprocessing capabilities. To develop these capabilities, CIGB has established a pilot plant. Two groups work with this plant: one specializing in the fermentation process and doing research to optimize productivity, and the other working on questions of purification. Both of these groups face the difficulties inherent in scaling-up bioprocessing by using larger bioreactors. A major problem confronted by both groups is that there is little experience in Cuba in bioprocessing and scale-up. Furthermore, unlike many of the core scientific capabilities, where research is done in universities and the results are usually made public, a good deal of research on bioprocessing is done by private companies and the findings are kept commercially secret. Bioprocessing, requiring sophisticated engineering skills and specialized inputs, frequently constitutes more of a constraint in developing countries than mastery of the core scientific capabilities.

The same point was stressed by senior officials involved in biotechnology planning in the People's Republic of China during my visit there in 1987. In China, in strong contrast to the Cuban example, the core scientific capabilities were acquired rapidly, largely as a result of scientific interchange with the United States. However, major constraints exist in China in downstream bioprocessing, which depends on the capabilities of Chinese industrial and engineering enterprises.

2.4.5 Biotechnology and Information/Communication Technology

A number of points may be made in addressing this complex and controversial topic.

There is no doubt that biotechnology, as an interrelated set of technologies, is having, and will continue to have, a pervasive effect on a large number of industrial sectors. It is perhaps best to analyse biotechnology as a set of process technologies with application to a large number of product areas. The process technologies include classical methods of selection, recombinant DNA techniques, cell fusion, tissue culture, protein engineering, and bioprocessing. Combinations of these technologies may be applied to the research and development of a large number of products. Examples referred to in this chapter include pharmaceuticals (such as insulin, interferon, and vaccines), industrial chemicals (such as enzymes, other proteins, and ethanol), and new plant varieties.

One implication of the pervasive effects of biotechnology is that important economies of scope may be reaped. In other words, investment in the capabilities and assets necessary to create an effective biotechnology system may be rewarded by high rates of return resulting from the widespread applicability of biotechnology. This possibility emerged clearly from the case study of Cuba, where the capabilities and assets built up in CIB and later CIGB were being applied across a wide range of areas, all of which contributed directly to Cuban development goals and priorities.

For the reason mentioned in the last paragraph, there would appear to be ample justification for establishing biotechnology programmes in developing countries. However, careful attention will have to be paid to the particular circumstances of each country in order to understand the limitations and constraints confronting any such programme (as discussed in Section 2.3).

Notwithstanding this general pervasiveness of biotechnology, there are a number of important differences between biotechnology and information/communication technology (ICT). For example, the link between process technology, product technology, and product characteristics is much closer for ICT than in biotechnology. Furthermore, ICT displays much stronger tendencies towards integration. For instance, the convergence of computing and communication technologies as a result of the digital 'common currency' has meant that ICT products tend relatively easily to become part of broader integrated systems. An example is the integration of personal computers, minicomputers, mainframes, robots, computer-controlled machinery, and local and even national communication systems into a broader technological system. The same integrative tendencies are not apparent for biotechnology.

At the same time there is an important process of convergence between biotechnology and ICT. On the one hand ICT is having a significant impact on the development of biotechnology process and product technologies. Examples are the use of microprocessors and computers in automated controls for bioreactors and DNA synthesizers, and in other areas such as sequencing. On the other hand, biotechnology is beginning to have an effect on ICT, although this effect is not yet as great as the other way round. For instance, one area of application for protein engineering is in the field of biosensors and biochips where integrated circuit technology is fused with protein engineering technology.

It is worth stressing that the current entry barriers into biotechnology are significantly lower than those into ICT, a point that was stressed earlier. Very few developing countries will be able to become significant producers of ICT products such as semiconductors, smaller computers, and communications products, including optical fibre or PBXs, although these types of products are being produced by countries such as the Republic of Korea, India, and Brazil. Most developing countries will be users rather than producers of ICTs. However, many more developing countries will be able to make a successful entry into the field of biotechnology. The qualifications surrounding the possibility for successful entry were examined in more detail in Section 2.4.3. From a policy point of view, therefore, whether the pervasiveness of ICT is greater than that of biotechnology is of little significance. Rather, the policy question ultimately boils down to an analysis of the social returns that may be derived from investing in a biotechnology-creating system, given the circumstances and constraints of the country concerned.

2.5 RECENT ADDITIONS TO THE LITERATURE

There have been many notable contributions recently to the field of biotechnology. This section will mention briefly a few recent studies that augment our current understanding of the generation, diffusion, and policy in the area of biotechnology.

Two recent books provide a panoramic overview of areas of application of biotechnology with particular relevance for Third World countries. These are Sasson's (1988) *Biotechnologies and Development* and Walgate's (1990) *Miracle or Menace? Biotechnology and the Third World*. Both of these books are concerned primarily with the technical development of biotechnology, with special reference to the Third World. They are extremely useful for those wishing to keep abreast of some of the huge quantity of biotechnology-related research that is being done. However, since this research is an ongoing phenomenon, it is necessary to be kept informed about current research developments. To facilitate this, two publications are extremely helpful. The first is UNIDO's (various) *Biotechnology and Genetic Engineering Monitor*, which tracks events in the field of biotechnology in both rich and poor countries. The second is the *Biotechnology and Development Monitor*, published jointly by the Dutch Government and the University of Amsterdam, which provides current information on scientific and technical developments, companies, regional developments in the Third World, and activities of international organizations. Finally, *The Biotechnology Revolution?* (Fransman et al., forthcoming) is a reader with contributions examining the major areas of science and technology in biotechnology, their various areas of application, and their implications.

Two studies of particular relevance to this chapter should also be mentioned. The first is Christopher Freeman's short chapter on the time-scale for the diffusion of biotechnology, published in *Biotechnology: Economic and Wider Impacts* (OECD, 1989). Freeman argues that

> For a new technological system to have major effects on the economy as a whole it should satisfy the following conditions:
> i.   A new range of products accompanied by an improvement in the technical characteristics of many products and processes. ...
> ii. A reduction in costs of many products and services. ...
> iii. Social and political acceptability. ...
> iv. Environmental acceptability. ...
> v.   Pervasive effects throughout the economic system.
>
> (pp. 49-50)

Regarding the 'revolutionary' nature of biotechnology (or in the terminology used by Freeman and Perez (1988), whether or not biotechnology constitutes a new 'technoeconomic paradigm'), Freeman is cautious:

> Whether [biotechnology] is such an important trajectory that it will ultimately come to affect management decision-making in most branches of the economy remains an open question. The new biotechnology has undoubtedly led to

enormous excitement in the research community and many new companies were established with venture capital to pursue R&D. This 'research explosion' was without parallel. Both the pervasiveness of a new trajectory or technical system depends on the range of profitable opportunities for exploitation. Until recently, despite its undoubted importance for the future, biotechnology had led to profitable innovations in only a relatively small number of applications in a few sectors and in a few countries. In Schumpeter's model, the profits realised by innovators are the decisive impulse to surges of growth, acting as a signal to the swarms of imitators. Biotechnology is a very long way from this mature stage and the main interest is in when it will enter the 'swarming' phase and on what scale.

(ibid, p. 49)

This conclusion is in line with that of this chapter.

Also relevant to this chapter is the research programme developed under the auspices of the International Federation of Institutes for Advanced Study (IFIAS) and the African Centre for Technology Studies (ACTS) in Nairobi on the international diffusion of biotechnology. Of particular interest is the 'SWOT methodology' (strengths, weaknesses, opportunities, and threats) developed under this programme for the formation of policies for the adoption and development of biotechnology in Third World countries. See Clark and Juma (1990) for further details.

This brief discussion addresses only some of the more important contributions that should be added to the survey in this chapter.

2.6 TOWARDS A GENERAL RESEARCH AGENDA

While it is not appropriate here to attempt to spell out a detailed research agenda for the biotechnology area, it is possible, on the basis of the information discussed in this chapter, to identify three broad themes that might form part of such an agenda.

2.6.1 Evolution of Biotechnology in Industrialized Countries

Research addressing the evolution of biotechnology in the advanced industrialized countries could be focused on three topics:

1. The science and technologies upon which biotechnology is based;
2. Biotechnology-related companies (small and large); and
3. Government policies.

It is assumed that a desirable research programme on biotechnology would be concerned both with the determinants of the major scientific and technological changes in the biotechnology field as well as with their socioeconomic effects. In order to analyse these determinants it is necessary to understand the overall trends in the evolving science and technology. While there is a huge literature reporting developments in the science and technology, there are far fewer attempts to identify the major trends. To take an example discussed earlier, what are the implications of current trends in bioprocessing for minimum firm size? The answer to this question has important consequences for the barriers to entry into biotechnology.

Closely related to the need to understand the continuing evolution of the science and technology is the need to analyse biotechnology-related developments in the major companies, both large and small, in the advanced industrialized countries. These companies are both the 'carriers' and the developers of the new technologies. The structure of their industry and their activities, both nationally and internationally, will have important implications for the future of biotechnology in the industrialized countries as well as the Third World. For example, the failure of Genentech, by far the largest of the American new biotechnology firms, to develop its complementary assets sufficiently, as signalled by its takeover by Hoffman La Roche, is a significant indication of a tendency towards increased concentration in the biotechnology sector. This has important consequences for entry into this sector and for the location of future technical change. It also suggests that Third World countries are increasingly likely to be dealing with larger rather than smaller companies in their private dealings in the field of biotechnology. A further example is the increasing use of strategic alliances in marketing, production, clinical trials, and, to a lesser extent, research by biotechnology-related companies in the advanced industrialized countries. These alliances, presenting both opportunities as well as, in some instances, threats, have important implications for Third World countries.

Finally, it is also necessary to analyse government policies, including the role of universities, in the major industrialized countries. Government policies and programmes will influence the evolution of science and technology in the biotechnology field and will have an effect on the relative international competitiveness of these countries. An example is the area of protein engineering, which is likely to become increasingly important as a new biotechnology, and which is being further developed in important programmes in countries such as Japan and Britain. The policies and programmes of governments in industrialized countries will also present opportunities and threats for Third World countries. A particularly important question relates to the evolving role of universities in the future biotechnology. Will biotechnology in the future continue to be university based to the extent that it has been or will trends in both product and process innovation mean that, as in some areas of telecommunications, information technology, and microelectronics, the locus of innovation will move increasingly into private companies? This is an extremely important question for Third World countries in view of the comparatively easy access that they have to universities in the industrialized countries. It also relates closely to the more general issue of barriers to entry into biotechnology.

2.6.2 Biotechnology Policies in Third World Countries

A series of major questions relates to the development in Third World countries of 'biotechnology systems' that will facilitate the generation and particularly the application of biotechnology. How should such a system be structured in view of the country's existing strengths and weaknesses? What roles should be played by large and small private companies, by universities, and by government programmes? What kinds of interactions should take place with foreign companies and foreign biotechnology systems? These are very large questions requiring detailed analyses that go beyond the general objectives of the conclusion to this chapter. But the usefulness of envisaging from the outset the development of a biotechnology *system* is worth stressing. Such a conceptualization focuses attention on the kinds of organizational structures that are required and on the interactions within and between organizations that are necessary. These are essential adjuncts to any study of the generation and application of biotechnology.

It is also worth noting that although a great deal of (mainly descriptive) literature exists on the experience of Third World countries with biotechnology, the appropriate approaches and methodologies required to assess the effectiveness of the generation and application of biotechnology in these countries are still lacking. The development of such approaches and methodologies must inevitably constitute a crucial part of any coherent research programme on biotechnology and its implications for the Third World. At the same time interest in the application of biotechnology must also imply concern with the complex issues of regulation.

2.6.3 Socioeconomic Effects of Biotechnology

One of the notable facts to emerge from this chapter is the extreme scarcity of rigorous studies analysing the economic and social effects of biotechnology in advanced industrialized and Third World countries. While studies on the use of biotechnology in various applications and countries abound, few good studies examine the effects of biotechnology. This is due in part to the complexities inherent in any rigorous study of effects, some of which, such as the need for economy-wide studies which take account of the interactions and interdependencies, have been mentioned in this chapter. Again the task that lies ahead is in significant measure one of refining approaches and methodologies. But just as an important start has been made in related areas, such as attempts to analyse the effects of the Green Revolution, so a similar start will have to be made for biotechnology.

It has become commonplace to tout biotechnology, together with information and communication technologies and new materials, as the 'new technologies' that individually and collectively will have profound consequences for our economy and society. However, this chapter has shown that we still have a long way to go before we can be satisfied that we have a reasonably robust understanding of the causes of the major scientific and technological changes in the biotechnology field as well as with their socioeconomic effects.

Furthermore, these are still early days in the development of biotechnology. It is, after all, worth reminding ourselves that it was only in the mid-1970s that the major new biotechnologies were invented. The history of all other major scientific and technological change cautions us to expect a long time-lag before major consequences occur, if indeed they are to occur. One of the tasks of the UNU/INTECH research programme, therefore, will be to analyse in 'real time' the causes and effects of biotechnology as they evolve.

ACKNOWLEDGEMENTS

In attempting to understand this new field I have received generous assistance from a large number of people, all of whom cannot be mentioned here. Nevertheless mention must be made of the help given by the following, none of whom bear any responsibility for the ideas and assertions contained in this chapter. The members of the United Nations University, Institute for New Technologies (UNU/INTECH) Feasibility Study, namely Charles Cooper, Jeffrey James, and Luc Soete, were particularly helpful in serving as a sounding board to clarify ideas and in providing conceptual and empirical input. Wilma Coenegrachts was invaluable as an administrator and source of efficiency and support. Edward Yoxen, of Manchester University, and Gerd Junne and Annemieke Roobeek of Amsterdam University, were extremely generous, not only in providing an introduction to the literature, but also in providing continuous guidance and support. Margaret Sharp of the Science Policy Research Unit, Sussex University, and Wendy Faulkner, of Stirling University, similarly provided valuable help. Mark Cantley of the European Community's Concentration Unit for Biotechnology in Europe (CUBE) in Brussels was an important source of ideas, contacts, and literature, and his colleague Ken Sargeant also gave useful advice. Wafa Kamel, in charge of UNIDO's initiative with the new International Centre for Genetic Engineering and Biotechnology (ICGEB), and his colleagues Ricardo Castro-Gonzales and Dianne Brown, provided a helpful insight into UNIDO's activities as did David McConnell. Ajit Bhalla and Susumu Watanabe of the Technology and Employment Branch of the International Labour Organization (ILO) in Geneva shared with me their growing interest in the area of biotechnology. Vinson Oviatt, at the World Health Organization (WHO) in Geneva, provided information about the WHO's biotechnology-related programmes.

In the United States Alfred Hellman, biotechnology adviser to the U.S. Department of Commerce, was a particularly important source of stimulation and information. I am especially grateful to him for having arranged numerous meetings for me in Washington, D.C. Judy Kosovich and Gary Ellis of the Office of Technology Assessment also provided useful information, while Charles Banbrook of the Board on Agriculture of the National Academy of Sciences opened my eyes to a number of important biotechnology issues in the area of agriculture. Chester Dickerson of Monsanto was particularly helpful in giving me an insight into the perspective of one of the largest corporations, heavily committed to biotechnology. Tony Robbins made me aware of the concerns of some members of the U.S. Congress with the need to regulate biotechnology. At Cornell University, Fred Buttel and Tad Cowan stimulated me with their ideas and together with Loren Tauir gave me an insight into the important work being undertaken on biotechnology from a social science perspective at the University. Martin Alexander, also of Cornell University, unravelled with great clarity the complex issues surrounding the questions of regulation, risk-assessment, and the deliberate release of genetically engineered organisms and vectors.

In the United Kingdom, Geoff Potter of the Biotechnology Directorate of the Science and Engineering Research Council (SERC) gave me an excellent overview of the difficulties of policy-making in the science and university side of biotechnology while Roy Dietz of the Biotechnology Unit in the Department of Trade and Industry did likewise in the area of national policy-making in biotechnology. Gerard Fairtlough, managing director of Celltech, shared with me not only his detailed knowledge of the difficulties facing new biotechnology firms but also his broader perspective on appropriate ways of conceptualizing the biotechnology industry and its science base. Bruce Haddock of Bioscot gave me an early insight into the nature of new and small biotechnology firms that have 'spun off' from university research. Jonathan Bard of the Medical Research Council's Cytology Laboratory in Edinburgh helped me to understand some of the implications of biotechnology in medical research. Richard Wakeford and Sabine Brandon-Cross of the British Library's European Biotechnology Information Project made me understand how essential a reliable and complete source of information is to scientists and social scientists alike. Finally, I am extremely grateful to Dr. Luis Herrera and all his colleagues involved in Cuban biotechnology for their extremely generous hospitality and rare insight that they gave me into their country's impressive performance. Some of these insights, I hope, are accurately reflected in the case study section on Cuban biotechnology.

To all these people, and others not mentioned here, I am indebted for having expanded my horizon by giving me insights and information of various kinds to help me to understand a little better this evolving field of biotechnology. To repeat, none of them is responsible for the ideas and contents of this chapter.

NOTES

1. This discussion draws on the useful paper by Teece (1986).
2. This part of the survey is based largely on an interview with a senior Monsanto executive held in Washington, D.C. in July 1986.
3. Later in this survey we will look at the implications of sugar-free sweeteners for international trade patterns and Third World countries. See Ruivenkamp (1986) and Bijman et al. (1986).
4. 'University—Industry Cooperation in Biotechnology' an investigation by the Science and Technology Sub-Committee of the Investigations and Oversight Committee, U.S. Congress, June 1982 (publication number 225-6275). The issue of university—industry links and their effects in the case of biotechnology is treated in more detail in Kenney (1986).
5. For further details on Monsanto see *Biotechnology and Development Monitor*, No.1, September 1989, pp. 19-20.
6. Further details on Genentech are given in *Biotechnology and Development Monitor*, No. 3, June 1990, pp. 3-5.
7. It should be noted that this section is not self-contained in that the discussions in a number of other parts of this survey have a strong bearing on Third World countries.

REFERENCES

Abernathy, W.J., Clark, K.B. and Kantrow, A.M. (1983), *Industrial Renaissance: Producing a Competitive Future for America*, Basic Books, New York.

Abernathy, W.J. and Utterback, J.M. (1975), 'A Dynamic Model of Product and Process Innovation', *Omega*, Vol. 3, pp. 639-656.

ACARD (Advisory Council for Applied Research and Development) (1980), *Biotechnology: Report of Joint Working Party of ACARD and Advisory Board for the Research Councils and Royal Society* (The Spinks Report), HMSO, London.

Anderson, A.M. (1984), *Science and Technology in Japan*, Longman, Harlow.

Arrow, K. (1962), 'Economic welfare and the allocation of resources for invention', in Rosenberg, N. (ed.) (1971), *The Economics of Technological Change*, Penguin, Harmondsworth.

Barnes, B. and Edge, D. (1982), *Science in Context. Readings in the Sociology of Science*, The Open University Press, Milton Keynes.

Beier, F.K., Crespi, R.S. and Straus, J. (1985), *Bio-Technology and Patent Protection. An International Review*, Organization for Economic Cooperation and Development, Paris.

Bialy, H. (1986), 'Cuban Biotechnology: Interferon as a Model', *Biotechnology*, Vol. 4, April, pp. 265-266.

Bijman, J., Van den Doel, K. and Junne, G. (1986), 'The Impact of Biotechnology on Living and Working Conditions in Western Europe and the Third World', Unpublished Manuscript.

Biotechnology and Development Monitor, Government of The Netherlands & University of Amsterdam, The Hague and Amsterdam.

Biotechnology and Genetic Engineering Monitor, United Nations Industrial Development Organization, Vienna.

Birch, J.R. et al. (1985), 'Large Scale Production of Monoclonal Antibodies', Paper presented at the Biotech 85 Conference, Washington, D.C., October.

Borrus, M. and Millstein, J. (1984), 'A Comparison of the US Semiconductor Industry and Biotechnology', Paper prepared for the U.S. Office of Technology Assessment, Appendix C of U.S. Congress, Office of Technology Assessment (1984), *Commercial Biotechnology: An International Analysis*, U.S. Congress, Washington, D.C.

Bull, A.T., Holt, G. and Lilly, M.D. (1982), *Biotechnology. International Trends and Perspectives*, Organization for Economic Cooperation and Development, Paris.

Butler, L.J. and Marion, B.W. (1985), *The Impacts of Patent Protection on the US Seed Industry and Public Plant Breeding*, N.C. Project 117, Monograph 16, Research Division, College of Agricultural and Life Sciences, University of Wisconsin — Madison, Madison, Wisconsin.

Buttel, F.H. (1986), 'Biotechnology and Public Agricultural Research Policy: Emergent Issues', in Dahlberg, K.A. (ed.) (1986), *New Directions for Agriculture and Agriculture Research*, Rowman and Allanheld, Totowa, New Jersey.

Buttel, F.H. (1986), 'Biotechnology and Public Agriculture Research Policy', Unpublished Manuscript, Cornell University, Ithaca, New York.

Buttel, F.H. and Kenney, M. (1985), 'Biotechnology and International Development: Prospects for Overcoming Dependence in the Information Age', Bulletin No. 143, Dept. of Rural Sociology, Cornell University, Ithaca, New York.

Buttel, F.H., Kenney, M. and Kloppenburg, J. (1985b), 'From Green Revolution to Bioevolution: Some Observations on the Changing Technological Bases of Economic Transformation in the Third World', *Economic Development and Cultural Change*, pp. 31-55.

Buttel, F.H., Kloppenburg, J. and Belsky, J. (1985a), 'Biotechnology, Plant Breeding, and Intellectual Property: Social and Ethical Dimensions', Unpublished Manuscript, Department of Rural Sociology, Cornell University, Ithaca, New York.

Celltech (UK) (1985), *Annual Report*.

Chemical and Engineering News (1984), 'Chief Scientist Schneiderman: Monsanto's Love Affair with R&D', December, 24.

Cherfas, J. (1982), *Man Made Life. A Genetic Engineering Primer*, Basil Blackwell, Oxford.

Chesnais, F. (1986), 'Some Notes on Technical Cumulativeness, the Appropriation of Technology and Technological Progressiveness in Concentrated Market Structures', Unpublished Manuscript.

Clark, N. and Juma, C. (1990) 'Biotechnology for Sustainable Development: Policy Options for Developing Countries', Unpublished Report, The

International Federation of Institutes for Advanced Study and African Centre for Technology Studies, Nairobi.

Clark, R.B. (1985), 'The Interaction of Design Hierarchies and Marketing Concepts in Technological Evolution', *Research Policy*, Vol. 14, pp. 235-251.

Cowan, J.T. (1986), 'An Emerging Structure of Technological Domination: Biotechnology, the Organisation of Agricultural Research, and the Third World', *International Journal of Contemporary Sociology* (forthcoming).

Crespi, R.S. (1985), 'Microbiological Inventions and the Patent Law — The International Dimension', *Biotechnology and Genetic Engineering Reviews*, Vol. 3.

Daly, P. (1985), *The Biotechnology Business: A Strategic Analysis*, Frances Pinter, London.

Davies, D. (1986), *Industrial Biotechnology in Europe: Issues for Public Policy*, Frances Pinter, London.

Dembo, D., Dias, C. and Morehouse, W. (1985), 'Biotechnology and the Third World: Some Social, Economic, Political and Legal Imports and Concerns', *Rutgers Computer and Technology Law Journal*, Vol. 11, No. 2, pp. 431-468.

Dunnill, P. and Rudd, M. (1984), *Biotechnology and British Industry*, Science and Engineering Research Council, Swindon.

Elkington, J.B. (1984), 'Cloning of palm trees in Malaysia', in *Blending of New Traditional Technologies: Case Studies*, Geneva, International Labour Office.

Fortune (1984), 'Monsanto's Brave New World', 30 April.

Fransman, M. (1986a), *Technology and Economic Development*, Wheatsheaf, Brighton.

Fransman, M. (1986b), 'A New Approach to the Study of Technological Capability in Less Developed Countries', World Employment Programme Research Working Paper, WEP 2-22/WP 166, International Labour Office, Geneva.

Fransman, M. (ed.) (1986c), *Machinery and Economic Development*, Macmillan, London.

Fransman, M. (1986d), 'The Japanese System and the Acquisition, Assimilation and Further Development of Technological Knowledge: Organisational Form, Markets and Government', Paper presented to conference on 'Technology and Social Change', University of Edinburgh, June 1986.

Fransman, M., Junne, G. and Roobeek, A. (forthcoming), *The Biotechnology Revolution?*, Blackwell, Oxford.

Freeman, C. and Perez, C. (1988), 'Structural Crises of Adjustment: Business Cycles and Investment Behaviour', in Dosi et al. (eds), *Technical Change and Economic Theory*, Pinter, London.

Goodman, D., Sorj, B. and Wilkinson, J. (1987) *From Farming to Biotechnology. A Theory of Agro-Industrial Development*, Blackwell, Oxford.

Hicks, J. (1981), 'The Mainspring of Economic Growth', *American Economic Review*, pp. 23-29.

Hughes, T.P. (1983), *Networks of Power: Electrification in Western Society 1880—1930*, Johns Hopkins University Press, Daltimore and London.

Kenney, M. (1986), *Biotechnology: The University—Industrial Complex*, Yale University Press, New Haven.

Kloppenburg, J. (1988), *First the Seed. The Political Economy of Plant Biotechnology, 1492—2000*, Cambridge University Press, New York.

Lesser, W. (1986), 'Patenting Seeds: What to Expect', Dept. of Agricultural Economics, Cornell University, Ithaca New York (mimeo).

Levin, R.C., Klevorick, A.K., Nelson, R.R. and Winter, S.G. (1984), 'Survey Research on R&D Appropriability and Technological Opportunity, Part 1: Appropriability', Yale University, New Haven (mimeo).

Lewis, H.W. (1984), *Biotechnology in Japan*, National Science Foundation, Washington, D.C., p 84.

Lipton, M. and Longhurst, R. (1986), 'Modern Varieties, International Agricultural Research and the Poor', Consultative Group in International Agricultural Research, Study Paper No. 2.

Mackenzie, D. and Wajcman J. (eds) (1985), *The Social Shaping of Technology*, The Open University Press, Milton Keynes.

Mang-ke Q. and Yong-Hui, L. (1986), 'Biotechnology in China: Walking on Two Legs', *Biotechnology*, Vol. 4.

McConnell, D.J., Riazuddin, S., Wu, R. and Zilinskas, R.A. (1986), 'Capability Building in Biotechnology and Genetic Engineering in Developing Countries', Report No. UNIDO/IS 608, United Nations Industrial Development Organization, Vienna.

Monsanto (1985), *Annual Report*.

Nelson, R.R. (1986), 'The Generation and Utilisation of Technology: A Cross Industry Analysis', Paper presented to Conference on 'Technology and Social Change', University of Edinburgh, June.

Nelson, R.R. and Winter, S.G. (1977), 'In Search of Useful Theory of Innovation', *Research Policy*, p. 36-76.

Nelson, R.R. and Winter, S.G. (1982), *An Evolutionary Theory of Economic Change*, The Belknap Press of Harvard University Press, Boston, Mass.

OECD (1989), *Biotechnology. Economic and Wider Impacts*, Organization for Economic Cooperation and Development, Paris.

Pisano, G.P., Shan, W. and Teece, D.J. (1989), 'Joint Ventures and Collaboration in the Biotechnology Industry', in Mowery, D.C. (ed.), *International Collaborative Ventures in U.S. Manufacturing*, Ballinger, Cambridge, Massachusetts.

Rosenberg, N. (1976), *Perspectives on Technology*, Cambridge University Press, Cambridge.

Rosenberg, N. (1982), *Inside the Black Box: Technology and Economics*, Cambridge University Press, Cambridge.

Rothman, H., Greenshields, R. and Calle, F.R. (1983), *The Alcohol Economy: Fuel Ethanol and the Brazilian Experience*, Frances Pinter, London.

Ruivenkamp, G. (1986), 'The Impact of Biotechnology on International Development: Competition between Sugar and New Sweeteners', *Vierteljahres Berichte*, No. 103.

Sasson, A. (1988), *Biotechnologies and Development*, United Nations Educational Scientific and Cultural Organization, Paris.

Schumpeter, J.A. (1966), *Capitalism, Socialism and Democracy*, Unwin, London.

Scientific American (1981), Special section on biotechnology, Vol. 245, No. 3.

Scientific American (1985), Special section on biotechnology, Vol. 253, No. 4, October/November?

Sharp, M. (ed.) (1985a), *Europe and the New Technologies*, Frances Pinter, London.

Sharp, M. (1985b), *The New Biotechnology, European Governments in search of a Strategy*, Sussex European Paper, No. 15, Science Policy Research Unit, Brighton.

Sharp, M. (1986), 'National Policies towards Biotechnology', Science Policy Research Unit, University of Sussex, Brighton (mimeo).

Sigurdson, J. (1986), *Industry and State Partnerships in Japan. The Very Large Scale Integrated Circuits (VLSI) Project*, Research Policy Institute, Lund, Sweden.

Tanaka, S. (1985), 'Japan's Policy for High Technology: The Case of Biotechnology', Department of Government, Cornell University, Ithaca, New York (mimeo), p. 54.

Teece, D.J. (1986), 'Capturing Valuation from Technological Innovation: Integration, Strategic Partnering and Licensing Decisions' *Research Policy* (forthcoming).

UNIDO (1981), 'The Establishment of an International Centre for Genetic Engineering and Biotechnology (ICGEB). Report of a group of experts', UNIDO (UNIDO/IS/254), Vienna.

UNIDO (1986), Report of specialized workshop, prepared by the UNIDO Secretariat, ICGEB/PREP Comm/18/2/ADD3, UNIDO, Vienna.

U.S. Congress, Investigations and Oversight Committee (1982), 'University—Industry Cooperation in Biotechnology', Investigation by the Science and Technology Sub-Committee, Washington D.C., U.S. Government Printing Office.

U.S. Congress, Office of Technology Assessment (1986), *Public Policy and the Changing Structure of American Agriculture* (OTA-F-285), U.S. Government Printing Office, Washington D.C.

U.S. Congress, Office of Technology Assessment (1984), *Commercial Biotechnology: An International Analysis* (OTA-BA-218), U.S. Government Printing Office, Washington D.C.

U.S. Department of Commerce (1985a), 'Biotechnology in Japan', Unpublished Report, U.S. Department of Commerce, Washington, D.C., 12 pp.

U.S. Department of Commerce (1985b), *Biotechnology in Japan*, Japanese Technology Evaluation Program, U.S. Department of Commerce, Washington, D.C.

Utterback, J.M. (1979), 'The Dynamics of Product and Process Innovation in Industry', in Hill, C.T. and Utterback, J.M. (eds), *Technological Innovation for a Dynamic Economy*, Pergamon Press, New York.

Voss, V.C. (1984), 'The Management of New Manufacturing Technologies', Australian School of Management.

Walgate, R. (1990) *Miracle or Menace? Biotechnology and the Third World*, The Panos Institute, London:.

Warhurst, A. (1985), 'Biotechnology for Mining: The Potential of an Emerging Technology, the Andean Pact Copper Project and some Policy Implications', *Development and Change*, Vol. 16, pp. 93-121.

Williamson, O.E. (1975), *Markets and Hierarchies: Analysis and Antitrust Implications*, The Free Press, New York.

Yanchinsky, S. (1986), 'Spearhead of a Second Green Revolution', *Financial Times*, 17 September.

Yoxen, E. (1983), *The Gene Business. Who shall Control Biotechnology?*, Pan Books, London.

ANNOTATED BIBLIOGRAPHY

Alexander, M. (1985), 'Ecological Consequences: Reducing the Uncertainties', *Issues in Science and Technology*, Vol. 1, No. 3, pp. 57-68.
Examines a number of hypotheses that have been proposed in assessing the risks associated with biotechnology. Goes on to propose a method for risk assessment and concludes that further research is necessary to examine rigorously the ecological consequences.

Assaad, F. (1985), 'World Health Organization's Programme for Vaccine Development', Unpublished Report, World Health Organization, Geneva, pp. 1-10.
Examines *inter alia* the relevance of recombinant DNA and cell fusion technology for the development of vaccines.

Beier, F.K., Crespi, R.S. and Straus, J. (1985), *Bio-Technology and Patent Protection. An International Review*, OECD, Paris.
Provides a background discussion on patents and biotechnology and reports on the results of a survey of OECD countries regarding differences in their patent systems. Ends with a number of recommendations for changes in patent legislation.

Bhalla, A.S. and James J. (1984), 'New Technology Revolution: Myth or Reality for Developing Countries?', *Greek Economic Review*, Vol. 6, No. 3, pp. 387-423.
Examines the relevance of new technologies, including biotechnology, for developing countries. Concludes that biotechnology has important implications.

Bifani, P. (1968), 'Biotechnology for Agricultural and Food Production in Africa', Unpublished Report, International Labour Office, Geneva.
Examines the applicability of tissue culture, nitrogen fixation bioprocessing, and single cell protein production in the context of African countries.

Bifani, P. (1986), 'New Biotechnology for Food Production in Developing Countries with Special Reference to Cuba and Mexico', Unpublished Report, International Labour Office, Geneva.
Discusses the application of biotechnologies to food production in developing countries, with special reference to the production of single cell proteins.

Birch, J.R. et al. (1985), 'Large Scale Production of Monoclonal Antibodies', Paper presented at the Biotech 85 Conference, Washington, D.C., October.
This paper, written by employees of Celltech (UK), discusses *inter alia* the importance of economies of scale, media design, and separation technology.

Borrus, M. and Millstein, J. (1984), 'A Comparison of the US Semiconductor Industry and Biotechnology', Paper prepared for the U.S. Office of Technology Assessment and used under this title in Appendix C of Office of Technology Assessment (1984), *Commercial Biotechnology: An International Analysis*, U.S. Congress, Washington, D.C.
An authoritative source for the comparison of the semiconductor and biotechnology industries.

Bull, A.T., Holt, G. and Lilly, M.D. (1982), *Biotechnology. International Trends and Perspectives*, OECD, Paris.
One of the major early studies, this book also surveys research priorities.

Butler, L.J. and Marion, B.W. (1985), *The Impacts of Patent Protection on the US Seed Industry and Public Plant Breeding*, N.C. Project 117, Monograph 16, Research Division, College of Agricultural and Life Sciences, University of Wisconsin — Madison, Madison, Wisconsin.
Examines the impact of the Plant Variety Protection Act (1970) in response to a request by the U.S. Senate Agriculture Committee after hearings on amendments to this Act held in 1980. Concludes that the Act has resulted in modest private and public benefits at modest public and private costs.

Buttel, F.H. (1986), 'Biotechnology and Public Agricultural Research Policy: Emergent Issues', in Dahlberg, K.A. (ed.) (1986), *New Directions for Agriculture and Agriculture Research*, Rowman and Allanheld, Totowa, New Jersey.
Examines the impact of biotechnology including a comparison with the Green Revolution and the implications for the Third World.

Buttel, F.H. (1986), 'Biotechnology and Public Agriculture Research Policy', Unpublished Manuscript, Cornell University, Ithaca, New York.
Examines the implications for the public sector, including the U.S. Land Grant Colleges, of the increasing tendency for the privatization of biotechnological knowledge.

Buttel, F.H. and Kenney, M. (1985), 'Biotechnology and International Development: Prospects for Overcoming Dependence in the Information Age', Bulletin No. 143, Dept. of Rural Sociology, Cornell University, Ithaca, New York.
Argues that while biotechnology has the potential to benefit Third World countries and improve the material situation of the majority of their populations, its development in these countries is likely to be constrained by social and political factors. The result is that ties of dependence will tend to be reproduced.

Buttel, F.H., Kloppenburg, J. and Belsky, J. (1985a), 'Biotechnology, Plant Breeding, and Intellectual Property: Social and Ethical Dimensions', Unpublished Manuscript, Department of Rural Sociology, Cornell University, Ithaca, New York.
Examines the increasing privatization of plant breeding technology in the U.S. and discusses the implications.

Chemical and Engineering News (1984), 'Chief Scientist Schneiderman: Monsanto's Love Affair with R&D', December, 24.
Examines the new increased role of R&D in Monsanto, particularly in the biological sciences, as the company restructures its activities away from its traditional area of commodity chemicals.

Chesnais, F. (1986), 'Some Notes on Technical Cumulativeness, the Appropriation of Technology and Technological Progressiveness in Concentrated Market Structures', Unpublished Manuscript.
Contains tables giving information on biotechnology agreements signed by Western and Japanese companies.

Cowan, J.T. (1986), 'An Emerging Structure of Technological Domination: Biotechnology, the Organisation of Agricultural Research, and the Third World', *International Journal of Contemporary Sociology* (forthcoming).
Examines current trends in the application of biotechnology in agriculture and concludes that the ability of Third World countries to benefit from these developments is limited by their lack of capacity to influence the activities of agribusiness transnational corporations.

Crespi, R.S. (1985), 'Microbiological Inventions and the Patent Law — The International Dimension', *Biotechnology and Genetic Engineering Reviews*, Vol. 3.
Surveys the current legal situation with regard to the patenting of microbiological inventions.

Daly, P. (1985), *The Biotechnology Business: A Strategic Analysis*, Frances Pinter, London.
Takes a strategic view based largely on the work of Porter in examining the experience of large firms and new biotechnology firms in the area of biotechnology.

Dingell, J.D., 'Benefits for the Developing World', *Biotechnology*, Vol. 3.
Argues that the development of biotechnology in the U.S. is not favourable to the long term interest of Third World countries. Suggests that a programme for biotechnology be created analogous to the orphan drug programme to ensure that the absence of short-term profit does not prevent the development of socially useful applications of biotechnology.

Doyle, J. (1985), *Altered Harvests: Agriculture, Genetics and the Fate of the World's Food Supply*, Viking, New York.
Examines the potential positive and negative effects of biotechnology in agriculture.

Elkington, J.B. (1984), 'Cloning of Palm Trees in Malaysia', in *Blending of New Traditional Technologies: Case Studies*, International Labour Office, Geneva.
Examines the application of tissue culture technology in Malaysia.

Fortune (1984), 'Monsanto's Brave New World', 30 April.
Analyses the new strategies being adopted by Monsanto which has been forced by declining profits to move away from its traditional base in commodity chemicals. Documents the company's move into biotechnology.

Hardy, R.W.F. and Glass, D.J. (1985), 'Our Investment: What is at Stake?', *Issues in Science and Technology*, Vol. 1, No. 3, pp. 69-82.
Argues from the point of view of private industry that the risks of biotechnology are not very great and that the U.S.'s competitive position could be harmed by too tight a regulatory framework.

Humphrey, A.E. (1982), 'Biotechnology: The Way Ahead', *J. Chem. Techn. Biotechnol.*, Vol. 32, pp. 25-33.
Argues that biotechnology opportunities have arisen out of crisis-oriented problems and looks at the implications of advances in related areas such as computer-aided automation.

Klyosov, A.A. (1984), 'Enzymatic Conversion of Cellulosic Materials to Sugars and Alcohol: The Technology and its Implications', Report No. UNIDO/IS/476, United Nations Industrial Development Organization, Vienna.
A useful and detailed survey of the research that has been done worldwide in this area and the policy implications for developing countries. Concludes that acid and enzymatic hydrolysis process hold the most promise.

Lesser, W. (1986), 'Patenting Seeds: What to Expect', Unpublished Report, Department of Agricultural Economics, Cornell University, Ithaca, New York. Discusses the likely effects of the legislation passed in September 1985 according to which open pollinated seeds become patentable. Concludes that seed patents are likely to provide moderate private and social benefits at moderate costs.

Lewis, H.W. (1984), *Biotechnology in Japan*, National Science Foundation, Washington, D.C., p. 84.
A detailed examination of the state of biotechnology in Japan in 1984. Examines also the role played by the universities in basic and applied research and the part played by government, particularly MITI, in stimulating the advance and diffusion of biotechnology. Concludes *inter alia*, that the MITI-established research association has not facilitated much genuinely cooperative research.

Lipton, M. and Longhurst, R. (1986), 'Modern Varieties, International Agricultural Research and the Poor', Consultative Group in International Agricultural Research, Study Paper No. 2.
Argues that 'The bio-economic impact of modern varieties should be specially favourable to smaller farmers, hired workers, and poor consumers, yet much of this "pro poor potential" has been lost due to a) insertion of modern varieties into social systems favouring urban groups and the big farmers who supply them, b) demographic dynamics making labour cheaper relative to land, and c) research structures practising fashionable topics rather than genuine needs of the poor'.

Mang-ke Q. and Yong-Hui, L. (1986), 'Biotechnology in China: Walking on Two Legs', *Biotechnology*, Vol. 4.
Examines the state of Chinese biotechnology outlining both areas of specialization and weakness.

McConnell D.J., Riazuddin, S., Wu, R. and Zilinskas, R.A. (1986), 'Capability Building in Biotechnology and Genetic Engineering in Developing Countries', Report No. UNIDO/IS 608, United Nations Industrial Development Organization, Vienna.
Provides an interesting account of the background to the establishment of the International Centre for Genetic Engineering and Biotechnology. Discusses some of the requirements for building biocapabilities in developing countries.

McGarity, T.O. (1985), 'Regularity, Biotechnology', *Issues in Science and Technology*, Vol. 1, No. 3, pp. 40-56.
Argues that the potential hazard from the application of biotechnology is great and examines the regulatory framework in the U.S.

Magrath, W.B. and Tamur, L.W. (1985), 'The Economic Impact of bGH on the New York State Dairy Sector: Comparative Static Results', *Cornell Agricultural Economics Staff Paper* 85-22, Cornell University, Ithaca, New York.
Uses a partial equilibrium framework in order to examine under a number of different technical assumptions the impact of bovine growth hormones on milk price, milk output, farm and cow numbers.

Nayudamma, Y. (1985), 'An Alternative Pathway for Industrialisation: A Biomass-based Strategy', Report No. UNIDO/IS/-532, United Nations Industrial Development Organization, Vienna.
Discusses the policies that are necessary, and the alternatives that exist, in implementing a biomass-based industrialization strategy.

Oviatt, V.R. (1982), 'Biotechnology — An International Viewpoint', in Whelan, W.J. and Black, S. (eds) (1982), *From Genetic Engineering to Biotechnology — The Critical Transition*, Wiley, London.
Argues that there are no unique or special risks associated with recombinant DNA research and discusses the WHO's safety measures in microbiology programmes.

Perpich, J.G. (1985), 'Export Controls on Biotechnology', *Biotechnology*, Vol. 3.
Argues for biotechnology export rules which do not interfere with international exchanges on which the scientific community and the biotechnology industry depend.

Sakaguchi, K. (1972), 'Historical Background of Industrial Fermentation in Japan', in Terui, G. (ed.) (1972), *Fermentation Technology Today*, Society of Fermentation Technology, Japan.
Analyses the development of fermentation technology in Japan starting with soy-bean paste and sake.

Scobie, G.M. (1979), 'Investment in International Agricultural Research: Some Economic Dimensions', *World Bank Staff Working Paper*, No. 361, The World Bank, Washington, D.C.
Examines the impact of Green Revolution research on output growth, income distribution, employment and nutrition.

Sargeant, K. (1984), 'Biotechnology in Japan', Unpublished Report, CUBE, Commission of the European Communities, Brussels.
Reports on a two-week visit to Japan in March 1984 at the invitation of MITI.

Sharp, M. (1986), 'National Policies Towards Biotechnology', Unpublished Report, Science Policy Research Unit, University of Sussex, Brighton, U.K.
Examines policy in the U.S., Japan and major European countries towards biotechnology.

Steinkraus, K.A. (1984), 'Biotechnology Applications to some African Fermented Foods', in Blending of New and Traditional Technologies, ILO, Geneva.
Using a wide definition of biotechnology, examines the traditional use of microorganisms mainly in the fermentation of beer.

Sun, M. (1986), 'UN Biotechnology Centre Mired in Politics', *Science*, Vol. 231, February.
Examines the political background to the establishment of the International Centre for Genetic Engineering and Biotechnology by UNIDO in Trieste and New Delhi.

Tanaka, S. (1985), 'Japan's Policy for High Technology: The Case of Biotechnology', Unpublished Report, Cornell University, Department of Government, Ithaca, New York, p. 54.
Examines the strengths and weaknesses of Japanese biotechnology and the role of various government ministries and programmes in promoting biotechnology.

Tauer, L.W. (1985), 'The Impact of Bovine Growth Hormone on the New York Dairy Sector: An Example using Sector Linear Programming', *Cornell Agricultural Economics Staff Paper*, Cornell University, Ithaca, New York, p. 17.
Examines the impact of bovine growth hormone under a number of conditions on: number of farms, milk prices, milk output, and dairy income.

UNIDO (1985), *Biotechnology in Agriculture: Evolving a Research Agenda for the ICGEB*, United Nations Industrial Development Organization, Vienna.
Proceedings of an international workshop to help develop a biotechnology programme in agriculture for the New Delhi component of the International Centre for Genetic Engineering and Biotechnology.

UNIDO (1986), Preparatory committee on the establishment of the International Centre for Genetic Engineering and Biotechnology (Eighth Session), Vienna, June, ICGEB/PREP COMM/8/10, United Nations Industrial Development Organization, Vienna.
Refers to the appointment of Professor I.C. Gunsalus as Director of the ICGEB and some of the related initial decisions taken.

UNIDO (1986a), Report of specialized workshop, prepared by the UNIDO Secretariat, ICGEB/PREP Comm/18/2/ADD3, United Nations Industrial Development Organization, Vienna.

Presents the main conclusions of the International Centre for Genetic Engineering and Biotechnology workshops on biotechnology and industrial commodities held in Trieste in March. The workshop examined possible priorities for research for the Trieste part of the UCGEB. The priorities for the New Delhi part are discussed in a separate publication (ICGEB/PREP COMM/7/2/ADD3). The paper also defines the required 'basic capabilities' needed to support all scientific aspects of the ICGEB's research.

UNIDO (Various), *Genetic Engineering and Biotechnology Monitor*, United Nations Industrial Development Organization, Vienna.
Summary of current biotechnology news taken from many of the major biotechnology publications.

UNIDO Secretariat (1985), 'The Promise of Biotechnology and Genetic Engineering for Africa', Report No. UNIDO/IS/513, Secretariat of United Nations Industrial Development Organization, Vienna.
A general paper giving an account of possible application areas in African countries. Does not go beyond a very general level.

UNIDO Secretariat (1986), 'The Role of UNIDO in Technological Advances in the Latin American—Caribbean Area', United Nations Industrial Development Organization, Vienna.
Analyses the role of UNIDO in microelectronics and biotechnology in the Latin American—Caribbean area.

U.S. Congress, Office of Technology Assessment (1984), 'Commercial Biotechnology: An International Analysis', Report No. OTA-BA-218, U.S. Government Printing Office, Washington, D.C.
A major comparative report assessing the international competitiveness of U.S. biotechnology.

U.S. Congress, Office of Technology Assessment (1986), 'Public Policy and the Changing Structure of American Agriculture', Report No. OTA-F-285, U.S. Government Printing Office, Washington, D.C.
A major report assessing the combined effects of biotechnology and information technology on U.S. agriculture.

U.S. Department of Commerce (1985a), 'Biotechnology in Japan', Unpublished Report, U.S. Department of Commerce, Washington, D.C., 12 pp.
A preliminary investigation of biotechnology in Japan drawing attention, *inter alia*, to Japanese strength in fermentation and downstream processing and to the importance of Japanese research contracts with U.S. firms and universities.

U.S. Department of Commerce (1985b), *Biotechnology in Japan*, Japanese Technology Evaluation Program, U.S. Department of Commerce, Washington, D.C.
Contains evaluations by a number of U.S. scientists of Japanese developments in the following areas: biochemical process technology; biosensors; cell culture; protein engineering; recombinant DNA technology. Concludes, *inter alia*, that the U.S. faces its most serious competitive challenge from Japan, particularly from the large companies with a strong base in conventional biotechnologies (e.g. fermentation) and longer planning horizons.

Warhurst, A. (1985), 'Biotechnology for Mining: The Potential of an Emerging Technology, the Andean Pact Copper Project and some Policy Implications', *Development and Change*, Vol. 16, pp. 93-121.
A study of the development of bacterial leaching in Andean Pact countries.

World Health Organization (1983), 'Quality Control and Biologicals Produced by Recombinant DNA Techniques', *Bulletin of the World Health Organization*, Vol. 61, No. 6, pp. 897-911.
Outlines the tests that would be appropriate for the control of the safety and efficiency of recombinant DNA products in the pharmaceutical industry.

World Health Organization (1983), *Laboratory Biosafety Manual*, World Health Organization, Geneva.
Provides guidelines and details regarding appropriate laboratory practice and management.

World Health Organization (1984), 'Health Impact of Biotechnology', Report on a WHO Working Group, Dublin, November 1982, *Swiss Biotech*, No. 5.
Examines the risk of accidental production or escape of pathogens. Concludes that the risks are small provided reasonable safety measures are followed.

Yanchinski, S. (1985), *Getting Genes to Work: The Industrial Era of Biotechnology*, Penguin Books, Harmondsworth.
A general introduction to biotechnology.

Yanchinsky, S. (1986), 'Spearhead of a Second Green Revolution', *Financial Times*, 17 September.
Discusses the implications of new rice varieties developed by the International Rice Research Institute and the relevance of new biotechnologies.

Yuan, R. (1985), 'Interim Report on Biotechnology in France', Unpublished Report, U.S. Department of Commerce, Washington, D.C.
Examines the state and international competitiveness of biotechnology in France and concludes that due to fragmentation, isolation and the small size of research

units, French biotechnology does not in general pose a threat to the competitive position of the U.S.

FOR FURTHER READING

Barnes, B. (1977), *Interests and the Growth of Knowledge*, Routledge and Kegan Paul, London.

Barnes, B. (1982), *T.S. Kuhn and Social Science*, Macmillan, London.

Bennett, D., Glasnor, P. and Travis, D. (1986), *The Politics of Uncertainty: Regulating recombinant DNA research in Britain*, Routledge and Kegan Paul, London.

Cantley, M.F. (1983), *Plan by Objective: Biotechnology*, European Commission FAST Project, Commission of the European Communities, Brussels.

Chandler, A.D. (1977), *The Visible Hand: The Managerial Revolution in American Business*, Harvard University Press, Cambridge, Massachusetts.

Chandley, A.D. (1962), *Strategy and Structure: Chapters in the History of the American Industrial Enterprise*, MIT Press, Cambridge, Massachusetts.

Commission of the European Communities, *Developments in the Biotechnology Industry: Prospects for US—EC Co-operation*, Commission of the European Communities, Brussels.

Coombs, J. (1984), *The International Biotechnology Directory*, Macmillan, Basingstoke.

Cooper, C. (1973), 'Science Technology and Production in the Underdeveloped Countries: An Introduction', in Cooper, C. (ed.), *Science, Technology and Development: The Political Economy of Technical Advance in Underdeveloped Countries*, Frank Cass, London.

Cooper, C.M. (1981), 'Policy Intervention for Technological Innovations in Developing Countries', *World Bank Staff Working Paper*, No. 441, The World Bank, Washington, D.C.

Dore, R. (1983), *A Case Study of Technology Forecasting in Japan: The Next Generation Base Technologies Development Programme*, Technical Change Centre, London.

Dore, R.P. (1985), 'Why Japanese Firms can take a Long-term View', *Financial Journal of Sociology*, Vol. XXXIV, No. 4, pp. 459-482.

Dore, R.P. (forthcoming), *'Flexible Rigidities'*, *Structural Adjustments in the Japanese Economy*, Athlone Press, London.

Doyle, J. (1985), 'Biotechnology's Harvest of Herbicides', *Genewatch*, Vol. 2.

European Federation of Biotechnology Newsletter (various), Frankfurt, Germany.

Fairtlough, G. (1980), 'How Systems Thinking Might Evolve', *Journal of Systems Analysis*, Vol. 7, pp. 13-21.

Fairtlough, G.H. (1982), 'Innovation and Biotechnology', *Journal of the Royal Society of Arts*, August, pp. 565-576.

Fairtlough, G.H. (1984); 'Can We Plan for New Technology?', *Long Range Planning*, Vol. 17, No. 3, pp. 14-23.

Faulkner, W.R. (1986), 'Linkages Between Industrial and Academic Research: The Case of Biotechnology Research in the Pharmaceutical Industry', Ph.D. Dissertation, University of Sussex.

Fransman, M. (1985), 'Conceptualizing Technical Change in the Third World in the 1980s: An Interpretative Survey', *Journal of Development Studies*.

Fransman, M. and King, K. (1984), *Technological Capability in the Third World*, Macmillan, London.

Gilbert, R. (1982), *Pharmaceuticals and Biotechnology in Japan*, James Capel and Co., London.

Japanscan: Bio-industry Bulletin (1983—), Mitaka, Leamington Spa.

Jasanoff, S. (1985), 'Technological Innovation in a Corporatist State: The Case of Biotechnology in the Federal Republic of Germany', *Research Policy*, Vol. 14, pp. 23-38.

Krimsky, S. (1982), *Genetic Alchemy: The Social History of the Recombinant DNA Controversy*, MIT Press, Boston.

Lesser, W., Magrath, W. and Kalter, R. (1985), 'Projecting Adoption Rates: Application of an Ex Ante Procedure to Biotechnology Projects', *Cornell Agricultural Economics Staff Paper*, Cornell University, Ithaca, New York.

Magrath, W.B. (1985), 'Factors Affecting the Location of the US Biotechnology Industry', *Cornell Agricultural Economics Staff Paper*, Cornell University, Ithaca, New York.

Magrath, W.B. (1986), 'Patent and Technology Transfer Issues in Biotechnology', *Cornell Agricultural Economics Staff Paper*, Cornell University, Ithaca, New York.

Okimoto, D.I., Sugano, T. and Weinstein, F.B. (1984), *Competitive Edge: The Semiconductor Industry in the US and Japan*, Stanford University Press, Stanford.

Randall, P. (1986), 'Recombinant Virus may be useful in Studying the AIDS virus and as Potential Vaccine', *News and Features from NIH*, Vol. 86, No. 4.

Roobeek, A.J.M. (1986), '*The Crisis in Fordism and the Rise of a New Technological System*', Department of Economics, University of Amsterdam, Amsterdam.

Rothman, H., Stanley, R., Thompson, S. and Towalski, Z. (1981), *Biotechnology: A Review and Annotated Bibliography*, Frances Pinter, London.

Ruivenkamp, G. (1984), 'Biotechnology. The Production of New Relations Within the Agro-industrial Chain of Production', Unpublished Manuscript.

Sasson, A. (1984), *Biotechnologies, Challenges and Promises*, United Nations Educational, Scientific and Cultural Organization, Paris.

Schneiderman, H.A. (1985), *Genetic Engineering in Agriculture — Will it Pay?*, Monsanto Co., St. Louis.

Schonberger, R.J. (1982), *Japanese Manufacturing Techniques: Nine Hidden Lessons in Simplicity*, The Free Press, New York.

Stankiewicz, R. (1981), 'The Single Cell Protein as a Technological Field', Report by the Research Policy Institute, University of Lund, Lund, Sweden.

Straus, J. (1985), *Industrial Property Protection of Biotechnical Inventions: Analysis of Certain Basic Issues*, World Intellectual Property Organization, Geneva, July.

Ubell, R.N. (1982), 'Cuba's Great Leap', *Nature*, Vol. 302, pp. 745-748.

Ubell, R.N. (1983), 'High-tech Medicine in the Caribbean', *The New England Journal of Medicine*, Vol. 309, pp. 1468-1472.

UNIDO (1984), 'Draft Work Programme for the First Five Years of Operation of the International Centre for Genetic Engineering and Biotechnology', Report No. ICGEB/PREP COMM/5/2, United Nations Industrial Development Organization, Vienna.

UNIDO Secretariat (1984), *'Biotechnology and the Developing Countries: Applications for the Pharmaceutical Industry and Agriculture'*, United Nations Industrial Development Organization, Vienna.

U.S. Government, Interagency Working Group on Competitive and Transfer Aspects of Biotechnology (1983), *Biobusiness World Data Base*, McGraw—Hill, Washington, D.C.

Utterback, J.M. and Abernathy, W.J. (1975), 'A Dynamic Model of Process and Product Innovation', *Omega*, Vol. 3, No. 6, pp. 639-656.

Warhurst, A. (1984), *'The Applications of Biotechnology in Developing Countries: The Case of Bacterial Leaching with Particular Reference to the Andean Pact Copper Project'*, United Nations Industrial Development Organization, Vienna.

Watanabe, S. (1985), 'Employment and Income Implications of the "Biorevolution": A Speculative Note', *International Labour Review*, Vol. 124, No. 3, pp. 281-297.

Watson, J.D. (1983), *A Short Course in Recombinant DNA*, Freeman, New York.

Williamson, O.E. (1979), 'Transaction Cost Economics: The Governance of Contractual Relations', *Journal of Law and Economics*, October, pp. 233-261.

Williamson, O.E. (1980), 'The Organization of Work. A Comparative Institutional Assessment', *Journal of Economic Behaviour and Organization*, pp. 5-38.

Zimmerman, B.K. (1984), *Biofuture — Confronting the Genetic Era*, Plenum Press, New York.

Zimmerman, B.K. (1984), *Trends in World Biotechnology*, a review and analysis of advances in technology and industrial development.

3. Microelectronics and the Third World

Jeffrey James

3.1 INTRODUCTION

This survey will be guided by recognition of two points which I hope will facilitate understanding of the impacts that innovations in microelectronics have on developing countries. The first is that the social impacts of technical change in general, and thus of microelectronic innovations in particular, are importantly influenced by the way in which innovations are generated and diffused. The second is that a wider range of economic and social analysis than is usually considered is in fact relevant to understanding the innovation processes and impacts associated with microelectronics. With reference to these two points, this chapter will attempt an integrative focus.

The purpose is not, however, to meet all the formidable integrative requirements imposed by this general framework. The purpose, rather, is to undertake part of the integration and to urge a far greater effort along similar synthetic lines than is typical of the existing literature. Perhaps mainly because it tends to emphasize the singular features of microelectronics-based innovations, this literature is inclined to disassociate itself methodologically from the economics of technical change on the one hand and from development economics on the other.

Yet, in our view, these bodies of thought can contribute greatly to understanding the economic impact of microelectronics on the Third World. Thus, the first part of this chapter (Section 3.2) will attempt to show how aspects of the literature on technology transfer, choice of technology, multinational enterprises (MNEs), and the diffusion of innovations can be used to help explain prevailing patterns of adoption and diffusion of microelectronics in developing countries. On the basis of these findings and with reference to an equally broad range of literature, the discussion is led, in Section 3.3, to identify the major development issues to which these patterns give rise, to suggest ways in which they may be tackled, and to assemble the evidence that bears on each of them. Emerging from the arguments of both these sections are issues for policy and for research directions. These are taken up in Section 3.4.

3.2 PATTERNS OF ADOPTION AND DIFFUSION IN THE THIRD WORLD

Understanding *generation* of new technology is concerned with the forces that determine the rate at which new technologies are created and the form that they take. *Diffusion*, in contrast, concerns the spread of new technologies so created. As such, it deals, on the one hand, with the conditions in which the owner of a new technology chooses to make his innovation (which may be a new process or a new product) available to potential users (who are firms in the case of new processes and households in the case of new products). We shall refer to these conditions as constituting the *supply side* of the diffusion of new technologies. In addition, there is a *demand-side* component, which relates to the factors that underlie demands for the new technologies by relevant groups of potential users.

In relation to the agricultural sector, the literature tends to focus almost entirely on the question of diffusion and, in particular, on the demand side of the problem (for example, the characteristics that predispose individual agents to accept or reject innovations). This preoccupation is mainly a reflection of the public goods character of many of the innovations introduced into this sector. For example,

> With the exception of a few countries, seed varieties are not effectively protected by licenses. In the case of many varieties, once a farmer has bought a single lot he can reproduce the seed himself and sell it to neighbours without

having to pay more to the plant-breeding firm. ... It was necessary to create a public agricultural research system to do research in the biological area in order to overcome the lack of incentive brought about by this situation.

(Binswanger and Ruttan, 1978, p. 117)

Once created, the innovations of such public research become freely accessible: that is, nonproprietary. Diffusion of such innovations, therefore, depends only on the side of demand, namely, whether and to what extent the innovations are taken up by the relevant groups of adopters.

Literature on the industrial sector focuses a great deal more attention on the generation of new technologies, because in this sector (unlike agriculture) innovations tend to be proprietary in character. With respect to many microelectronics-based innovations, for example, 'whether final goods or components, vital technical information regarding design, engineering specifications, process know-how, testing procedures etc., is proprietary in nature, covered by patents or copyrights, or closely held within various electronics firms from developed countries' (O'Connor, 1985b, p. 12). There is relatively little discussion, however, of the circumstances that govern the way owners of proprietary knowledge in microelectronics, or indeed new technologies in general, choose to exploit these assets (that is, on the supply-side aspects of diffusion). Yet, in the case of developing countries — for most of whom the generation of microelectronics innovations takes place entirely exogenously — it is precisely this question that one needs to answer to determine the availability of new technologies. Accordingly, we devote the first part of this section to a discussion of supply-side factors in the diffusion of microelectronics technologies in the Third World. Thereafter, we will examine the major determinants of demand for these innovations.[1]

3.2.1 Supply-Side Factors

It is convenient to discuss the supply-side determinants of diffusion of microelectronics to developing countries under the two broad headings of foreign direct investment and arm's-length markets. We shall begin with the issues raised under the former and then proceed to define the circumstances in which certain new technologies become available to the Third World without the accompaniment of foreign investment (e.g., through licensing).

3.2.1.1 Foreign direct investment

Literature on the activities of multinational corporations in developing countries tends to distinguish sharply between exporters on the one hand and firms producing for domestic markets on the other (Caves, 1982). This same distinction is necessary also as a starting point for explaining the presence of multinational subsidiaries in the electronics-based industries of the Third World.

Export-oriented foreign investment   There is a sizeable literature describing the evolution of competitive forces within markets in developed countries that compel multinational electronics corporations to locate production for export in the Third World (Plesch, 1979; ESCAP, 1979; Ernst, 1983; O'Connor, 1985a,b; Henderson, 1989). Many of the most important of these forces — ease of entry, the threat of internal and external competition and the rapidity of technical change — are illustrated with particular clarity in the history of the computer industry.

What is interesting, in particular, is the contrast between the mainframe and the later, smaller, computers. Thus,

> Mainframe computer manufacture has historically been concentrated almost exclusively in the advanced industrialised countries. Since the demand for mainframes has not generally been price elastic, lowering production costs through offshore assembly has not been considered a requirement of competition in that product range. Demand for smaller computer systems, however, tends to be more price sensitive, with the result that computer firms have had to economise on production costs in whatever way possible so as to expand their market shares. In addition to this fact, in the low end of the computer market ... firms have employed aggressive market entry pricing strategies which have resulted in periodic rounds of steep price reductions. Combined with the rapid pace of product innovation in this segment of the industry, the intense price competition has forced a number of computer manufacturers to shift production to low wage locations as a short term survival strategy.
>
> (O'Connor, 1985b, p. 6)

Somewhat less numerous than the explanations of why MNEs choose to undertake export-oriented investments in the Third World (such as that quoted in the previous paragraph) are attempts to account for the particular countries selected. One approach employs a cross-country framework to identify the common characteristics of the countries selected (for example, Nayyar, 1978).[2] Wheeler and Mody (1988) used this approach to investigate location decisions by U.S. MNEs in manufacturing. What they found, in the case of export-oriented electronics firms, is that these decisions are not a function of labour costs alone: the quality of infrastructure and agglomeration economies appear to be equally important. These results, in turn, help to explain the popularity of East Asian locations among U.S. electronics firms, as reflected, for example, in the fact that in 1983 the vast majority of semiconductor imports under sections 806.30/807.00 of the U.S. Tariff Schedule came from assembly plants in four East Asian countries.[3] On the one hand, many countries in the region have a well-developed infrastructure: 'In fact, some Far East locations today have an excellent infrastructure which, more so than in OECD [Organization for Economic Cooperation and Development] countries, is geared to the requirements of global sourcing in electronics' (Ernst, 1985, p. 31). On the other hand, the newly industrialized countries (NICs) appear to have benefited from what Wheeler and Mody refer to as an 'historical first-mover advantage', that is the agglomeration economies that accrued to these countries from the substantial offshore assembly investment undertaken by U.S. firms during the 1970s in the face of strong Japanese competition.

While one can progress reasonably far on the basis of this sort of cross-country analysis, it is apparent that in many cases an adequate explanation needs to invoke a much more specific set of factors. Consider, for example, the case of computer disk drives, in which Singapore has become the principal location for production by multinational subsidiaries (O'Connor, 1985b; UNCTC, 1987). This has occurred, according to O'Connor (1985b), for reasons associated with the presence in that country, because of its industrial history, of a well-developed machining industry. Television assembly, in contrast to semiconductor assembly, is space intensive, which could explain in part why Hong Kong and Singapore do not figure as centrally in this segment of the electronics industry as their more 'land-rich' neighbours, Korea and Taiwan. ... In addition, Hong Kong and Singapore lack domestic manufacturing capacity for cathode ray tubes (CRTs), which put them at a competitive disadvantage not only in TV production but in the production of computer terminals and monitors, since the CRTs used in such products are bulky and costly to transport' (ibid., p. 6 of notes and references).

What these examples suggest is the need for an approach to the study of the location of foreign electronics investment which can, on the one hand, specify in detail the requirements of each of the new technologies (for components, infrastructure, managerial skills, and so on) and, on the other, discern the extent to which different developing countries can satisfy these diverse requirements. Though clearly highly demanding of data and research input, such an approach is often likely to be highly rewarding. It enables one to bring out, for example, the relevance of the pattern of past industrial (and other) development in a developing country to the determination of its present comparative advantage (and, by extension, points to the way in which current patterns might impinge on its future endowment).[4]

Henderson (1989) made a systematic effort along these disaggregated lines to explain the changed (and changing) pattern of foreign investment in semiconductor production in East Asia. In particular, he suggests that a 'specifically East Asian division of labour has developed' (ibid., p. 55). This new pattern of foreign investment is essentially one in which 'more and more of the investment in assembly plants for large-batch standardised outputs tended to go to an increasing degree to Thailand, Malaysia, the Philippines, and so on, while Hong Kong, Singapore and now, seemingly Malaysia, have tended to be upgraded as to the quality and complexity of their production technologies and labour processes' (ibid., p. 59). Henderson also offered a very detailed explanation of these important changes, to which we will refer in later sections.

Local-market oriented foreign investment The model of the multinational firm which (as we shall see) underlies much of the literature on the impact of microelectronics on the Third World is the export-oriented subsidiary. This model applies best to the semiconductor industry, in which there is a preponderance of direct foreign investment that is heavily oriented towards production for export. Yet in many other sectors it is manufacturing subsidiaries with an orientation to the local, rather than the export market, that tend to dominate.[5] In fact, 'Like investments by computer and consumer electronics TNCs [transnational corporations] in developing countries, those by telecommunications TNCs tend to be oriented largely toward local or regional markets' (O'Connor, 1985b, p. 37). Fragmentary data for Japanese MNEs operating in consumer electronics suggest that local-market-oriented investment may have comprised roughly 50% of total global investment in the mid-1970s (ESCAP, 1979). A recent study of the electronics industry in Brazil concludes that foreign computer firms were 'much more interested in Brazil's market than in the price of its labour' (Hewitt, 1988, p. 170).

At a general level, it is important to recognize that the location of local-market-oriented investment needs to be viewed, as Vernon (1973) has pointed out, from a different realm of economic theory than that which governs the export-oriented variety. Whereas 'the classical model provides a fairly good basis for the description of locational behaviour' for export-oriented investment, one may often need to look to oligopoly theory to explain patterns of domestic-market-oriented foreign investment. To illustrate this important point, consider the locational decisions prompted by the local substitution of imported consumer electronics goods in most of developing Asia after 1960. The sequence of events has been described as follows:

> The erection of protective trade barriers compelled the foreign exporters to commence local production if their market was not to be lost. The Japanese in particular stood to lose as they had been very active in the export field. *Moreover, there appears to have developed a 'bandwagon effect' whereby Japanese firms upon witnessing the relocation of their competition, perceived a threat to their market share and subsequently followed the move.*
> (ESCAP, 1979, p. 29, emphasis added)

It is plainly not standard comparative cost theory that lies behind this concentration of foreign investment for the local markets, which appears to be explicable instead in terms of a 'follow-the-leader' type of reaction function in oligopolistic markets (Vernon, 1973). That is, 'the decision of one firm in an international oligopoly to establish a new producing facility outside its home country often seems to trigger the establishment of similar facilities in that country by others'[6] (ibid., p. 21).

Although very little is known about the inter-country distribution of local-market-oriented investment (which, as in the case of export-oriented production, will vary according to the specific fiscal and other attractions offered by particular developing countries), a few general observations can be made. The first is that insofar as economies of scale are a significant aspect of the new technologies, large [in the sense of having a high gross domestic product (GDP)] countries will be favoured. Since, for example, 'there are substantial economies of scale in the production of many pieces of telecommunications equipment, only those developing countries with the largest potential markets have attracted substantial investments' (O'Connor, 1985b, p. 37). A second observation is that adaptation of new technologies to serve particular user needs will tend to be profitable only if the size of the market is sufficiently large.[7] It seems plausible, for example, to view the specialized development efforts that have been undertaken by computer MNEs to overcome the language processing requirements in Korea, China, and Taiwan (ibid.) in terms of the potential afforded by the combined market size of these countries. The last observation is that the market size for different products in a developing country is likely to depend on the pattern of income distribution, as well as on per capita income. When a given average income is evenly distributed, large markets are created for relatively simple goods (e.g., radios). But if income is highly unequally distributed, a small market is created for more sophisticated, 'high-income' products (such as VCRs).

Taken together, these general observations suggest a broad pattern of local-market-oriented investment that will tend to comprise individual countries with a relatively high GDP, a high per capita GDP, or groups of countries which possess one or both of these characteristics. Combined with the types of countries that appear to be favoured by export-oriented investments in microelectronics described above, several tentative generalizations about the overall distribution of foreign investment in the Third World may be offered. The first is that many countries (such as the Asian NICs, Mexico, parts of the Caribbean, etc.) will be favoured by both forms of foreign investment. Insofar as (is broadly the case) these are among the more affluent developing countries, an inegalitarian bias in the distribution of foreign investment within the Third World is created. And this bias is not generally likely to be offset by the relatively low incomes of countries that fall in only one or other of the two investment categories (though of course, there are such cases, such as India and the Philippines). On the contrary, the income levels of countries forming part of these categories may well be such as to contribute to, rather than ameliorate, the tendency to inequality.[8] Though there are no data that can throw any conclusive light on these hypotheses, some very crude supportive evidence for the computer industry is given in Table 3.1. Though the classification of countries according to the stance that they adopt *vis-à-vis* MNEs ('assertive' versus 'accommodating') is somewhat questionable, the table is useful in showing that the total involvement of American computer MNEs in the Third World was concentrated among a narrow group of countries during the late 1970s.

Table 3.1   U.S. computer enterprises in upper-tier developing countries, late 1970s

Category of developing country[a]	Number of units[b]	Percentage of units in all LDCs
Assertive	12	40.0
Accommodating	11	36.6

[a]Assertive LDCs are defined to include India, Brazil, Mexico, Colombia, Indonesia, Nigeria, and Venezuela; accommodating LDCs are defined to include Hong Kong, Malaysia, the Philippines, Singapore, Taiwan, South Korea, and Thailand.
[b]No manufacturing subsidiary was operating at this time in Indonesia, Nigeria, or Venezuela.
Source: Grieco (1984, p. 65).

In particular, 76% of the total was invested in India, Brazil, Mexico, Colombia, Hong Kong, Malaysia, the Philippines, Singapore, Taiwan, South Korea, and Thailand.[9] The predominance of relatively affluent segments of the Third World (namely, the groups of large Latin American countries and East Asian NICs) in this list of countries also bears on the arguments presented immediately above.

Another piece of evidence is provided by the global distribution of overseas subsidiaries of Japanese electronics firms. Of the total number of these subsidiaries, 46% are found in four Asian countries (Singapore, Korea, Taiwan, and Malaysia), while another 11% are located in Latin America (Humbert, 1988). When these tendencies towards concentration are combined with the finding that agglomeration economies appear to be very important to the location decisions of multinational firms, the likelihood of a future pattern of cumulative causation emerges (Wheeler and Mody, 1988). That is, 'newcomer' countries will find it increasingly difficult to attract foreign investment in microelectronics-related industries, while countries already in the location 'tournament' will become increasingly attractive.

Distinctions between export- and import-oriented investment   An interesting and important question is whether any systematic differences can be found in the behaviour of subsidiaries engaged in production for export as opposed to those that are oriented to the local market. Unfortunately, however, only one study — of the consumer electronics industry in a group of developing Asian countries — has addressed this question systematically. On the basis of a sample of 63 firms drawn from Malaysia, Korea, Singapore, and Thailand, this study 'suggests the existence of a tendency for outward-looking foreign investments vis-à-vis domestic market-oriented businesses to have larger production volumes, a higher degree of product specialization, greater foreign equity participation, a lower percentage of domestic value-added and a higher proportion of expatriate management' (ESCAP, 1979, p. 50). In several respects, such as differences in ownership and value added, these findings match those of other studies that have compared the behaviour of inward- and outward-looking manufacturing subsidiaries (see, e.g., Reuber et al., 1973).

They are also confirmed in part by a more recent study of MNEs in the electronics industries of some of the same economies (UNCTC, 1987). But because they were not subjected to tests of statistical significance, the results of the Asian survey need to be treated with the corresponding degree of caution.

3.2.1.2 Transfer mechanisms not involving foreign investment

So far, our review of the factors that determine the availability of microelectronics technologies to developing countries has relied in effect upon two assumptions: (1) that some degree of monopoly control over these technologies is held by agents in the advanced countries and (2) that these agents choose to exploit their proprietary rights in the form of foreign direct investment in the Third World. The fact that these assumptions are not always applicable, however, gives rise to a set of alternative mechanisms through which the new technologies become available to certain developing countries. To begin, we will consider the circumstances in which, though proprietary rights in these technologies are held, they are exploited in forms that do not involve foreign direct investment.

Arm's-length licensing From the general literature on technology transfer, it is possible to identify the variables that seem to govern the firm's choice between establishing a foreign subsidiary and licensing its proprietary assets at arm's length. This literature suggests, first, that 'companies do contemplate foreign investment and licensing as direct alternatives, preferring foreign investment for its greater rent-extracting potential, turning to licensing only if that potential cannot be realized' (Caves, 1982, p. 204). In the semiconductor industry, for example, the preference of American firms for wholly owned subsidiaries in East Asia continues to be reflected in the predominance of this form of production in the region (Henderson, 1989, p. 55).

It is accordingly mostly to the circumstances that are relatively unconducive to foreign investment that one must look in predicting when licensing will occur. In particular, 'Arm's-length licensing is encouraged by risks to foreign investors and barriers to entry of subsidiaries, by short economic life of the knowledge asset, by simplicity of the technology, by high capital costs for the potential foreign investor, and by certain types of product market competition that favor reciprocal licensing' (Caves, 1982, p. 224).

Tigre's (1983) study of the computer industry in Brazil throws some degree of light on these propositions in the context of transfers of microelectronics technologies to the Third World. Among the foreign computer firms operating in that country in 1980, Tigre found a tendency for foreign investment to be associated mainly with very large firms. 'Smaller firms either licensed their technology or entered into joint ventures in order to compete in the Brazilian market' (Tigre, 1983, p. 143). His explanation of this finding is that while foreign ownership was the preferred mode of transfer for most firms 'only very large firms could actually afford to pursue this strategy' (ibid.). Underlying this distinction between actual and desired behaviour is the finding that several of the circumstances mentioned in the previous paragraph as being unfavourable for foreign investment (or favourable to licensing) bore in this case differently on firms of different size. In particular, these factors appeared to be so arranged as to make licensing the preferred option only for firms that were relatively small.

The absence of direct investment by all except large firms arose because 'medium-size firms usually lacked the managerial and financial resources to compete directly in overseas markets. A licensing agreement did not require any additional investment and helped the firms recover previous R&D expenditure' (ibid., p. 144). A second reason was that the smaller firms appeared to be less able than their very large counterparts to resist demands by the Brazilian authorities to share technology. (The same point is made by Evans and Tigre, 1989, in relation to 'super-mini' computers in Brazil.) Finally, the competitive forces to which the smaller firms were subjected, to an apparently greater degree, meant that Brazil obtained access to some of the new technologies in the computer industry relatively early in the product cycle and on terms other than through foreign investment. For example, in 1979 the Brazilian firm Flexidisk tried to obtain a licence from Shugart to manufacture floppy-disk drives in Brazil. Shugart refused on the grounds that its corporate policy was not to sell newly developed technology. Later, however, when Flexidisk was on the brink of signing a technology transfer agreement with another American manufacturer (Pertec), Shugart realized that its policy could cause it to lose the fast-growing Brazilian market. Thus it changed its policy and agreed to license floppy-disk drives to Flexidisk (Tigre, 1983, p. 165).[10]

Though there is very little hard evidence on the subject, one suspects that this last example constitutes an exception to the more general rule that licensed technology is available to developing countries only at fairly advanced stages of the product cycle.[11]

Clarke and Cable, for example, observed that

> Japanese firms (even in the case of joint ventures) have displayed a reluctance to sell licenses for more advanced technology. ... Japanese firms prefer to transfer know-how only for simple products such as black and white sets and simple colour portables, using older technology in tubes and semiconductors. ... Japanese producers have also been unwilling to provide Korean firms with technical know-how for new products such as VCRs and video discs.
>
> (Clarke and Cable, 1982, p. 31)

Much is likely to depend, however, on the prevalence of small firms which are innovative but unable to gain access to the resources required for direct investments. These firms will tend to license their innovations early, because there is no alternative way to exploit the market (Evans and Tigre, 1989).

Subcontracting Just as licensing arrangements may, under some circumstances, replace foreign investment as a mechanism of 'horizontal' transfer of microelectronics technology (i.e., between firms producing the same line of goods), so too may subcontracting sometimes serve as a substitute for the multinational subsidiary in production that is vertically integrated (e.g., semiconductors). This latter phenomenon has been noted by several authors (Plesch 1979; ESCAP, 1979), and, not surprisingly, it seems to be facilitated by several of the same factors that were described above as tending to favour licensing over foreign investment. Plesch, for example, cites the following specific determining factors:[12]

- If a company's production ... is too small to justify offshore production and take advantage of possible economies of scale, subcontracting an independent

LDC manufacturer would seem a more economical solution, especially so when it requires lower investment;[13]
- If a company's production volume is subject to fluctuations, subcontracting may be a short-term solution during peak production periods;
- Subcontracting may involve less risks than offshore investment;[14] products or processes that are subcontracted are generally the most standardised and unsophisticated.

(Plesch, 1979, pp. 87-88)

The first two of these factors appear also to explain the emergence of a network of subcontracting relationships in the overwhelmingly foreign-owned semiconductor industry in East Asia. Such arrangements have emerged particularly in the Philippines and to a lesser extent in Korea (Henderson, 1989).

Loss of effective proprietary rights   In the discussion above, the availability to developing countries of the new microelectronics-based innovations was shown to be circumscribed by the various mechanisms that owners of proprietary rights in the innovations choose to exploit them. But insofar as these rights may themselves become ineffective, further possibilities of access are opened up to developing countries. The replication in the Third World of microcomputers developed by MNEs is undoubtedly one of the most important manifestations of these possibilities.[15]

In part, this phenomenon appears to have resulted from the reliance of MNEs on outside sourcing which, by disclosing technical information to supplier firms, 'made the replication of standard computer architectures somewhat simpler' (O'Connor, 1985a, p. 320). But the loss of proprietary control over this technology also has to be viewed against the particular industrial structure in the developed countries from which it emerged. This structure was one in which the innovation of the microprocessor (the central element of the microcomputer) occurred in firms that happened to have no incentive to exploit the innovation as proprietary knowledge. Specifically, 'Because microprocessors were produced by semi-conductor companies, like Zilog, Intel and Motorola, which did not themselves produce computers, they were available on a merchandise basis *rather than being incorporated in final demand products as proprietary technology*[16] (Evans, 1985, p. 21, emphasis added). Countries with the relevant technological capabilities (such as Brazil, Taiwan, and Korea) were thereby enabled to use the microprocessor (purchased on the open market) as a basis upon which to imitate existing models, such as Apple.[17] Indeed, 'It was the micro computer that really generated a dynamic set of locally-owned hardware producers in Brazil' (ibid., p. 21). More recently, Brazil and Korea have also used the availability of microprocessors on international markets as a basis for some of their attempts to promote an indigenous 'super-mini' computer industry (Evans and Tigre, 1989).

It bears emphasizing, however, that access by developing countries to the new technologies may often continue to depend on the behaviour of suppliers even when the technologies themselves are internationally available. In their study of the diffusion of flexible automation techniques, Edquist and Jacobsson (1988), for example, refer to this uncertainty as an important constraint on the adoption of these techniques in the newly industrializing countries. As they see it, the general problem is that 'in the fast-growing industries which are intensive in the use of service and/or application engineering, the suppliers may not be interested in sending scarce service or application engineers to marginal markets' (ibid., pp. 155-156).

3.2.2 Demand-Side Factors

Even in the absence of the supply-side constraints described in Section 3.2.1 — that is, even if the new technologies were freely accessible to the developing countries — demand-side factors alone are capable of preventing any generally rapid and widespread diffusion of these technologies in the Third World. The experience of the 'early follower' countries after the Industrial Revolution is well worth citing in this regard: at that time, from many points of view, the forces of demand were much more conducive to rapid adoption of the then-new technologies (which were apparently also easily accessible). These relatively favourable circumstances on the side of demand in the early follower countries (of continental Europe) have been described by Landes.

Their supply of capital and standard of living were substantially higher than in the 'backward' lands of today. And with this went a level of technical skill that, if not immediately adequate to the task of sustaining an industrial revolution was right at the margin. Culturally, of course, the outlook was even brighter. The continental countries were part of the same larger civilisation as Britain; and they were certainly her equals, in some respects her superiors, in science and education for the elite. In short if they were in their day 'underdeveloped', the word must be understood quite differently from the way it is today. ... Nevertheless, their Industrial Revolution was substantially slower than the British. *Although they were able to study the new machines and engines from the start and indeed acquire them in spite of prohibitions on their export, they were generations in absorbing them. ... In view of the enormous economic superiority of these innovations, one would expect the rest to have followed automatically.*

(Landes, 1969, pp. 125-126, emphasis added)

As we turn in this section to review the major determinants of demand for the current microelectronics technologies by the contemporary developing countries, it is worth noting that, in at least one major respect, the composition of this demand will differ from that prevailing during the historical experience just cited. This distinctive feature of today's situation arises from the very considerably enlarged role of the state in contemporary latecomers *vis-à-vis* the 'early followers' of the Industrial Revolution (ibid.).[18] In addition to these (now more numerous) agencies of the state, however, we shall also need to consider the demands for new technologies that arise from the other major groups of agents in the developing economies, namely, privately owned firms and individual households. The necessity for a classification of this kind arises not merely from the fact that each group generally pursues a different set of objectives within a diverse set of constraints,[19] but also because the demands of each may often relate to a quite different set of microelectronics-based innovations. Whereas, for example, the public sector has to take decisions about the 'public goods' aspects of the new technologies (such as telecommunications), individual household demands relate mainly to consumer electronics products.[20]

3.2.2.1 Agents on the demand side: the public sector

The state plays an indirect role in determining the nature and extent of demand for the new technologies through the overall development strategy that it chooses to pursue. For example, an outward-looking strategy generally imposes greater pressures to acquire the latest innovations than do inward-looking strategies, in which older vintages tend to be more prevalent. Governments also vary in the strategic role that they assign to the electronics complex in the modernization process as a whole (see Jacobsson and Sigurdson, 1983). Nochteff (1985, p. 42), for example, has noted that

> The strategic character which the Brazilian State assigned to national development in the field of data processing ... contrasts with a much less precise and aggressive attitude in the other two countries [Argentina and Mexico] where, historically speaking, the position in this sector had not been regarded as one of the nerve centres in the pattern of capital accumulation in modern societies.

More specifically, government policy towards importation of microelectronics technologies influences the range of and price at which these technologies are available domestically. For example, 'The nature of the protective policies for the machine tool industries in the NICs restricts access to, and therefore the scope for the introduction of, NCMTs' (Edquist and Jacobsson, 1988, p. 149). Government policy with respect to infrastructure, education, and skill formation also impinges in an important way on demand, since these variables often seem (as noted below) to be relevant to decisions to adopt the new techniques.

Governments influence demand in a direct way, however, through the agency of the state-owned enterprise, an institution that is currently of considerable importance in many parts of the Third World (see James, 1989). A series of studies has thrown considerable light on the factors that govern the technological choices of these firms. What emerges from this research, essentially, is a view of the decision-making process that is substantially at odds with the traditional theory of the firm (see James, 1989; Deolalikar and Sundaram, 1989; Fleury, 1989). For instance, managers appeared to use highly simplified decision rules, were often poorly informed, and were subjected to a variety of subtle motivations that led neither to profit maximization nor to fulfilment of the goals of the state.

While it is evident that state-owned enterprises also play a prominent role in the demand for microelectronics technologies,[21] it is not yet clear what underlies these demands. The reason for the uncertainty is that much of the literature focuses on the applications of microelectronics technologies by various government agencies, rather than on the nature of the institutional decisions that underlie these applications.[22] Several observations, however, suggest the need to examine the role of foreign (i.e., developed country) influences on these decisions. 'At present', for example 'much of the importation of microcomputer systems is done with donor agency funding' (Munasinghe et al., 1985, p. 37). Lahera and Nochteff (1983, p. 172) contend that 'computers and related systems were introduced in Latin America as a result of impulses which may be considered to be exogenous. The suppliers of computers ... pressured customers into buying products for which there was no local demand'.[23] Other evidence points to the need to examine deficiencies in the process by which decisions for the purchase of microelectronics technologies are made by state-owned firms in developing countries. For example, during the 1960s and early 1970s, 'a principal cause of India's inability to obtain more efficient computer systems was the information-gathering and -analysis problems of the government institutions responsible for the acquisition of computers by major Indian users' (Grieco, 1984, p. 108).

3.2.2.2 Private-producing units

Profitability is obviously a very important goal of private units and considerable literature attests to the fact that the speed of adoption of innovations is positively related to their impact on profits (see, e.g., Davies, 1979; Rogers, 1983; Stoneman, 1983). To examine patterns of adoption of microelectronics innovations by private units in developing countries, it is accordingly essential to identify the factors that determine the profitability of these innovations and it is to this task that we now turn.

Factor costs   Critical to the question of profitability is whether new technologies entirely dominate the old (i.e., when they are more profitable at all relevant factor price ratios) or whether they are profitable only at the factor prices prevailing in developed countries (Bhalla and J. James, 1986). What evidence that exists on this important question[24] suggests (in the case of electronic capital goods) that dominance is not a *pervasive* aspect of new technologies, although there are cases in which this phenomenon does seem to occur. One important source of evidence was derived as part of a complicated simulation exercise conducted by Mody and Wheeler (1990) to determine changes in international competitive advantage in three different industries (semiconductors, automobiles, and textiles/garments). For one of these industries, textiles and garments, the study reveals that the efficiency of new technologies depends very directly on relative wage levels across countries. Thus, 'The new microelectronics technology does offer savings in labor and time related costs, but these currently seem sufficient for dominance only in garment pre-assembly activities. In garment assembly and post-assembly, by contrast, sites in countries like China seem to retain a substantial cost advantage' (ibid., p. 64).

This finding is interesting because it mirrors in a broad way the outcome of previous generations of technological progress in this industry, which did not lead to the widespread disappearance of older techniques in developing countries.[25] The findings are also illuminating from the standpoint of the contrast that they present with the semiconductor industry, in which the highly automated technology did appear to be dominant at all relevant factor price ratios.

Other detailed research on the effects of new technologies on factor costs has been conducted in relation to computer numerically controlled (CNC) machine tools (CNCMTs) (Chudnovsky, 1984; Edquist et al., 1985; Jacobsson, 1986) and in relation to four flexible automation techniques (Edquist and Jacobsson, 1988). Of this work, Jacobsson's (1986) and Edquist and Jacobsson's (1988) contains the most detailed quantification of factor-saving bias and it is especially important in drawing attention to the extent of skilled labour that appears to be saved through the use of both CNC machine tools and computer-aided design (CAD).

Product characteristics Product characteristics may have an important bearing on the returns that can be expected from the adoption of a new process. The reason is that process innovations usually cause changes in the product. And as Davies (1979) points out, this influence can cut both ways, by either raising or reducing profitability.

In the development context, the literature has focused predominantly on increased profits. For a variety of countries and innovations [e.g., CAD, computer-aided manufacturing (CAM), and CNC machine tools], enhancement of product quality is a well-documented phenomenon (see Chudnovsky, 1984; Tauile, 1984; Edquist et al., 1985; Kaplinsky, 1982a, 1985; Hoffman and Rush, 1988; O'Connor, 1989). What also seems clear is that this phenomenon is most important to firms competing in markets in developed countries (particularly those in which the basis of competition is quality rather than price) and in developing countries where competition is on much the same basis (for example, in market segments dominated by the affluent minorities in these countries) (see James, 1987a).

Boon (1986a,b) has drawn detailed attention to the manner in which product characteristics of new technologies may constrain the adoption in developing countries of the process innovations with which they are associated. In a study of the adoption of CNC machine tools by firms in Mexico, he shows that these machines are suited to a particular degree of piece complexity and heterogeneity (and one that is characteristic of production in the developed countries). Plants that produce to a different pattern (for example, with more simple and homogeneous pieces) were found to be less attracted to the new machines. Boon's argument, however, has been questioned by Edquist and Jacobsson, who contend that 'there is really no empirical evidence showing that the NICs have a radically different output mix than the developed countries' (Edquist and Jacobsson, 1988, p. 147). They conclude, correctly, that the issue can be settled only on the basis of far more empirical evidence than is currently available.

The changing economics of time Closely related to the discussion of products is the question of the changing economics of time: that is, the more rapid production response (or shortened production cycle) that is possible with new technologies. This consideration allows, on the one hand, a reduction in working capital costs, and, on the other, it affords the competitive advantage of a more rapid response to consumer demands.[26] The latter is, of course, particularly relevant to industries (such as textiles and automobiles) in which demand tends to change relatively rapidly. Tauile's study of the Brazilian automobile industry, for example, shows that 'The need to assure uniformity of quality and respond quickly to modifications to orders (both regarding quantity and specifications) is definitely a powerful factor inducing auto parts makers to adopt more flexible and efficient production methods, i.e. ME [micro-electronic] equipment' (Tauile, 1984, p. 20). Moreover, insofar as rapid taste change is more typically a phenomenon of high-income societies (in these and other industries), this advantage of new technologies may again be most relevant to firms in developing countries that export to markets in the developed world.

The connection between product characteristics and flexibility on the one hand, and (developed country) export markets on the other, emerges strikingly from a set of recent case studies conducted for the International Labour Organization (ILO) (Pyo, 1986; Schmitz and Carvalho, 1987; Dominguez-Villalobos, 1988; Onn, 1989). These studies cover a range of industries, such as electronics, electrical, automobiles, general machinery, and ship-building, and they sought to determine, among other things, the reasons for adoption of flexible automation techniques. The results indicate that product quality and flexibility of production were uniformly among the most important factors in adoption decisions. These considerations, in turn, appear from the ILO studies to be closely related to exports, not only through quality requirements for competition in final goods, but also through the more stringent standards for inputs that such goods often induce.

Findings such as these are not unfamiliar in the literature on choice of technology. On the contrary, the need to produce to international standards is one of the reasons most commonly cited for adopting capital-intensive techniques in developing countries, especially in the case of relatively large firms (Stewart, 1987). Some of the issues that have been raised in this context may therefore also be relevant to new microelectronics technologies. From a policy point of view, for example, 'the extent and benefits from exporting must be clearly assessed and weighed against the cost of adopting inappropriate technology' (ibid., p. 291). Policy-makers also ought to consider whether exports could be directed towards markets that are less demanding in terms of product quality and which may thus lessen the degree of automation that is required. Trade between developing countries, perhaps on a regional basis, is one way in which this could occur.

Complementary infrastructure and skills   The profitability of many innovations in microelectronics depends heavily on the availability of skilled labour and complementary infrastructure. Hoffman (1984) has described the design, maintenance, and managerial skill requirements that are often both essential, and lacking, in the Third World.[27] Much the same can usually be said of infrastructure requirements;[28] in the case of microcomputers, for example, maintenance support, existing telephone systems, and erratic electrical power supply all act as severe constraints on expanded adoption (Munasinghe et al., 1985; Munasinghe, 1989).

Other factors   The factors considered above are those that appear to be *generally* relevant to the profitability of new techniques. A wide range of other variables also arise in specific contexts. Edquist and Jacobsson's (1988) study of flexible automation techniques, for example, contains an extensive discussion of a large number of factors that influence the adoption of these techniques in NICs. Only some of these factors fall into the four previous categories.

Taken together, the various factors that influence the speed of adoption through their effects on profitability tend to reinforce, on the demand side (and for some of the same reasons), the conclusion that was reached on the supply side: namely, that the bigger, more developed countries of the Third World are mostly better placed to take advantage of microelectronics-based innovations. For, except where they are dominant, these innovations tend to be more efficient at relatively high wages, when the product mix with which they are associated approximates patterns observed in developed countries (in the case of CNC machine tools), and when they are combined with a well-developed infrastructure (including technical and other skills).[29] It is no doubt at least partly for these reasons that the diffusion of many of the flexible automation techniques is confined largely to the more advanced developing countries (Edquist and Jacobsson, 1988; Onn, 1989). The diffusion of computers appears to follow a similar pattern.[30]

Information imperfections   Profitability is not the only factor that influences adoption, as Edquist and Jacobsson emphasized in their study of flexible automation techniques in the engineering industries in the OECD and NICs (Edquist and Jacobsson, 1988). Indeed, the finding that these techniques are generally being diffused less rapidly in the latter than in the former group can, according to this study, be explained only to a limited extent by differences in potential profitability (especially with regard to CNC machine tools and CAD, which, because of their skill-saving features, are often attractive from this point of view). Edquist and Jacobsson point instead to information imperfections — about and how to use the new techniques — as being 'especially important' for the developing countries and 'above all' for firms that are not subsidiaries of MNEs (ibid., p. 187). It follows from this conclusion that there is considerable scope for policy to provide information, especially to national firms, in these (and also, by extension, in other) developing countries.

3.2.2.3 Household demand
Corresponding to the literature on new processes are numerous studies that deal with the diffusion of product innovations (mostly consumer durable goods). These studies (see Davies, 1979; and Stoneman, 1983, for reviews) suggest that although the economic agents involved are different in the two cases (households as opposed to firms), a number of important parallels can nevertheless be drawn. First, it is clear that

diffusion of new products, as with new processes, often requires a considerable period of time. Ironmonger's (1972) study of the diffusion of more than sixty new commodities in the United Kingdom, for example, found that although diffusion sometimes takes only about twenty years, in other cases it may take much longer. As a determinant of these disparate durations, moreover, factors akin to the role of profitability in the diffusion of new processes seem to be important. In particular, the cheaper is the new product and the greater the extent to which it constitutes an improvement over existing versions, the more rapid is its diffusion likely to be (Davies, 1979; see also Rogers, 1983).

In the specific context of developing countries, a small but quite separate literature has sought to explain the patterns of demand for new (and imported) products in terms of factors such as advertising and international demonstration effects (see James and Stewart, 1981; James, 1987b). This literature emphasizes the role that MNEs and other foreign influences play in shaping patterns of demand in the Third World. The relevance of this literature (as well as of that described in the previous paragraph) to the comparative speed with which consumer electronics products have been diffused within (and between) developing countries, has not, however, yet been explored. Indeed, the whole question of household demand has suffered from considerable neglect compared to the demands of producing units. Such neglect is especially serious in the light of the fact that household demand tends to be fairly substantial, even in the very poorest developing countries which do not undertake any productive activities in the electronics field.[31]

3.3 IMPACTS OF MICROELECTRONICS

The impacts of new technologies in general, and thus of microelectronics in particular, can be thought of in terms of two main categories: effects on output and income, and effects on income distribution. In analysing these effects, we shall pursue the integrative theme of this chapter by relating them, on the one hand, to the patterns of diffusion discussed above, and on the other hand to a broad range of relevant literature.

3.3.1 Sectoral Versus Economy-Wide Impacts on Output and Employment

Sectoral (or partial) analysis attempts to explain the behaviour of producers and consumers in determining price and output in a given market. For this purpose, it is necessary to assume that there are no major changes in any of the other sectors of the economy. In this type of framework, the forces that determine the output and employment response to technical change may be briefly described as follows (James 1985, 1988). *Technical change*, by definition, increases output per unit of input. If output remains constant, then the derived demand for at least one factor input (e.g., labour) must necessarily fall. But since increased productivity lowers costs, *more* output will be produced at a given price by the profit-maximizing firm. This incremental supply will mean that output is higher and price lower than prior to the technical change. The *extent* of the increase in output depends on the degree of cost reduction and on the elasticity of demand. (The greater these are, the stronger will be the tendency towards expanded output.)

To determine the new factor demands, whether these have increased or decreased as a result of technical change, the increase in output has to be compared to the increase in productivity. In some cases — if, for example, the increase in output is large and the technological change is not strongly biased towards saving a particular factor — demand for that factor will increase. (In other circumstances, such as when output growth is constrained and technological change is strongly biased, demand for that factor will tend to fall.) Assuming that demand for the factor does increase, this will be reflected (to an extent that depends on the elasticity of the supply curve of the factor) in either increased employment (in the case of labour) or a rise in wages (or some combination of these).

This discussion is based on the assumption that technical change does not alter the market structure and, in particular, that competitive conditions continue to prevail after the change. But insofar as temporary market power is created for the innovating firm, this power will tend to cause a reduction in output compared to the competitive situation. This, in turn, will lead to a reduction in the demand for inputs in general, and labour in particular. Alternatively, if several firms adopt the innovation at a similar time, some form of oligopoly will be created and in this case the effect on the volume of output (and hence the demand for inputs) is less clear.

It is apparent that applying partial analysis to understanding the employment effect of microelectronics innovations in a particular sector requires knowledge of not only the factor-saving bias of the particular innovation and its effect on market structure, but also the elasticity of final demand and the elasticity of (the various types of) labour supply. Although, as we noted earlier, progress has been made in estimating the first of these requirements (mostly in relation to CNC machine tools), no sectoral studies have combined these estimates with those for the other requirements. Some ILO case studies, however, do attempt to relate the labour-saving bias of flexible automation techniques (such as CNCMTs and CAD) to an increase in export demand that adoption of these techniques often seemed to induce (in large part because of changes in the characteristics of the products associated with the new techniques). In fact, several studies (Dominguez-Villalobos, 1988; Onn, 1989) suggest that for some firms increased export demand may have more than offset the labour-saving effect, thus leading to a net increase in labour demand. It is clear, however, that much more empirical research is needed to determine the effects on output and employment at the partial equilibrium level.[32]

A similar need arises in relation to impacts on income distribution at this level. A conceptual essay on these impacts by James (1985) concludes that they are likely to be inegalitarian, but the data required to support this view are almost entirely lacking. Nevertheless, what needs to be emphasized is that this type of research would be relevant only to certain instances in which microelectronics technologies have been diffused in the Third World. In particular, partial methods make methodological sense in those developing countries where diffusion of technologies is confined to a very limited part (sector or region) of the economy (such as, for example, an electronics assembly enclave), since under those circumstances, the various effects of the given sector or region on others in the economy (and the effects that these, in turn, have on the original location) can quite reasonably be ignored. That is, under those circumstances, one is entitled to neglect the economy-wide effects of the diffusion of microelectronics-based innovations. But in countries (such as India, China, the NICs, etc.) where this is not the case — where, instead, these innovations are widely diffused across sectors — it becomes imperative to incorporate these effects into the analysis of impacts.

Because this task has not yet been undertaken in a modelling exercise, we are able only to offer insights from some existing economy-wide models of developing countries as to how these economy-wide effects might operate and how they may yield results that differ from those obtained using partial analysis. Binswanger's (1980) model, for example, suggests and quantifies several important mechanisms through which the economy-wide effects of technical change are transmitted. In particular, that model demonstrates how technical change that occurs in one sector affects the demand for output (and thus inputs) of other sectors, via so-called 'price' and 'income' effects. Technical change in a given sector, that is to say, increases per capita income (the 'income' effect) and tends to decrease the price of the good (the 'price' effect). If the former outweighs the latter, output in sectors in which technical change does not occur will increase, despite the relative rise in prices of the goods produced in that sector. In Binswanger's two-sector model, which simulates the effects of labour-saving technical change in the nonagricultural sector (representing, broadly, some of the likely technological and sectoral features of microelectronics innovations), the income effect is shown to outweigh the price effect so that agricultural output actually falls.[33]

Another important set of economy-wide mechanisms is incorporated in the well-known dual-economy model of Kelley et al. (1972). These authors criticize the framework within which the effects of technical change in developing countries were considered in the early dual-economy literature. In particular, they criticize the attempt by Fei and Ranis (who formulated one of the first such models) to examine the conflict between the output-enhancing effects of technical change and the employment effect '*while holding both the rate of capital formation and the rate of population growth constant*'[34] (Kelley et al., 1972, p. 205, emphasis in the original). Kelley et al. (ibid., pp. 205-206) contend instead that 'any meaningful analysis of the conflict must take account of the impact on capital accumulation of population growth and the manner in which these variables interact with the improvement of technology'. They seek to demonstrate quantitatively, in the context of their simulation model, that the dynamic effects of technical change on these variables may be considerable, leading to conclusions very different from those based on the early dual-economy literature. Specifically, 'the advantage of rapid rates of technical change in developing economies now becomes much clearer. Rapid rates of technical change tend to raise achievable rates of capital accumulation and to lower rates of population growth by stimulating urban-industrial development' (ibid., p. 210).

The correct inference to be drawn from this conclusion is not that these economy-wide effects will necessarily accompany micro-electronics-based innovations that are widely diffused in a particular developing country. It is possible, for example, to think of applications of these innovations (e.g., in the health sector) that will *increase population growth rates*,[35] and it is equally reasonable to debate the favourable effects of technical change on investment in various Third World contexts.[36] The important point is that these critical issues ought to be the subject of a great deal more empirical attention than is currently the case.

The final economy-wide mechanism we shall consider is backward linkage, or input–output effects, in production.[37] Evidence from the United States based on a simulation exercise carried out by Leontief and Duchin (1985) points to powerful backward linkage effects associated with microelectronics, and highlights the additional employment created indirectly in sectors that produce new capital goods, especially computers. According to several observers, however (see Hoffman, 1985b; Schmitz, 1985), comparable effects cannot be expected in the Third World since most developing countries import rather than produce innovations in microelectronics. Hoffman (1985b,

p. 269), for example, argues that 'most Third World nations will be net importers of the new equipment and lack the strong software and capital goods sector that are the source of many new jobs in the developed countries'. While this distinction is important, it must be qualified in several ways.

First, as Schmitz (1985) and Edquist and Jacobsson (1988) have pointed out (and as was also apparent from the earlier discussion of the diffusion of the new technologies), there are important segments of the Third World in which production is important (though the extent of backward linkages from this will vary a good deal according to the specific form that it takes: assembly production, for example, is almost entirely devoid of linkage effects; see Lall, 1983). Second, the employment impact associated with an expansion in output depends not only on how integrated is the productive structure in the developing country — which determines the strength of linkages between sectors — but also on the labour:output ratios (or labour requirements per unit of output) in each of these sectors. The significance of this distinction has been stated lucidly by Stern and Lewis (1980, p. 39):

> In all industrial sectors the direct labour coefficients, or labour—output ratios, decline as an economy develops. This decline ... will tend to reduce the employment impact of an expansion in output. At the same time, however, the increasing interindustry linkages that accompany economic growth serve to increase the employment impact of output expansion.

Determining the relative size of these conflicting effects in the specific context of innovations in microelectronics is yet another economy-wide issue that warrants empirical investigation.[38]

3.3.2 Impact of Adoption on Non-Adopters of New Technologies

Section 3.3.1 stressed that differential adoption and diffusion of new technologies in the Third World could give rise to a correspondingly diverse pattern of economic impacts at the sectoral and economy-wide levels. This section addresses the general issue of the impact of adoption of these technologies on *non-adopters* (whether these are

individual units or aggregations of units into regions/countries, etc.).[39]
It is useful on analytical grounds to approach this issue in terms of a
broad taxonomy that incorporates the following elements:

1. Different types of adopting and non-adopting units (for example,
   consuming versus producing units);
2. The location of these units within or between different regions or
   countries; and
3. The different possibilities that arise from the combination of points
   1 and 2.

For example, the effects on the welfare of consumers in one
country arising from adoption of consumer electronics goods in
another country could be analysed in terms of the phenomenon of
international demonstration effects (see James, 1987b). Or one could
evaluate the effects on non-adopting firms in a given region arising
from the adoption of the new technologies by other firms in the same
region.[40] At the level of countries, questions are posed for the impact
on exports and imports by non-adopters due to adoption in other
countries. At each of these levels — national, regional and
individual — important distributional consequences are likely to arise.
In particular, to the extent that adopters have high initial levels of
income relative to non-adopters, the impact of new technologies on
income distribution will tend to be inegalitarian.

This possibility has been raised in the literature almost exclusively
in one particular context: the effects of the adoption of innovations in
microelectronics by firms in the advanced countries on the
comparative advantage of developing countries. Indeed, this theme has
been so dominant that special issues of two development journals were
devoted specifically to its exploration (see Hoffman, 1985a; Kaplinsky,
1982b). In what follows we first review this particular aspect of the
effects of microelectronics on the relationships between adopters and
non-adopters and then, in the light of the more general taxonomy
above, describe areas that seem to us to demand further attention.

3.3.2.1 Comparative advantage reversal

The central concern of the numerous authors who have addressed this question is that manufactured exports from the Third World will be undermined by the introduction of microelectronics in the developed countries from where, in general, the innovations originate.[41] Although rarely spelled out in any detail, the theoretical rationale of this concern seems to be that the nature of new technologies in general (and microelectronics in particular) is heavily conditioned by their origin (overwhelmingly) in the developed countries and that this, in turn, imparts a systematic tendency for diffusion of new technologies to take place in rich rather than poor countries.

The first part of this argument — that dealing with the endogenous nature of technical change — can be expressed concisely in terms of the theory of induced innovation. According to this approach, as espoused by Binswanger and Ruttan (1978), the direction of technical change in any economy tends to be based on prevailing factor scarcities. In developed countries, where labour is relatively scarce and the wage:rental ratio is accordingly relatively high, technical change will tend towards saving labour rather than capital. Thus, insofar as global technical change is concentrated in these countries, it will tend to be poorly suited to the generally very different factor endowments of the developing countries. Even if this tendency is acknowledged, it does not follow that the pattern of diffusion to which it gives rise will *automatically* induce trade reversals. The reason is that a general tendency to save labour is consistent with two different types of new technologies and these differences have contrasting implications for rates of diffusion between rich and poor countries.

In the first case, new technologies widen the range of technological options in a labour-saving direction, without dominating older technologies for similar products. That is, these technologies systematically save labour per unit of output while requiring more capital per unit of output in relation to the latter. Consequently, the cost-reducing effects of the new technologies can only be realized in countries where labour is sufficiently highly priced and capital sufficiently cheap. This condition will not necessarily hold in all advanced countries, and it may not hold in any. But it is evidently more likely to hold, in general, in rich than in poor economies.[42] To this extent, trade reversals might possibly arise; and for some forms of microelectronics technologies this possibility already appears to have been realized to some degree. For example, the differential in the diffusion of robots (which save mainly unskilled labour) between OECD and newly industrializing countries appears to reflect largely differences in wage costs in the two groups of countries (Edquist and Jacobsson, 1988).

The second form in which new technologies save labour, however, does not give rise to any such presumption of trade reversals. For in this case, the new technologies require no more *capital* per unit of output and for this reason are said to dominate older techniques.[43] That is, because they use fewer inputs (strictly, less of one and no more than the other) to produce any given level of output, the new techniques will be more profitable at *any* set of factor prices. Consequently, they will tend to replace the old in all new investments in the relevant lines of production in all countries. Insofar as adoption patterns are actually determined on this basis, there is accordingly no basis for expecting trade reversals to occur.

The question that is then immediately raised is which of these two forms do new microelectronics technologies tend to assume: that is, do they supplement or dominate the range of existing techniques? Some of the evidence cited above (for example, from the studies by Mody and Wheeler, 1990; and Edquist and Jacobsson, 1988) suggests that dominance is not a pervasive feature of new technologies. As yet, however, the debate on this question remains inconclusive (see Kaplinsky, 1984; Soete, 1985), and it is therefore difficult to assess the *empirical* basis of the reversals argument. But what can and should be emphasized is that the origin of microelectronics technologies in the advanced countries carries with it no general presumption in favour of this phenomenon.

This conclusion may, however, be challenged on the grounds that it is based on a simplistic two-factor model and that only in a more realistic 'three-factor' world do the systematic links between the origin of new technologies, the features that they embody, and the rates at which they diffuse in rich and poor countries become fully apparent.

Only in this broader context, therefore, is it possible (in this view) to establish an adequate rationale for the possibility of trade reversals. In the following discussion, accordingly, we shall examine three factors that constitute highly important aspects of microelectronics technologies, but which are not captured in the simple two-factor model: namely, skills, the organization of production, and flexibility of output.

Availability of skilled labour   In relation to skills, the implicit assumption of some versions of the reversals argument seems to be that these resources are available only in the developed countries, where adoption of new technologies will consequently tend to be concentrated. Unable, because of an absolute scarcity of relevant skills, to make use of these technologies, developing countries will then tend to be confronted with an erosion of their comparative advantage in international trade.

At the level of particular skills and countries, this argument may carry considerable force. But it would seem to have only limited relevance to the developing countries that are currently most heavily engaged in the production of manufactures for export, namely, the newly industrializing countries of East Asia.[44] There are several reasons for this. First, these countries do appear to possess at least some of the relevant skills; indeed, the price at which they are able to supply this factor of production may serve to attract foreign firms. For example, in the semiconductor industry, Ernst has observed that

> Even for increasing levels of automation, it still matters that, by and large, operators and maintenance personnel in developing countries receive significantly lower wages than their counterparts in the US, Western Europe and Japan. ... Caught in a severe 'human capital trap' and in order to reduce the cost of R&D personnel and highly skilled technicians, electronics firms will have to rely increasingly on cheap human capital available in some of the more advanced developing countries.
>
> (Ernst, 1985, p. 30)

Second, it is now becoming apparent that certain new technologies may actually *save* skilled labour. For example,

CNC lathes can be tremendously skill saving. Proportionately speaking, the savings in skills is greater than that of *undifferentiated* labour which in turn is far greater than that of capital. This means that the CNC lathe represents a technical change, the appropriateness of which is a function of the degree of scarcity of skilled labour compared to semi-skilled labour and to capital. If we assume that the scarcity of skilled labour in relation to semi-skilled labour is greater in the NICs than in the developed countries, we would be forced to the conclusion that *we are witnessing a technical change which has its origin in the developed countries but which is of a greater potential benefit to the NICs.*

(Jacobsson, 1986, p. 24, emphasis added)

On the other hand, as noted earlier in connection with adoption decisions, this 'potential benefit' of CNC machine tools (and also CAD) has not been fully exploited *in practice* by the NICs. For a variety of reasons — such as government policy and information imperfections — the rates of diffusion of CNC machine tools and CAD in the engineering industries of these countries, have lagged quite substantially behind the OECD countries (Edquist and Jacobsson, 1988).

In judging the extent to which this situation actually threatens the comparative advantage of the NICs, however, two things need to be considered. The first is that the product lines which have been most affected by the diffusion of flexible automation techniques are generally *not* those in which the NICs have been most successful in exporting (ibid.). The second is that (as noted previously) the new techniques often seem to be associated with changes in product characteristics and the implications of these changes for competition between adopters and non-adopters have still to be worked out (as we suggest in more detail below).

Finally, even if skilled labour is neither available nor saved by the new technologies, it may be supplied to the newly industrializing countries, either by foreign firms (seeking to make superior use of the factor abundances in these countries by supplying complementary factors, which are in short supply there), or by the governments of these countries themselves. The evidence presented below (when considering the acquisition of technological capabilities in microelectronics, Section 3.3) of the rapidity with which some of the relevant skills have been built up through state intervention in some of the NICs suggests that the possibility of trade reversals cannot realistically be made to rest on the assumption of fixed factor endowments. On the contrary, in the semiconductor industry, certain East Asian economies appear to have acquired a *new* source of comparative advantage through the intervention of the state, which has 'created conditions conducive not to investment in unskilled assembly processes, but rather to investment in relatively high-skill, capital-intensive production processes' (Henderson, 1989, p. 159). As a result, what Henderson refers to as a distinct regional division of labour has emerged in East Asia. It is reflected in the facts that:

> More and more of the investment in assembly plants for large-batch standardised outputs tended to go to an increasing degree to Thailand, Malaysia, the Philippines and so on, while Hong Kong, Singapore and now, seemingly Malaysia, have tended to be upgraded as to the quality and complexity of their production technologies and labour processes.
>
> (ibid., p. 59)

Organization of production A second aspect of new technologies that is not captured in the two-factor model is the radical change in the organization of production and the work practices that these technologies often seem to require. Exemplified by the Japanese ('just-in-time') system of production, the labour processes associated with best practice levels of productivity in microelectronics confers considerably more autonomy on workers (with respect, for example, to quality control) than is the case with mass-production methods based heavily on a rigid division of labour (see Kaplinsky, 1986, 1987, 1990). Because worker collaboration tends, on this account, to become more important in the new labour process, new forms of control over labour need to be exercised to replace methods (notably, machine-pacing and supervision of labour at the point of production) that were formerly relevant. In particular, as Kaplinsky (1986) has emphasized, social forms of organization, or what is known as 'habituation', come to assume much greater importance. 'Insofar as "culture" or politics determines the success with which labour is habituated to work in this way, the social context of innovation becomes increasingly important in the analysis' (ibid., p. 39).

This social context, however, is unlikely to be generally more favourable in the developed world than in the NICs. On the contrary, for many of the East Asian countries it may be easier, both politically (because of the strong control over labour that is normally exercised there) and culturally (because of an 'ethos' that is relatively close to the Japanese model), to introduce the new labour process than it is in some of the advanced countries. To this extent, far from precipitating a trade reversal, the new technologies may be more likely, in fact, to *enhance* the comparative advantage of certain NICs *vis-à-vis* some of the industrialized countries.[45]

Flexibility of output   A third aspect of new technologies that is neglected in the basic two-factor model is flexibility of output, which, as noted in a previous section, has come to assume increased importance in sectors where demand is prone to change rapidly. Insofar as this factor becomes the *decisive* element of competition in such sectors (of which garments and textiles are good examples), the location of production would tend to take place *entirely* in countries that constitute the final markets for the relevant products (which, for the most part, is likely to mean the developed countries and the rapidly growing markets of some large developing economies).

The actual behaviour of producers, however, suggests that this is not the case; that is to say, the time factor is not always (or even generally) the only competitive consideration, even in sectors especially prone to rapid alterations in demand. What firms often appear to seek, instead, is a combination of low wage costs and short turnaround time. In garments, for example, 'there are clear signs that the Caribbean is becoming an increasingly important site for production aimed at the US market' (Mody and Wheeler, 1990, p.61). What appears to be happening is that U.S. producers preassemble the garment (using relatively capital-intensive techniques), which is then sewn in the Caribbean (and exported to the United States under section 807 of the tariff code). In this way, producers are able to combine low production costs and quick turnaround time. A similar pattern can be discerned in the investment by West European firms in Mediterranean Basin locations close to the domestic market (ibid.).

Correspondingly, other locations in the Third World, notably those in the Far East, have tended to lose attractiveness from this point of view.[46]

Conclusions The conclusion of our discussion of trade reversals is that this phenomenon is a necessary outcome of neither the simple two-factor model nor of extensions to this model which embrace a number of 'third factors'. We have shown that while there may indeed be cases in which reversals seem likely (such as when the new technologies are profitable only at factor price ratios prevailing in developed countries), there are also cases in which the opposite effect may occur [such as when the new technologies save skills that are relatively scarce in the NICs; when they require a labour process that is more easily implemented in these countries than in developed societies; or when there is no systematic bias in adoption patterns between rich and poor countries (which will be the case when the new technologies are more profitable than the old at all price ratios)]. This variety of outcomes may help to explain why no substantial relocation of investment (to the developed countries) has yet taken place.[47] But this fact may also be explicable, in part, by the notion that reversals take time to be realized. For example, firms are not likely to scrap equipment in existing offshore locations immediately. Rather, they may behave in a manner consistent with the predictions of the vintage model of diffusion:

> It is perfectly rational for entrepreneurs to use old technology even when new best-practice techniques exist. Essentially, old machines can still yield a contribution to profits if price covers operating costs, and they are therefore worth using while this condition holds. Only as the appearance of new machines drives price below operating costs are they replaced.
>
> (Stoneman, 1983, p. 115)

For this and other reasons (that are given in the general literature on the diffusion of innovations), locational changes expected to follow from reversal of comparative advantage will tend to be more of a gradual, long-run process than a sudden, radical departure from past tendencies. This is the principal finding, for example, of Hoffman and

Rush's study of the impact of microelectronics on the clothing industry, which concludes that:

> Earlier predictions that the North's use of microelectronics would lead to an imminent and massive shift in competitive advantage against the Third World must now be tempered considerably. The requisite structural and technical changes for such a transformation in the international division of labor are far too complex to occur in only a few years. However, the equally important conclusion that stems from our analysis is that the clothing industry in the OECD will eventually be altered fundamentally by the developments and trends we have observed. One result of this transformation could indeed be a threat to the competitive advantage of developing countries.
>
> (Hoffman and Rush, 1988, p. 224)

An industry study of automobiles and components draws a similar distinction between short- and longer-term locational changes (Hoffman and Kaplinsky, 1988). Longer-term changes seem likely to comprise a reduction in both export-oriented foreign investment and in offshore sourcing by foreign-owned automobile and components firms (ibid.). The former changes, in contrast, present a much more complex picture. Indeed, what has to be explained is the phenomenon observed during the 1980s, of 'a sharp *rise* in the volume and value of components and whole vehicle exports originating from DCs [developing countries] and destined for the United States and Western Europe, often tied to TNC activity' (ibid., p. 294). Hoffman and Kaplinsky explain this seemingly paradoxical finding mainly in terms of the competitive response of U.S. firms to the Japanese success in adopting those elements of the new technologies that have been described as 'systemofacture'. In particular, 'fearful that they would not be able to reduce costs quickly enough in the short run, all United States assemblers have since the late 1970s and early 1980s been exploring a variety of conduits and mechanisms to source both finished units and components from offshore suppliers' (ibid., p. 298).

3.3.2.2 Neglected aspects of the relationship between adopters and non-adopters of new technologies

The nearly overriding concern with comparative cost reversal in the literature has led to the general neglect of several important aspects of the relationship between adopters and non-adopters of new technologies. These neglected aspects arise from the focus of this literature (1) on countries (rather than households or firms) as the relevant trading units; (2) on costs (or supply) as the sole determinant of comparative advantage (thereby neglecting demand-side considerations of product differentiation); and (3) on the effects of export contraction rather than changes in imports on the developing economies.

Firms competing within developing countries Taking the relevant unit to be the firm rather than the national economy raises a host of important questions for trade and inequality within the developing countries that deserve much more attention than they have hitherto received. There is a need, for example, to examine the various mechanisms through which losses may be imparted to non-adopting firms. One such mechanism may arise through the product enhancement effect of new technologies (which was emphasized in Section 3.2.2.2). In general, and depending on the extent of substitutability between them, product innovations tend to diminish the market for existing products (as when, for instance, the appearance of improved-quality colour televisions hastens a decline in the market for black and white televisions) (see James, 1985). Moreover, the initial entry of new products may set up barriers to the entry of (often smaller) firms to the market.[48] In instances where, on the other hand, innovations take the form solely of changes in processes, non-adopting firms will tend to be unfavourably affected by the decline in the price of existing products that the innovation may occasion. If these firms happen to be small relative to the adopting units, the result, again, may be to increase inequality in the developing country.

The relationship between firm size and adoption seems in fact to be rather complex. On the one hand, some new technologies (such as CNCMTs and CAD/CAM) are in important respects well suited to adoption by small-scale enterprises. On the other hand, questions of risk aversion and information availability tend to favour early adoption by large-scale firms (Edquist and Jacobsson, 1988). The nature of the relationships between the firms themselves must also be considered. For example, small-scale subcontractors may be encouraged to adopt new technologies by the requirements of their large-scale manufacturing clients for inputs of a particular quality (Onn, 1989).

Households within developing countries Because they are designed mostly for the high average-income levels prevailing in the advanced countries, product innovations in electronics (especially durable goods) tend to be adopted by the relative affluent minority of households in developing countries. The resulting 'demonstration effects' on non-adopting households in these countries may be very important, although they are totally neglected in the literature. For example, adoption by others of new products may induce non-adopting households to supply more labour, with favourable effects on economy-wide output.

Alternatively, non-adopting groups may increase consumption spending out of existing incomes, with corresponding negative effects on savings and economic growth.

The role of product characteristics in international trade Discussion of comparative advantage reversal tends to focus on supply and cost to the neglect of demand and product characteristics.[49] Yet product and demand factors are likely to have the most important bearing on the outcome of the relationship between adopters and non-adopters in international trade. It is possible, as noted above, that as the characteristics of products traded internationally change in a 'high-income' direction as a result of microelectronics (because of more consistent or higher quality), the developing countries are enabled to maintain (or even increase) their advantage in 'low-income' trade with other developing countries (see Boon, 1986b). Or again, certain forms of trade between developing countries (such as in cotton textiles) may be based on preferences[50] that are not readily eroded by product innovations in microelectronics in the developed countries.

It is worth stressing that if these hypotheses are to be tested, much more disaggregated data will be required than is available in international trade statistics. For even in their most disaggregated form, these data tend to conceal the subtle differences in product characteristics that in our view are so important to understanding the impact of microelectronics on global competition.

Imports, decline of local industry, and effects on employment As noted above, the literature on reversal of competitive advantage is concerned with only one side of the balance of payments problem posed by the adoption of microelectronics-based innovations in the developed countries: namely, the potentially reduced competitiveness of manufactured exports from the Third World. This literature largely ignores the change in *imports* that might also be occasioned and the effect that this change, in turn, could have on the domestic economy. That the implications of such neglect may be considerable is suggested first by the fact that 'developing countries' imports of manufactured goods exceeds their exports of manufactured goods by a factor of more than three. Nearly 85% come from developed market economies (Keesing, 1979, p. 17). And insofar as these imports from the rich countries gain in competitiveness as a result of microelectronics-based innovations, the potential for displacement of competing local production becomes obvious, a problem that, in other literature, has not gone unnoticed. Indeed, as Hagen (1982, p. 176) points out, 'the disastrous effect of imports on traditional handicrafts has frequently been noted'. The consequences of displaced traditional handicrafts producers for unemployment and poverty in the Third World have been frequently noted too.

Much depends, of course, on the extent of tariff protection in different developing countries. But to the extent that such displacement does occur, it is important to recognize that unemployment is the probable outcome.

> For example, if the introduction of video recorders, produced overseas, leads to expenditure being switched out of domestic products, in the absence of price changes, such a technological change may reduce labour demand. Only if reductions in domestic wages result and lead to import substitution for other goods can full employment be re-established.
>
> (Stoneman, 1983, p. 260)

Much also obviously depends on the extent to which goods affected by new techniques are actually produced in the Third World. In cases where local production is slight or non-existent, consumers or producers may benefit from the importation of products made cheaper by the introduction of new techniques. (On the case of capital goods, see Edquist and Jacobsson, 1988.)

3.3.3 Acquisition of Technological Capabilities

In the first part of the survey we distinguished between numerous modes of transfer of microelectronics innovations to the Third World. This section examines how these different modes bear on the process by which domestic technological capabilities are acquired. Then, in Section 3.3.4, we take up the question of how (certain of) these capabilities are actually applied in the developing countries and ask, among other things, whether the result is a more appropriate pattern of innovation than would result from dependence on imports.

3.3.3.1 Acquisition of user capabilities

Much of the Third World (especially the poorest parts) relates to microelectronics innovations from the point of view of users (i.e., importers) rather than producers.[51] It follows that an important part of any adequate analysis of the effects of microelectronics on local technological capabilities needs to be concerned with various *user capabilities,* such as 'to follow instructions, to learn how to service it, [an imported good or machine] and eventually to replace parts and repair it' (Teitel, 1984, p. 51).

Unfortunately, there is not a great deal in the literature that specifically addresses this question. What fragments of evidence that do exist point to the role of the supplier in determining whether, and to what degree, user capabilities are fostered by the importation of the new technologies. From this point of view, the role of the supplier is often painted somewhat negatively.[52] Narasimhan (1984, p. 50), for example, observes that, in the Third World as a whole,

> To a very large extent the needs of the information processing sector are met through imports; ... The import and sale of systems (hardware and software)

are done at the initiative of multinationals, their subsidiaries, or their agents. Quite often systems are over-sold, remain under-utilised or unutilised due to lack of proper training, and after-sales service to maintain these systems in satisfactory operation.[53]

A similar point has been made by Carroll (1985, p. 110) in relation to microcomputers in development assistance projects:[54]

Microcomputer activities in projects for sector energy planning and management usually include ... an expressed intent that developing country staff will enhance their analytical skills and ability to use microcomputers effectively in decision analysis. However, under the pressure of time and resources, such good intentions often suffer. Many of the U.S., Canadian and European professionals interviewed ... feel 'more could have been done' either in training or analytical work with developing country staff. The complaint is heard that 'since we left, the computer isn't used much'.

Some authors have discerned much the same problem of inadequate supplier support in relation to electronic capital goods.[55]

Taken together, these examples point to what may be a quite pervasive problem with the importation of microelectronics technology.[56] However, this same problem may, under certain circumstances, lead to substitution of domestic for foreign sources of supplier support. Future research in this area ought to identify the circumstances under which this form of substitution is likely to occur.

3.3.3.2 Acquisition of production capabilities

This section will discuss research on the roles of various technology diffusion mechanisms in the acquisition of production capabilities in the Third World. (The diffusion mechanisms were discussed in Section 3.2.)

Export-oriented direct foreign investment Much of the literature in this area addresses two related questions. The first is whether and to what extent local technological capabilities are fostered by export of assembly forms of production. The second concerns the transferability of any capabilities thus acquired to other areas of domestic production. With respect to the first question, it seems extremely doubtful (as one might perhaps expect) that any significant degree of local capability is generally engendered in the assembly of products for export. With respect to the semiconductor industry, for example, which, as noted earlier, is dominated by foreign investment, Ernst (1985, p. 16) argues that 'export-oriented chip assembly has played a very minor role in establishing an effective transfer of technology to developing countries'. He contends that this form of assembly production has fostered neither 'the skills, knowledge and learning capabilities' of the production workers, nor the engineering capabilities of the domestic economy (see also O'Connor, 1989). Even if this is not the case, that is even if capabilities do happen to be acquired, doubts have been raised about the transferability of these capabilities to other areas of production. In this respect, it appears to be necessary to distinguish the semiconductor from the consumer electronics industry.

> Whatever technology and skills are transferred to developing countries through ... offshore semiconductor assembly may be applicable to other assembly-type industries but are not apt to foster the development of a more technologically sophisticated electronics industry *per se*. By way of contrast, the technology transferred through offshore investments in consumer electronics production would appear to embody certain skills and technical know how which are more directly applicable to the electronics industry. In part at least this can be explained by the fact that in consumer electronics a larger portion of the production process is transferred abroad. Certain developing countries which have perfected manufacturing techniques for components of consumer electronics products have been able to apply their experience ... to the production of peripheral equipment for computers.[57]
>
> (O'Connor, 1985b, p. 22)

A third strand of literature, like the first, concerns foreign investment in the semiconductor industry. But whereas the latter emphasizes the generally limited contribution made by foreign investment to domestic capabilities, the former addresses the question of why, in countries such as Korea, Taiwan, and Singapore, foreign investment in this industry *has* been effectively used as the basis for indigenous technological development (as reflected, among other ways, in the emergence of locally owned production complexes and in higher levels of local expertise employed in foreign-owned firms). Henderson's study of this important question stresses a variety of explanatory factors, ranging from 'the changing structure of the world economy and markets and corporate priorities in those contexts, to the development strategies of the national states in question' (Henderson, 1989, p. 163).

Local-market-oriented direct foreign investment Hobday's (1986b) study of telecommunications in Brazil provides the most detailed evidence available related to this type of foreign investment (see also Göransson, 1984). Hobday's research (which we shall mention again below) is extremely important in demonstrating how subsidiaries of multinational telecommunication companies operating in Brazil imparted highly favourable impacts on Brazilian technological capabilities. Hobday adduced considerable evidence of '(a) strategic investments and efforts in local technology, (b) falling technology imports, and (c) developments in management and technological organisation at the firm level'. Hobday suggests that this evidence 'points to a major shift by the MNCs [multinational corporations], from the passive subsidiary role under electromechanical technology, to a positive technology developing role under microelectronic technology' (Hobday, 1986b, p. 301). These new and more favourable technological efforts appear to be explicable in part by government policies, and partly by competition among subsidiaries for the growing market in microelectronic exchanges.

Because they appear to conflict with the conclusions of other studies,[58] Hobday's findings pose a fundamental empirical question for future research: Did the successful acquisition of technological capabilities in this case result from an inherent aspect of the telecommunications sector (as opposed to other areas of local-market-oriented investment in microelectronics),[59] or is it due instead to some exceptional circumstances of the case?

Licensing Systematic evidence of the impact of arm's-length licensing on technological capabilities in developing countries seems to be confined to Tigre's (1983) study of the Brazilian computer industry. His findings suggest that the short-run impact of licensing may conflict with some of the long-run effects. On the one hand, 'licenses substantially reduced the time required to start up local production of data-processing equipment and helped to avoid mistakes both in product and process design' (Tigre, 1983, p. 113). On the other hand, 'product policy, including product changes and competition, is widely used by licensers as an instrument to restrict licensees' managerial and technical independence' (ibid., p. 169).

A case study of the 'super-mini' computer industry in Brazil indicates that the drawbacks of licensing as a mode of acquiring technological capabilities were not confined to competitive problems with the licensor, although these were still very much in evidence (Evans and Tigre, 1989). The study shows that the effectiveness of licensing in this respect also depends heavily on the specific institutional context in which it takes place: in Brazil's case the 'nationalist environment', based on locally developed technology, often seemed to be in conflict with efforts to acquire technological capabilities through licensing agreements. Evans and Tigre illustrate this conflict with examples that fruitfully combine political economy, industrial organization, and a thorough grasp of the technologies in question. They also use the same methodology in a most instructive comparison of Brazil's attempts to acquire 'super-mini' capabilities with those of Korea, which, for the most part adopted a very different (and generally more successful) strategy.

Loss of effective proprietary rights: role of the microprocessor   In Section 3.2.1.2 we saw how the circumstances under which the microprocessor was invented enabled some developing countries to gain access to the new technologies without involvement by MNEs. As one might expect, this development also contained some profound implications for the development of indigenous production capabilities in these countries. Some countries seem to have received a considerable and favourable impact. Brazil, for example, 'has created locally controlled manufacturing capacity in a technologically complex industry. It has shifted its reliance on imports from final products to components. *And, most impressive of all, it has generated local capacity for product innovation'* (Evans, 1985, p. 27; emphasis added). A similar pattern can also be discerned for India (Grieco, 1984).[60]

These authors have described these two country cases in detail.[61] It is essential, however, to recognize that in both cases, development of local capabilities did not result solely from changes that had occurred on the supply side. Rather, 'it was the emergence of relatively strong governmental institutions in the specific field of computing which in Brazil, as in India, made possible the initial domestic exploitation of these international opportunities' (ibid., p. 162).

Two factors related to the government's role warrant emphasis because both seem to have been necessary conditions for the successful interventions that occurred. One involves the configuration of political and economic forces that permitted the governments in these countries to undertake the policies that they did (among the most important of which were the protection of the local microcomputer industry from foreign competition).[62] The second relates to the availability of what Evans calls the 'pre-existing infrastructure'. In the Brazilian case, the availability of this administrative infrastructure was made possible by the fact that 'the development of the people and skills necessary to take an initiative in the computer industry had been going on for at least a decade before the initiatives were taken' (Evans, 1985, p. 38). India, too, is well known for a long tradition of governmental controls and an unusually well-developed administrative structure. It is worth emphasizing that these two necessary conditions are unlikely to be satisfied *simultaneously* in many developing countries. For even if the political will to make the necessary interventions exists, the required infrastructure often does not.[63]

3.3.4 Applications of Technological Capabilities

At several points we have mentioned the role of government in the processes by which technological capabilities in microelectronics are acquired.[64] This role is no less important in determining the types of innovations that flow from these capabilities and it is exercised broadly in two (often closely related) ways. The first is indirect, through the influence of the country's overall development strategy, and the second is in the form of direct interventions.[65] We shall discuss each of these in turn.

3.3.4.1 The role of development strategy

One extremely important aspect of development strategy is that large countries have a much greater potential for independence from international trade than small countries. This distinction has powerful implications for the pattern of technical change in general and of innovations in microelectronics in particular.

For example, large 'inward-looking' developing countries have the opportunity to produce a set of innovations that is more appropriate to local circumstances and needs than technologies imported from advanced countries. Achieving this possibility, however, often seems to be hindered by the high degree of protection behind which the technological capabilities themselves are created. India's protected microcomputer industry is an important, albeit perhaps somewhat extreme, example of this problem. In that case, 'so much protection' was granted to the local microcomputer manufacturer that there was no incentive for this firm to produce products that were in any sense appropriate to local needs. In the Brazilian microcomputer case, a more favourable outcome of protection seems to have emerged: 'Despite sometimes higher prices than those in the developed countries, products are more appropriate to the local needs because they are designed to match local requirements' (Tigre, 1983, p. 173).

These examples highlight the possibility that microelectronics innovations in 'inward-looking' developing countries may be appropriate in some dimensions (such as adaptations to the local environment) but inappropriate in others (such as cost). And both examples raise the crucial policy question of how to secure innovations that are appropriate in *all* relevant dimensions. This is apparently unlikely to occur either with excessive protection, or (for a different reason) with too little (or no) protection.

Small countries, as noted above, are generally much more dependent than large countries on international trade.[66] It is sometimes argued that the need to conform to international export standards robs these countries (such as the East Asian NICs) of an incentive to generate appropriate innovations. Fransman's (1986b) study of CNCMT producers in Taiwan and Japan, however, suggests that there may be important ways in which this view fails to capture the reality of the innovation process in 'outward-looking' developing countries. Using a four-dimensional index of product quality, he tries to 'quantify the price and quality differential that existed between Taiwanese CNC machine tools and the best quality competing product in export markets' (Fransman, 1986b, p. 1391). He concluded that the mean price differential was 70%, while the quality differential ranged from 82 to 93% of the performance of the best competing machine. Thus, the adaptive innovations evolved by Taiwanese producers enabled purchasers of these machines to obtain a somewhat diminished performance (relative to the best competing product), but for a more than proportionate reduction in price. The explanation of this pattern of innovations seems to be that Taiwanese producers are competing principally in the less exacting markets of other developing countries (ibid., Table 5B) and in those markets in developed countries that are highly sensitive to price.[67]

These few examples are probably enough to suggest that the pattern of innovation in microelectronics is not any simple derivative of a country's development strategy. These examples also raise the issue of precisely *which* technical capabilities are required for appropriate innovations. For many such innovations (which are often incremental or adaptive in character)[68] it would seem, for example, that a full 'own-capability' in microelectronics (in the form of domestic production of semiconductors) is neither a necessary nor a sufficient condition.

3.3.4.2 Direct government interventions

The question of whether microelectronics capabilities can be used to promote the welfare of those who live in poverty (mostly in the rural areas) in the Third World arises more directly in regard to institutions owned by the state itself. For, while privately owned firms respond only indirectly to government policies, the state intervenes *directly* in many areas of most developing countries (such as telecommunications, health, education, and so on).[69] For many of the poorest people in these countries, it is only in such areas that any direct contact with new microelectronic technologies may conceivably come about. To understand the effects these technologies have on income distribution, it is of the utmost importance to recognize the numerous innovations in the public domain that have been designed expressly to make this contact possible.

One example is described by Hobday (1986b) in a study of the Research and Development Centre of Telebras (the Brazilian Telecommunications Administration). He shows how a small-scale, low-capacity, public exchange system for rural and low-density urban use evolved (among numerous other innovations) out of the research activities of this Centre. Another example is the Project for Strengthening Health Delivery Systems in Central and West Africa, which uses microcomputers 'to improve regional and national disease surveillance, health and demographic data systems, and to integrate these systems into national health planning systems' (Munasinghe et al., 1985, p.121). Further examples can be drawn from the ongoing research area known as technological 'blending', which in a narrow sense refers to the possibility of combining elements of new and traditional technologies, but which, more generally, deals with applications of new technologies in traditional sectors (see Bhalla et al., 1984; Bhalla and D. James, 1986, 1988; Rosenberg, 1988). Among the most interesting cases that this research has uncovered are the System for Computer-Aided Agricultural Planning and Action to assist rubber small-holders in Malaysia and the use of electronic load-controllers in micro-hydro projects in a number of tropical developing countries.[70]

The major question that arises from these direct applications in the public sector is whether (and under what circumstances) they are likely to be replicable on a scale that is significant at the macroeconomic level of developing countries. The answer to this question will depend in part, of course, on the purely technical ease with which these types of applications can be made (see Rosenberg, 1988). But the answer will also depend heavily on political factors, and in this regard much can be learned from the available literature that attempts to explain why so many past efforts to secure more appropriate technologies appear to have been unsuccessful. A major finding of this literature is that past failures are 'to a considerable extent ... the consequence of the political economy of the required policy changes' (Stewart, 1987, p. 295). More specifically, 'many of the policies necessary to promote AT [appropriate technology] would strongly conflict with the interests of dominant groups' (ibid., p. 295).

Two conclusions for policy may be drawn from this overall finding (ibid.) and both of them would appear to condition in a powerful way the feasibility of microelectronics innovations that are designed to benefit those groups living in poverty in the Third World. The first is that any *widespread* introduction of appropriate technologies will not normally occur without a fundamental shift in political power in favour of these groups.[71] The second is that there is (nevertheless) likely to be scope for *particular* interventions in specific country circumstances depending, for example, on the degree to which processes designed to assist certain disadvantaged groups also threaten the interests of the dominant groups in society.

3.4 POLICY IMPLICATIONS AND FUTURE RESEARCH DIRECTIONS

Formulation of policy towards microelectronics in developing countries requires a sound understanding of the impacts of these technologies. The findings of this chapter suggest, however, that this understanding is lacking in many areas of the existing literature.

The first of these areas is adoption and diffusion of new technologies. In particular, to the degree that the impact of new microelectronics technologies is influenced by the form and rate of their diffusion in developing countries, it becomes essential to throw additional light on the factors that condition these processes. Some excellent case studies provide a start in this direction for specific sectors and regions, but considerable scope remains for further research.

This chapter suggests that it might be helpful to base such research on a distinction between factors of supply and demand. It was suggested, further, that in regard to supply factors, much depends on the degree to which new technologies give rise to a set of proprietary assets and (when they do) on the mechanisms that owners of these assets choose to exploit them. There is some evidence, for example, that this choice depends on whether multinational firms (as the major owners of proprietary knowledge in microelectronics innovations) are oriented towards production for domestic markets in developing countries or for export.

On the demand side, attention was drawn to the need to distinguish different groups of agents involved in the adoption process, namely, privately owned firms, state-owned enterprises, and individual households (or groups of households). The necessity for this distinction was shown to arise not only from the fact that each group generally pursues a different set of goals within a diverse set of constraints, but also because the demands of each tend to relate to a quite different set of microelectronics-based innovations. In explaining the behaviour of these various groups (as well as those on the supply side), this survey took pains to emphasize that, in relation to each, one can point to a substantial literature on which future research can and should draw. We find, tentatively, that on both the supply and demand sides, the bigger and more developed countries of the Third World are generally best placed to benefit from microelectronics-based innovations. In some respects, moreover, this tendency towards polarization may be cumulative, leading to even further divisions in the future.

A second major component of a future research effort will need to address systematically the economic impacts of the diffusion patterns revealed by the research advocated in the previous paragraph. Unlike many studies on the impact of the Green Revolution (cf. Binswanger and Ruttan, 1978; Scobie, 1979; Lipton and Longhurst, 1989), literature on microelectronics has become remarkably dissociated from economic analysis in general and development economics in particular. This tendency has led to neglect (in varying degrees of completeness) of a wide variety of potentially important economic relationships. These can be categorized into three main groups.

The first set of relationships concerns the distinction between sectoral (or partial) and economy-wide (or general equilibrium) impacts in analysis of major government initiatives to address factors such as output, employment, and income distribution. The former method applies when the impact of microelectronics on a sector or region in the Third World is sufficiently small as to be marginal in relation to other sectors (as will tend to be the case, for example, if the relevant region or sector is very small in relation to the rest of the economy). There is not much evidence to draw on at this level. What few studies do exist suggest that unemployment is by no means an inevitable consequence of adopting new techniques. On the contrary, export demand may have more than offset the labour-saving effects of these technologies in several cases, leading to a net increase in labour demand.

I am aware of no studies, however, at the general equilibrium level of analysis. This type of analysis is relevant when the impact of microelectronics in a sector or region is nonmarginal relative to the economy as a whole (a major new investment in a fully automated shipyard, for example, might fall into this category). The point is that in these cases it becomes essential to consider various economy-wide effects of new technologies. Our review of economy-wide models of developing countries that incorporate technical change pointed to some of the forms that these effects are likely to take. One such model, for example, showed how technical change in one sector affects the demands for inputs and outputs of other sectors. Another economy-wide model draws attention to the likely effects of technical change on capital accumulation and population growth in developing countries. To what extent (and in which directions) these (and other) macro-economic effects are likely to occur in the specific case of technical change in microelectronics is a question that will demand considerable theoretical and empirical analysis.

A second (and related) area of research on economic impacts concerns the relationships between adopters and non-adopters of new technologies. As shown in Section 3.3.2, the literature in this area focuses overwhelmingly on just one aspect of these relationships, namely, the possibly negative effects that adoption of new technologies by developing countries may have on the comparative advantage of developing countries. Our examination of this possibility showed that the (usually implicit) microeconomic model that underlies it is far too simple to capture the variety of adoption patterns and locational tendencies that can be observed in different branches of microelectronics. More complex models of investment behaviour need, accordingly, to be applied to the question. There is also a need to consider other neglected aspects of the relationship between adopters and non-adopters: (1) to consider *firms and households* (as well as countries) as the relevant trading units; (2) to incorporate *demand-side* factors of product quality (as well as costs and *supply*) in analysing the relationships between trading units; and (3) to include the effects of changes in *imports* (as well as changes in *exports*) on developing countries. It bears emphasizing that study of these neglected areas will (in most cases) depend upon more data than are currently available on patterns of adoption by the various economic agents identified earlier in this section.

The final aspect of impacts that was addressed in this chapter deals with the acquisition of technological capabilities and the nature of innovations that arise from them. In regard to acquisition, emphasis was again placed on the proposition that the outcome depends on the specific form in which the new technologies are diffused to different parts of the Third World. More specifically, some rather sketchy evidence was cited to suggest that the acquisition of capabilities in microelectronics is sensitive to the form (such as licences, foreign investment, imports of consumer durable goods and machinery) in which the new technologies are actually transferred to the developing countries. Evidence is also available to support the contention that some developing countries have acquired substantial production, as distinct from user, capabilities in electronics. And with respect to these countries, we posed the important question of whether the acquired capabilities have led to a different — and more specifically, to a more appropriate — pattern of innovation than would result from reliance on technology imports from the developed countries. Although there is little systematic evidence on this question, it seems clear to us that in formulating an answer to it, particular attention will need to be focused on the direct and indirect role of government in the developing countries concerned.

3.4.1 Normative Aspects of Policy Formulation: 'What Governments Ought to Do'

Even if a substantial amount of research on the impacts of microelectronics was to be conducted in the areas described above, there would still be an inadequate empirical basis for the formulation of policy. One major reason is that the study of impacts tends to provide only partial information about the *social* gains and losses from different policies, and it is on the basis of these magnitudes that governments 'ought to behave'. But since governments often have different objectives (or objectives with different weights), and since these differences influence what is considered socially desirable, there is no universally applicable policy prescription. Countries which regard technological self-reliance as highly important, for example, are likely to consider as socially optimal a very different set of policies than countries which accord little or no weight to this objective. Particularly because the rate of technical change in (some areas of) microelectronics is very rapid, moreover, the question of what governments 'ought to do' in this sense has an important dynamic (as well as a static) dimension. For example, Dahlman et al. have suggested that:

> A static comparison of the choice of technology to make mechanical watches or electronic watches in a labour-abundant economy may show that the technology for mechanical watches has the highest benefit–cost ratio among existing technologies. But because electronic watches probably will soon make mechanical watches and their technology obsolete, the better choice may be electronic watches, despite their lower apparent benefit–cost ratio. This choice is more apposite if little of the experience acquired by producing mechanical watches can be transferred to the production of electronic watches. Moreover, producing electronic watches from the start may enable the building of skills that will later be useful for more complicated electronic watches and other products that have electronic components. ... choosing the right technology involves simultaneously optimising the static and dynamic elements of the choice.
>
> (Dahlman et al., 1985, p. 13)

Dynamic issues arise, too, in relation to policies designed to protect local technological capabilities. In particular, it is important to be able to establish (albeit somewhat crudely) the differential social costs and benefits of intervening in alternative areas of microelectronics (such as microcomputers, telecommunications, and computer software). However, in part because the literature on what governments 'ought to do' is typically rather general (see, e.g. Wad, 1982; Hoffman, 1984; Commonwealth Secretariat, 1985), there is very little solid empirical evidence available to answer specific questions such as these.[72]

Part of the problem is that the information needed to address this and similar questions relates to the difficult area of 'dynamic externalities' between sectors, and more specifically to the idea that positive externalities may be created by a certain sequence of policies. Concentration on a particular 'leading' sector, for example, may confer advantages on, and opportunities for, other related sectors (Mody, 1989). Part of the success achieved by Taiwan and Korea in electronics production is thought by some economists to be due precisely to the emphasis that was paid by these countries to policy sequencing in general, and to the role of consumer electronics as a leading sector in particular (ibid.). Much more needs to be known, however, about the circumstances in which particular sequences and packages of policies are likely to yield different types of external effects (and how large these effects are likely to be).

Policy-making would benefit also from a heavier research focus on the problem of uncertainty that is so pronounced in the rapidly changing world of microelectronics. For, in these circumstances, what governments 'ought to do' is often far from clear, especially when scale economies and other forms of cumulative causation are also present (ibid.).

Beyond the related problems created by the pace of technological change, by the specific policy sequences, and by uncertainty, the circumstances under which different policies towards electronics are likely to be *feasible* needs to be considered. One dimension of feasibility is economic, and in this context it is useful to consider the advocacy of small-scale, decentralized production based on new technologies in developing countries (see, for example, Sabel, 1984; Perez, 1985; Schmitz, 1990; and Kaplinsky, 1990). Though the *potential* for this type of production does indeed seem inherent in certain aspects of microelectronics (namely, those that reduce the importance of plant-level economies of scale, and allow greater flexibility in production),[73] few authors have identified the specific circumstances under which it is likely to be *achieved*. A notable exception, however, is Maxwell's (1983) study of economies of scale in Argentina. On the basis of detailed case-study evidence, he suggests that small-scale firms are likely to possess a competitive advantage in several specific areas of microelectronics, including industrial process control, office automation, medical electronics equipment, educational computing, and applications software in general. Small firms appear to possess an advantage in these areas, mainly because they are especially well placed to meet what are described as 'idiosyncratic' local needs. But this advantage, as Maxwell is concerned to stress, is inherently self-limiting.

> For if the volume of business started to grow to the point where large series manufacture (e.g. of microcomputers) was involved, the business would then be likely to become obvious and attractive for entry by the 'big battalion' companies. ... Their strategy would then be to adapt one of their standard-range models in the required direction and proceed greatly to undercut the small local manufacturer in terms of cost and price.
>
> (Maxwell, 1983, pp. 236-37)

Whether findings similar to those described by Maxwell apply also to other developing countries is an important priority for future research.[74]

Another dimension of feasibility is political. Since so many of the impacts that we reviewed were heavily conditioned by government policies (either directly or indirectly), it is essential to understand the forces of political economy that underlie these actions. Only three of the case studies that we cited (those by Grieco, 1984; Evans, 1985; Evans and Tigre, 1989) sought to undertake this task in a systematic way and there is considerable scope for research along similar lines in other contexts.

Not all the constraints confronting the various policy-making institutions in the sphere of microelectronics, however, are related to political economy factors. Some of them appear instead to involve problems connected with analysis of industrial organization (though, of course, these problems may themselves be intertwined with political economy factors). To this extent, there is additional scope for detailed analysis of how organizational constraints bear on different types of institutions (such as government ministries and state-owned enterprises) involved in making policy towards the electronics sector. In many countries, research of this kind will probably include institutions entrusted with science and technology policy in general. Though they have often performed rather poorly, these institutions have all too rarely been the object of adequate social science research.

Closely related to the question of political and institutional feasibility is what Hirschman (1967, p. 130) called the 'basic dilemma of project design in an underdeveloped country'. This dilemma arises from the following type of technological policy problem.

> It could be argued that a country without much experience in solving technological problems should stay away from projects requiring a large capability in this regard. But the opposite course can also be defended: how will the country ever learn about technology if it does not tackle technologically complex and problem-rich tasks? In this reasoning a certain 'unfitness' of the project for a country becomes an additional and strong argument for undertaking it; for the project, *if it is successful*, will be valuable not only because of its physical output but even more because of the social and human changes it will have wrought.
>
> (ibid., p. 129, emphasis in original)

Because effective operation of so many microelectronics technologies seems to depend heavily on various types of capabilities, this type of policy dilemma is likely to be a very real one indeed for the countries of the Third World. In escaping from it, much can be learned, as Hirschman suggests, from the past experience of development projects.

ACKNOWLEDGEMENTS

Many people have contributed to the various stages involved in the preparation of this survey. I am especially grateful to Ajit Bhalla, Wilma Coenengracht, Charles Cooper, Martin Fransman, Gerd Junne, Raphael Kaplinsky, Ashok Mody, Luc Soete, and Rob van Tulder.

NOTES

1. The separate question of whether it is predominantly supply- or demand-side factors that determine diffusion is not, however, addressed.
2. See also O'Connor (1985b).
3. See Table 2 in Castells and Tyson (1988).
4. For a general discussion of this approach see Stewart (1982).
5. It is useful to recall here that 'in the past two decades the prime motive of direct foreign investment by transnationals in the Third World has been to secure the protected markets of these economies' (Nayyar, 1978, p. 772).
6. Vernon notes that this type of behaviour can occur even when import protection is not guaranteed. In particular, 'when the basis for an oligopoly is product and brand differentiation, as in food preparations and in drugs, the production facility that is in closest contact with the market generally operates at a major advantage over the others. As a result, if a leading competitor improves its contacts with the market by establishing a local production unit, others in the industry may feel threatened; hence the tendency to follow the leader' (Vernon, 1973, p. 22).
7. The general point is made in Hood and Young (1979).
8. Research by Reuber et al. (1973), which showed a strong positive correlation between the stock of foreign investment per head and gross national product per capita in developing countries, is worth noting in this context.
9. Many of these countries were among the world's fastest growing import markets in the late 1970s, according to a table presented by Ernst (1983, p. 153).
10. This example is interesting also in showing how supply-side factors may, in reality, be prompted by initiatives on the side of demand.
11. O'Connor, for example, contends that 'Developed country electronics firms are frequently unwilling to license their state-of-the-art technologies due to their concern that by so doing they could undermine their own competitive advantage' (O'Connor, 1985b, p. 42).
12. Plesch (1979, p. 87) cites numerous examples to support these conclusions.
13. This reason also appears to underlie the subcontracting relationships between firms in developed countries and local software institutes in developing countries. Indeed, partnerships or subcontracting arrangements are said to be 'the most common form of software-related activity undertaken by developed country-based computer firms in developing country markets. For, a TNC is not likely to make sizeable investments in its own software development subsidiary for a particular national market unless that market is sufficiently large to warrant it' (O'Connor, 1985a, p. 320).
14. See also Humbert (1988, p. 155).
15. The ineffectiveness of legal protection against copying and use of computer software is also a much discussed subject (Correa, 1985; Narasimhan, 1985), but it is not clear to what extent copying actually occurs in the Third World.
16. Evans also makes the important point that if IBM, Burroughs, or Digital had been the innovators of the microprocessor, they would have accordingly had a 'strong interest in restricting their use by third parties' (Evans, 1985, p. 21).
17. It is worth noting that the 'counterfeit' Apples produced by some Asian firms have been pursued legally by Apple Computer, which was able to have thousands of 'look-alikes' confiscated at ports in the United States. Apparently as a result, 'Taiwanese microcomputer manufacturers have begun to focus their efforts on developing and manufacturing IBM PC compatible systems, seeking to avoid legal problems by arranging to license IBM's operating system, design their own hardware, and write their own software onto memory chips' (O'Connor, 1985b, footnotes).

18. As measured by state ownership, the role of the state is especially pronounced in Africa. The public sector in Africa contributed no less than 33 % of investments in the 1970s (Hawkins, 1986) and the figure remains high even today.
19. See Stewart (1987) for a full discussion.
20. Though, of course, there will be overlapping demands (such as for computers), and hybridous cases (such as when the *government* decides to adopt a digital telecommunications network and *individuals* decide on the extent to which they will use it).
21. According to one estimate, for example, purchases by public administrations exceed 40 % of the total demand for electronics in Latin America. See Lahera and Nochteff (1983) and Correa (1989). A study of computerization in Indonesia found that 'the Government and quasi Government agencies have always been the dominant user of computers' (Pesik, 1981, p. 128). For some African evidence see Obudho and Taylor (1977).
22. Among the many references on applications are Munasinghe et al. (1985); Obudho and Taylor (1977); Teoh and Rasiah (1984); Tottle (1984); Bennett and Kalman (1981); Damachi et al. (1987); and Munasinghe (1989).
23. To support their contention, these authors point to the large numbers of different (and mostly incompatible) types of models purchased by public administration in at least one Latin American country.
24. Landes (1969, p. 542) makes a lot of relative factor cost differentials in explaining why the early follower countries took so long to assimilate the innovations of the Industrial Revolution.
25. Bhalla and J. James (1986, p. 160) quote Howard Pack to the effect that in the weaving industry 'research on improving production has not led to equipment that dictates the disregard of older methods of production in the developing countries'.
26. See Mody and Wheeler (1990) for some estimates of the extent of gains that are likely from these two sources.
27. For a discussion of skill requirements in relation to computer-aided design, see Kaplinsky (1982a), and in relation to four flexible automation techniques see Edquist and Jacobsson (1988).
28. Telecommunications appears to be exceptional in this respect, since 'in tropical and inhospitable climates solid state, digital equipment requires less maintenance than electromechanical technology which requires a high degree of insulation from the outside environment' (or 'tropicalization') (Hobday, 1986a, pp. 28-29).
29. The product quality argument itself contains no obvious bias in its implications for the income level of the adopting country, since many of the products are exported. There may, however, be a positive correlation with growth rates insofar as the latter are enhanced by outward-looking strategies (Chenery and Keesing, 1979). The growth-enhancing effects of such strategies have been examined in detail in the *World Development Report*, of the World Bank in 1987.
30. For the case of computers in Latin America, see Correa (1989) and with respect to microelectronics-based industrial machinery in the Association of Southeast Asian Nations (ASEAN) region, see Onn (1989).
31. See, for example, the demand for electronics products in Ethiopia as reported in Degefu (1985).
32. Kaplinsky's review of the employment effects of new technologies for the International Labour Organization concludes that 'although there has been extensive literature on the linkage between the new technology and employment in the industrially advanced economies the debate has, with the partial exception of Brazil, barely been raised at all with respect to developing countries, especially those with low-incomes and predominantly agricultural populations' (1987, p. 145). Another exceptional case is the study of the Philippines by Palafox and Casel (1985).

33. The model employs parameter values based on estimates for Japan in three different periods, namely, 1880, 1930, and 1960. See Binswanger (1980).

34. In the simplest dual-economy formulation, where labour-saving technical change occurs in the modern sector, the effect (unless output increases sufficiently rapidly) would be to postpone the 'turning-point' (i.e., the point at which the labour force in the nonmodern sector begins to decline). Calculations conducted by Birdsall provide some sense of the likely orders of magnitude of such postponement for selected countries. On the basis of assumptions about probable rates of population growth, she shows that a reduction in the demand for labour by the modern sector from 4 to 2 per cent per annum (due, we assume, to the effect of labour-saving technical change in the modern sector) would postpone the turning point by an average of about twenty years for the particular sample of countries. See Birdsall (1984).

35. Johnston and Kilby (1975) give a detailed discussion of how technical change affects the rate of population growth.

36. There is a brief allusion to this question in the debate between Hall and Heffernan (1985) and Hagen (1982, 1985).

37. This discussion draws heavily on James (1985).

38. The plea for more attention to economy-wide effects that has formed a major theme of this section is also made by Lipton and Longhurst (1989) in the context of assessing the impact of the new varieties on the poor. One of the few studies of the rural sector with an economy-wide focus is that by Bell et al. (1982). Their investigation of the impact of the Muda project in Malaysia revealed sizeable effects on the national economy: for every dollar of value added that was generated directly by the project, approximately another 80 cents were generated indirectly.

39. In practice, of course, the two concerns are related: impacts on developing countries depend not only on the degree to which the countries embrace the new technologies but also on the patterns of adoption and diffusion in the rich countries. Ideally, therefore, both issues should be tackled simultaneously in a systems-analytical framework. One approach of this kind is the global modelling exercise conducted by Bessant and Cole (1985). The demands of this level of aggregation, however, require the authors to make a set of often unrealistic assumptions.

40. This is an important focus of much of the literature on the Green Revolution. See, for example, Scobie (1979) and Binswanger (1980).

41. In some of the more extreme statements of this concern, the reversal of comparative advantage based on cheap labour (to which automation would give rise) would manifest itself in the sizeable and rapid relocation of export-oriented foreign investment to the developed countries. Rada (1980, p. 106) has observed that 'some key industries are returning to the developed countries'. More recently, in an UNCTAD document it was noted that 'many offshore assembly operations of transnational corporations that were previously profitable in developing countries, mainly because of low absolute costs of both unskilled and skilled labour, are now being transferred back to the home country or other developed countries to take advantage of contiguity to markets and of cost economies arising from the centralised location of production operations made possible by automation. The risk of a shift in comparative advantage away from developing countries reflects not only labour cost reduction but also the improved quality which automation permits' (UNCTAD, 1984, p. 22).

42. Although in some developing countries, factor prices may be 'distorted' enough (through, for example, minimum wage legislation and subsidies on capital) to make the new techniques as profitable to the private sector as in developed economies. Moreover, even if this is not the case, there may be developing countries that are capable of *adapting* the new techniques to their own factor endowments and prices.

43. The new technology may, of course, require *less* capital per unit of output (as well as less labour per unit). As long as the proportionate saving in capital requirements is less than that of labour, the optimal capital–labour ratio rises as a result of technical change, which is then defined as labour-saving in a Hicksian sense. See Binswanger and Ruttan (1978).

44. The concentration of manufactured exports from the Third World among the East Asian NICs is shown in Keesing (1979). For 1975, for example, the share of Hong Kong, Taiwan, and South Korea in this total amounted to nearly 40%.

45. This possibility is acknowledged by Kaplinsky (1986, p. 45), who suggests that the more 'class-ridden' of the developed countries will tend to suffer from it since they are least able to accommodate the new labour process. See also Hoffman and Kaplinsky (1988).

46. For a detailed, empirical assessment of this tendency see Mody and Wheeler (1990). According to these authors, the competitiveness of the NICs in the U.S. market for textiles and garments is likely to be threatened during the next decade not only by U.S./Caribbean joint operations but also by low-cost production in China.

47. As noted for example by Castells and Tyson (1988). Much depends, of course, on factors *other* than the technical change itself. For example, as O'Connor has pointed out, 'Factors like the protectionist policies of the OECD countries — and realignments of international exchange rates have had more profound implications for the second-tier NICs' economies in recent years than technological developments *per se*' (O'Connor, 1989, p. 3). The political economy of protectionism is discussed in many sectoral studies (such as Hoffman and Rush, 1988; Hoffman and Kaplinsky, 1988; Mody and Wheeler, 1990). Kaplinsky (1989) discusses the factors that tend to make protectionism more severe in some sectors than others.

48. Tigre's (1983) study of technology and competition in the Brazilian computer industry, for example, shows how entry barriers were created for domestic producers by the goodwill that the large multinational firms were able to engender for their own trademarks.

49. A point that is recognized by Mody and Wheeler (1990), who attempt to specify some differences in the characteristics of the products with which they are concerned.

50. See Keesing (1979). It is perhaps worth noting, in this context, that South–South trade in manufactures accounted for 36% of manufactured exports from the South to the world in 1979 (see Amsden, 1983).

51. This distinction is suggested by the earlier discussion on diffusion, although the data required to quantify it precisely are not available.

52. In relation to developed countries, Northcott (1985) points out that the reliance on suppliers is especially important for the smallest establishments.

53. Carroll (1985), however, suggests that as a result of a combination of expanded manufacturer and distributor outlets, and the provision of repair facilities in some major cities, the servicing of microcomputers is becoming more widespread in the Third World (though, as he also notes, it 'remains expensive').

54. Schware and Trembour (1985, p. 17) describe in detail an aid project, that, 'by its own assessment ... left behind ill-trained operators and a computer system that remained inadequately installed'. See also the report on computers in Sri Lanka by UNDP/ILO (1982).

55. As noted above. For a detailed discussion, see Edquist and Jacobsson (1988).

56. Khanna (1986) notes the presence of this problem in the early Chinese experience with the acquisition of foreign technology.

57. O'Connor (1985b) does, however, also observe that investments in semiconductor assembly in large markets are often followed with a lag by backward integration into wafer processing.

58. Tigre's study of computers in Brazil, for example, finds no evidence 'to support the hypothesis that majority local ownership in overseas subsidiaries facilitates technology transfer through access to technical knowledge generated abroad. On the contrary ... even majority local partnership in overseas subsidiaries of MNCs does not favour technology transfer' (Tigre, 1983, p. 89).

59. The government may, for example, be in a more monopsonistic situation in the telecommunications sector. This tends to strengthen its bargaining position with respect to the subsidiaries. See Hobday (1986b).

60. We consider below the *nature* of the innovations to which these capabilities gave rise: whether, for example, they were more appropriate to local conditions than imported technologies.

61. Evans (1985) and Grieco (1984) for Brazil and India, respectively.

62. Both Evans and Grieco raise, in an extremely interesting way, the issue of how their findings challenge the tenets of dependency theory.

63. Grieco's description of the evolution of the computer industry in Nigeria and Indonesia lends powerful support to this conclusion. He shows that these countries, unlike India and Brazil, did not formulate policies that enabled them 'to take advantage of international computer developments'. As a result, 'in Indonesia there was no sign at the end of the 1970s that an indigenous systems-engineering industry would soon emerge, and in Nigeria only one five-person firm ... had emerged to fabricate a few small ($1,000) micro-systems' (1984, p. 164).

64. A more extensive list of references on this subject would include Göransson (1984), Hoffman (1984), Erber (1985), Jacobsson and Sigurdson (1983), Nochteff (1985), O'Connor (1985b), Fransman (1986a), Junne (1986), Khanna (1986), Edquist and Jacobsson (1988), Mody (1989), Henderson (1989), Evans and Tigre (1989).

65. The distinction between direct and indirect forms of government influence on technology decisions is made by Stewart (1987).

66. In the context of microelectronics, O'Connor (1985b, p. 6) makes the interesting observation that 'countries whose industries are more export oriented tend to have a product mix more heavily weighted toward consumer electronics goods than those countries producing electronics goods largely for the domestic market'. There is also some evidence that the electronics sector in large, inward-looking countries, such as India and China, suffers from low-quality products. See Grieco (1984) and Sigurdson and Bhargava (1983).

67. This type of orientation of the export trade of East Asian NICs seems to apply quite generally. See Chenery and Keesing (1979).

68. It is these types of innovations that seem to have accounted for a good deal of technical change in the general development of the East Asian NICs. See, for example, Johnston and Kilby (1975).

69. Many of these areas are known to economists as 'public goods' (i.e., goods whose benefits are not reduced by an additional user and for which it is difficult to exclude people from its benefits, whether or not they are willing to pay).

70. These examples are contained in Bhalla and James (1988). Other useful cases are described in Munasinghe et al. (1985), Bhalla et al. (1984), Obudho and Taylor (1977), Kaplinsky (1990).

71. In the context of microelectronics, the strength of political economy factors is suggested in Hobday's study of telecommunications in Brazil. He shows that 'rural and regional TC [telecommunications] have not progressed to anywhere near the same level of coverage or quality as the major industrial centres or the capital Brasilia' (1986b, p. 232). He views this neglect of the rural areas as 'part of the wider problem of underdevelopment and inequality in Brazil'.

72. There are, of course, exceptions to this characterization. Hobday's (1986b) study of Brazil, for example, seeks to assess the costs and benefits to that country of investment in telecommunications technology and infrastructure.
73. See Kaplinsky (1990), Schmitz (1990), and Rosenberg (1988) for a discussion of these features of new technologies.
74. In the case of relatively poor developing countries, for example, it could be argued that domestic market 'niches' of the kind identified by Maxwell are less apparent. To this extent, the potential afforded by the small scale of some microelectronics production will be less available for exploitation. Problems may, of course, also arise on the supply side to limit the general applicability of this type of production.

REFERENCES

Amsden, A. (1983), 'De-skilling, Skilled Commodities and the NICs' Emerging Competitive Advantage', *American Economic Review*, Vol. 73, No. 2.

Bell, C., Hazell, and Slade, R. (1982), *Project Evaluation in Regional Perspective*, Johns Hopkins University Press, Baltimore.

Bennett, J.M. and Kalman, R.E. (eds) (1981), *Computers in Developing Nations*, North-Holland, Amsterdam.

Bessant, J. and Cole, S. (1985), *Stacking the Chips*, Frances Pinter, London.

Bhalla, A. and James, D. (eds) (1986), *New Technology Applications in Traditional Sectors*, International Labour Organization, Geneva.

Bhalla, A. and James, D. (eds) (1988), *New Technologies and Development: Experiences in 'Technology Blending'*, Lynne Rienner, London.

Bhalla, A., James, D. and Stevens, Y. (1984), *Blending of New and Traditional Technologies: Case Studies*, Tycooly Publishers, Dublin.

Bhalla, A.S. and James, J. (1986), 'New Technology Revolution: Myth or Reality for Developing Countries?', in Hall (1986).

Binswanger, H. (1980), 'Income Distribution Effects of Technical Change: Some Analytic Issues', *The South East Asian Economic Review*, Vol. 1, No. 3.

Binswanger, H. and Ruttan, V. (1978), *Induced Innovation*, Johns Hopkins University Press, Baltimore.

Birdsall, N. (1984), 'Population Growth and the Structural Transformation of the Labor Force', Paper prepared for Conference on Population Growth and Labour Absorption in the Developing World 1960–2000, Bellagio, July.

Boon, G.K. (1986a), *The Interrelated Impact of Microelectronic Technology on the First, Second and Third World*, The Technology Scientific Foundation, Noordwijk, The Netherlands.

Boon, G.K. (1986b), *Computer Based Techniques: Diffusion, Impact, Policy in the South–North Perspective*, Parts A and B, Draft final report, The Technology Scientific Foundation, Noordwijk, The Netherlands.

Carroll, T. Owen (1985), 'The Use of Microcomputer in the Energy Sector in Developing Countries', in Munasinghe et al. (1985).

Castells, M. and Tyson, L. (1988), 'High-Technology Choices Ahead: Restructuring Interdependence', in J. Sewell et al. (eds), *Growth, Exports and Jobs in a Changing World Economy: Agenda 1988*, Transaction Books, New Brunswick.

Caves, R.E. (1982), *Multinational Enterprise and Economic Analysis*, Cambridge University Press, Cambridge.

Chenery, H. and Keesing, D. (1979), 'The Changing Composition of Developing Country Exports', *World Bank Staff Working Paper*, No. 314, World Bank, Washington, D.C.

Chudnovsky, D. (1984), 'The Diffusion of Electronics Technology in Developing Countries: Capital Goods Sector: The Argentinian Case', Working Paper R 641, Centro de Economía Transnacional, Buenos Aires.

Clarke, J. and Cable, V. (1982), 'The Asian Electronics Industry Looks to the Future', *IDS Bulletin*, Vol. 13, No. 2.

Commonwealth Secretariat (1985), *Technological Change, Enhancing the Benefits*, Vols I and II, Commonwealth Secretariat, London.

Correa, C. (1985), 'Trends in Commercialization of Software in Developing Countries', UNIDO Report No. IS.574, United Nations Industrial Development Organization, Vienna.

Correa, C. (1989), 'Informatics in Latin America: Promises and Realities', *Journal of World Trade Law*, April.

Dahlman, C., et al. (1985), 'Managing Technological Development', *World Bank Staff Working Paper*, No. 718, World Bank, Washington, D.C.

Damachi, U., et al. (1987), *Computers and Computer Applications in Developing Nations*, Macmillan, London.

Davies, S. (1979), *The Diffusion of Process Innovations*, Cambridge University Press, Cambridge.

Degefu, G. (1985), 'Development of Electronics in Ethiopia', UNIDO Report No. ID/WG.437/2, United Nations Industrial Development Organization, Vienna.

Deolalikar, A.B. and Sundaram, A.K. (1989), 'Technology Choice, Adaption and Diffusion in Private- and State-owned Enterprises in India', in James (1989).

Dominguez-Villalobos, L. (1988), 'Microelectronics-based Innovations and Employment in Mexican Industries', ILO Technology and Employment Programme Working Paper No. 183, International Labour Organization, Geneva.

Edquist, C. and Jacobsson, S. (1988), *Flexible Automation*, Blackwell, Oxford.

Edquist, C., Jacobsson, S. and Jethanandani, K. (1985), 'Automation in Engineering Industries of India and Republic of Korea', *Economic and Political Weekly*, 13 April.

Erber, F. (1985), 'The Development of the "Electronics Complex" and Government Policies in Brazil', in Hoffman (1985a).

Ernst, D. (1983), *The Global Race in Microelectronics, Innovation and Corporate Strategies in a Period of Crisis*, MIT, Campus, Frankfurt a.M. and New York.

Ernst, D. (1985), *Automation, Employment and the Third World — the Case of the Electronics Industry*, Institute of Social Studies and IDPAD, The Hague.

214   *Technology and Innovation in the International Economy*

ESCAP (1979), 'Transnational Corporations in the Consumer Electronics Industry of Developing ESCAP Countries', UN Working Paper No. 5, January.

Evans, P.B. (1985), 'State, Capital and the Transformation of Dependence: The Brazilian Computer Case', Working Paper No. 6. Department of Sociology, Brown University.

Evans, P. and Tigre, P.B. (1989), 'Going beyond Clones in Brazil and Korea: A Comparative Analysis of NIC Strategies in the Computer Industry', *World Development*, Vol. 17, No. 11.

Fleury, A. (1989), 'The Technological Behaviour of State-Owned Enterprises in Brazil', in James (1989).

Fransman, M. (1986a), *Technology and Economic Development*, Wheatsheaf Books Ltd., Brighton.

Fransman, M. (1986b), 'International Competitiveness, Technical Change, and the State: The Machine Tool Industry in Taiwan and Japan', *World Development*, Vol. 14, No. 11, November.

Göransson, B. (1984), 'Enhancing National Technological Capability — The Case of Telecommunications in Brazil', Discussion Paper No. 158. Research Policy Institute, University of Lund, Lund, Sweden.

Grieco, J.M. (1984), *Between Dependency and Autonomy. India's Experience with the International Computer Industry*, University of California Press, Berkeley.

Hagen, E.E. (1982), 'Technological Disemployment and Economic Growth', *Journal of Development Economics*, Vol. 10.

Hagen, E.E. (1985), 'More on the Employment Effects of Innovation — More than a Response', *Journal of Development Economics*, Vol. 17.

Hall, P. (ed.) (1986), *Technology, Innovation and Economic Policy*, Philip Allan, Oxford.

Hall, P. and Heffernan, S. (1985), 'More on the Employment Effects of Innovation', *Journal of Development Economics*, Vol. 17.

Hawkins, A.M. (1986), 'Can Africa Industrialize?', in R. Berg and J. Whitaker (eds), *Strategies for African Development*, University of California Press, Berkeley.

Henderson, J. (1989), *The Globalisation of High Technology Production*, Routledge, London.

Hewitt, T.R. (1988), 'Employment and Skills in the Electronics Industry: The Case of Brazil', D. Phil. Thesis, University of Sussex, Brighton.

Hirschman, A. (1967), *Development Projects Observed*, The Brookings Foundation, Washington, D.C.

Hobday, M. (1986a), 'Telecommunications — A "Leading Edge" in the Accumulation of Digital Technology? Evidence from the Case of Brazil', *Information Technology for Development*, Vol. 1, No. 1.

Hobday, M. (1986b), 'Digital Telecommunications Technology and the Third World: The Theory, the Challenge, and the Evidence from Brazil', D. Phil. Thesis, University of Sussex, Brighton.

Hoffman, K. (1984), 'Managing Technological Change: The Impact and Policy Implications of Microelectronics', Report to Commonwealth Secretariat Working Group, London.

Hoffman, K. (ed.) (1985a), Special Issue of *World Development*, Vol. 13, No. 3, March.

Hoffman, K. (1985b), 'Microelectronics, International Competition and Development Strategies: The Unavoidable Issues', in Hoffman (1985a).

Hoffman, K. and Kaplinsky, R. (1988), *Driving Force: The Global Restructuring of Technology, Labour, and Investment in the Automobile and Components Industries*, Westview, Boulder, Colorado.

Hoffman, K. and Rush, H. (1988), *Micro-electronics and Clothing*, Praeger, New York.

Hood, N. and Young, S. (1979), *The Economics of Multinational Enterprise*, Longman, New York.

Humbert, M. (1988), 'Global Study on World Electronics', UNIDO Report No. ID/WG. 478/2 (SPEC), United Nations Industrial Development Organization, Vienna.

Ironmonger, D. (1972), *New Commodities*, Cambridge University Press, Cambridge.

Jacobsson, S. (1986), *Electronics and Industrial Policy. The Case of Computer Controlled Lathes*, Allen and Unwin, London.

Jacobsson, S. and Sigurdson, J. (eds) (1983), *Technological Trends and Challenges in Electronics*, Lund University, Lund, Sweden.

James, J. (1985), 'The Employment and Income Distributional Impact of Microelectronics: A Prospective Analysis for the Third World', World Employment Programme, Research Working Paper, No. 153, International Labour Organization, Geneva.

James J. (1987a), 'Population and Technical Change in the Manufacturing Sector of Developing Countries', in D. Gale Johnson and R.D. Lee (eds), *Population Growth and Development: Issues and Evidence*, University of Wisconsin Press, Madison.

James, J. (1987b), 'Positional Goods, Conspicuous Consumption and the International Demonstration Effect Reconsidered', *World Development*, Vol. 15, No. 4.

James, J. (1988), 'The Output and Employment Impact of Microelectronics in the Third World', in Wad (1988).

James, J. (ed.) (1989), *The Technological Behaviour of Public Enterprises in Developing Countries*, Routledge, London.

James, J. and Stewart, F. (1981), 'New Products: A Discussion of the Welfare Effects of the Introduction of New Products in Developing Countries', *Oxford Economic Papers*, March.

Johnston, B. and Kilby, P. (1975), *Agriculture and Structural Transformation*, Oxford University Press, Oxford.

Junne, G. (ed.) (1986), *'New Technologies and Third World Development'*, Special Issue of *Vierteljahresberichte: Problems of International Cooperation*, No. 103, Friedrich-Ebert Foundation, Bonn.

Kaplinsky, R. (1982a), *Computer Aided Design: Electronics, Comparative Advantage and Development*, United Nations Industrial Development Organization, Vienna.

Kaplinsky, R. (ed.) (1982b), *Comparative Advantage in an Automating World*, Special Issue of *IDS Bulletin*, Vol. 13, No. 2, March.

Kaplinsky, R. (1984), *Automation, the Technology and Society*, Longman, Harlow.

Kaplinsky, R. (1985), 'Electronics-based Automation Technologies and the Onset of Systemofacture: Implications for Third World Industrialisation', in Hoffman (1985a).

Kaplinsky, R. (1986), 'Technological Change, Employment and Comparative Advantage', Unpublished Report, Institute of Development Studies, University of Sussex, Brighton, U.K.

Kaplinsky, R. (1987), *Microelectronics and Employment — A Review of Evidence*, International Labour Organization, Geneva.

Kaplinsky, R. (1989), '"Technological Revolution" and the International Division of Labour in Manufacturing: A Place for the Third World', *European Journal of Development Research*, Vol. 1, No. 1.

Kaplinsky, R. (1990), *The Economies of Small: Appropriate Technology in a Changing World*, IT Publications, London.

Keesing, D. (1979), 'World Trade and Output of Manufactures: Structural Trends and Developing Countries' Exports', *World Bank Staff Working Paper*, No. 316, World Bank, Washington, D.C.

Kelley, A., Williamson, J. and Cheetham, R. (1972), *Dualistic Economic Development*, University of Chicago Press, Chicago.

Khanna, A. (1986), 'Issues in the Technological Development of China's Electronics Sector', *World Bank Staff Working Paper*, No. 762, World Bank, Washington, D.C.

Lahera, E. and Nochteff, H. (1983), 'Microelectronics and Latin American Development', *Cepal Review*, No. 19, April.

Lall, Sanjaya (1983), *The Multinational Corporation*, Macmillan, London.

Landes, D.S. (1969), *The Unbound Prometheus, Technological Change and Industrial Development in Western Europe from 1750 to the Present*, Cambridge University Press, Cambridge.

Leontief, W. and Duchin, F. (1985), *The Future Impacts of Automation on Workers*, Oxford University Press, Oxford.

Lipton, M. and Longhurst, R. (1989), *New Seeds and Poor People*, Unwin Hyman, London.

Maxwell, P. (1983), 'Specialisation Decisions in Electronic Production — Lessons from the Experience of Two Argentine Firms', in Jacobsson and Sigurdson (1983).

Mody, A. (1989), 'Strategies for Developing Information Industries', *The European Journal of Development Research*, Vol. 1, No. 1.

Mody, A. and Wheeler, D. (1990), *Automation and World Competition*, Macmillan, London.

Munasinghe, M. (ed.) (1989), *Computers and Informatics in Developing Countries*, Butterworths, London.

Munasinghe, M., Dow, M. and Fritz, J. (eds) (1985), *Microcomputers for Development: Issues and Policy*, Cintec-Nas Publication.

Narasimhan, R. (1984), 'Guidelines for Software Development in Developing Countries', Report No. UNIDO/IS.439, United Nations Industrial Development Organization, Vienna.

Narasimhan, R. (1985), 'The UNIDO Programme on Microelectronics: An Analytical Perspective', Report No. UNIDO/IS.529, United Nations Industrial Development Organization, Vienna.

Nayyar, D. (1978), 'Transnational Corporations and Manufactured Exports from Poor Countries', *The Economic Journal*, Vol. 88, March.

Nochteff, H. (1985), 'Government Policies for the Data Processing Industries in Argentina, Brazil and Mexico', UNIDO Report No. ID/WG.440/7 and Corr.2, United Nations Industrial Development Organization, Vienna.

Northcott, J. (1985), 'Microelectronics in Mexico: Applications in Mexico', UNIDO/IS, United Nations Industrial Development Organization, Vienna.

Obudho, R.A. and Taylor, D.R.F. (eds) (1977), *The Computer and Africa. Applications, Problems and Potential*, Praeger, New York.

O'Connor, D. (1985a), 'The Computer Industry in the Third World: Some Policy Options and Constraints', in Hoffman (1985a).

O'Connor, D. (1985b), 'Global Trends in Electronics: Implications for Developing Countries', Unpublished Report, World Bank, Washington, D.C.

O'Connor, D. (1989), 'Microelectronics-based Innovations: Strategic Implications for Selected Industries in the Second-tier Newly Industrialising Countries (NICs) of Southeast Asia', OECD Development Centre, Paris.

Onn, Fong Chan (1989), 'Employment and Income Implications of Microelectronic Industrial Machinery in ASEAN: The Case of Malaysia/Singapore', ILO Technology and Employment Programme, Working Paper No. 202, International Labour Organization, Geneva.

Palafox, J. and Casel, J. (1985), 'The Impact of New Technology on Employment in Selected Banking Electronics and Telecommunications Establishments in Metro Manila', Institute of Industrial Relations, University of the Philippines, Quezon City.

Perez, C. (1985), 'Microelectronics, Long Waves and World Structural Change: New Perspectives for Developing Countries', in Hoffman (1985a).

Pesik, R.J. (1981), 'Computerisation in Indonesia', in Bennett and Kalman (1981).

Plesch, P. (1979), *Developing Countries' Exports of Electronics and Electrical Engineering Products*, World Bank, Washington, D.C.

Pyo, H.K. (1986), 'The Impact of Microelectronics Technologies on Employment and Indigenous Technological Capability in the Republic of Korea', ILO Technology and Employment Programme, Working Paper No. 172, International Labour Organization, Geneva.

Rada, J. (1980), *The Impact of Microelectronics: A Tentative Appraisal of Information Technology*, International Labour Organization, Geneva.

Reuber, G.L. et al. (1973), *Private Foreign Investment in Development*, Clarendon Press, Oxford.

Rogers, E. (1983), *The Diffusion of Innovations*, 3rd edn, The Free Press, New York.

Rosenberg, N. (1988), 'New Technologies and Old Debates', in Bhalla and James (1988).

Sabel, Charles F. (1984), 'Yeoman Economics and Modern Technology: Rediscovering an Alternative Path to Industrialisation', Paper presented at the Conference on Economic Development and Democracy, Helen Kellogh Institute for International Studies, April.

Schmitz, H. (1985), 'Micro-electronics: Implications for Employment, Outwork, Skills and Wages', IDS Discussion Paper No. 205, June, Institute of Development Studies, Brighton, U.K.

Schmitz, H. (1990), 'Flexible Specialisation in Third World Industry: Prospects and Research Requirements', Industrialisation Seminar Paper No. 90/5, Institute of Social Studies, The Hague.

Schmitz, H. and De Quadros Carvalho, R. (1987), 'Automation and Labour in the Brazilian Car Industry', IDS Discussion Paper, No. 239, December, Institute of Development Studies, Brighton, U.K.

Schware, R. and Trembour, A. (1985), 'Rethinking Microcomputer Technology Transfer to Third World Countries', *Science and Public Policy*, Vol. 1, No. 1, February.

Scobie, G.M. (1979), 'Investment in International Agricultural Research: Some Economic Dimensions', *World Bank Staff Working Paper*, No. 361, World Bank, Washington, D.C.

Sigurdson, J. (1983), 'Forces of Technological Change', in Jacobsson and Sigurdson (1983).

Sigurdson, J. and Bhargava, P. (1983), 'The Challenge of the Electronics Industry in China and India', in Jacobsson and Sigurdson (1983).

Soete, L. (1985), 'International Diffusion of Technology, Industrial Development and Technological Leapfrogging', in Hoffman (1985a).

Stern, J. and Lewis, J. (1980), 'Employment Patterns and Economic Growth', *World Bank Staff Working Paper*, No. 419, World Bank, Washington, D.C.

Stewart, F. (1982), 'Industrialisation, Technical Change and the International Division of Labour', in G.K. Helleiner (ed.), *For Good or Evil*, University of Toronto Press, Toronto.

Stewart, F. (1987), *Macro-policies for Appropriate Technology*, Westview Press, Boulder, Colorado.

Stoneman, P. (1983), *The Economic Analysis of Technical Change*, Oxford University Press, Oxford.

Tauile, J. (1984), 'Employment Effects of Micro-electronic Equipment in the Brazilian Automobile Industry', ILO World Employment Programme Research, Working Paper No. 131, International Labour Organization, Geneva.

Teitel, S. (1984), 'Technology Creation in Semi-Industrial Economies', *Journal of Development Economics*, Vol. 16.

Teoh, S.T. and Raja I. Rasiah (1984), *The Use of a Microcomputer System at District Level Health Services*, Dept. of Social and Preventive Medicine, Faculty of Medicine, University of Malaya, Kuala Lumpur.

Tigre, P. (1983), *Technology and Competition in the Brazilian Computer Industry*, Frances Pinter, London.

Tottle, G. (1984), 'The Computer and Agricultural Management', *Far Eastern Agriculture*, May/June.

UNCTAD (1984), 'New and Emerging Technologies: Some Economic, Commercial and Developmental Aspects', UNCTAD Report TD/B/C.6/120, 2 August, United Nations Conference on Trade and Development.

UNCTC (1987), 'Transnational Corporations and the Electronics Industries of ASEAN Economies', *UNCTC Current Studies Series A*, No. 5.

UNDP/ILO (1982), 'Toward a National Computer Policy in Sri Lanka', Report of the United Nations Development Program/International Labour Organization Team, Colombo.

Vernon, R. (1973), 'The Location of Economic Activity', Unpublished Report, Harvard Business School, Cambridge, Massachusetts.

Wad, A. (1982), 'Microelectronics: Implications and Strategies for the Third World', *Third World Quarterly*, October.

Wad, A. (ed.) (1988), *Science, Technology and Development*, Westview Press, Boulder, Colorado.

Wheeler, D. and Mody, A. (1988), 'Risks and Rewards in International Location Tournaments: The Case of US Firms', Unpublished Manuscript.

FOR FURTHER READING

Acero, L. (1984), 'Technical Change in a Newly Industrialising Country: A Case Study of the Impacts on Employment and Skills in the Brazilian Textiles Industry', *SPRU Occasional Paper Series*, No. 22, Science Policy Research Unit, University of Sussex, Brighton, U.K.

Agarwal, S. (1985), 'Electronics in India: Past Strategies and Future Possibilities', *World Development*, Vol. 13, No. 3.

Aguirre, C. and Heredia, R. (1982), 'Elements for the Formulation of a Regional Programme of Action in the Area of Microelectronics', Report No. UNIDO ID/WG.372/10, United Nations Industrial Development Organization, Vienna.

Alfthan, T. (1985), 'Developing Skills for Technological Change: Some Policy Issues', *International Labour Review*, Vol. 124, No. 5, September—October.

Aslam, M. (1984), 'State-of-the-art Series on Microelectronics: No. 4, Pakistan', Report No. UNIDO/IS.493, United Nations Industrial Development Organization, Vienna.

Baal-Schem, J. (1983), 'The Information Revolution and its Societal Implications', in P. Fleissner (ed.), *Systems Approach to Appropriate Technology Transfer*, International Federation of Automatic Control, Vienna.

Bagchi, A.K. (1987), 'The Differential Impact of New Technologies on Developing Countries: A Framework of Analysis', ILO Technology and Employment Programme, Report No. WP. 176, International Labour Organization, Geneva.

Balassa, B. (1979), 'The Changing Pattern of Comparative Advantage in Manufacturing Goods', *Review of Economics and Statistics*, May.

Balassa, B. (1980), 'Structural Change in Trade in Manufactured Goods between Industrial and Developing Countries', *World Bank Staff Working Paper*, No. 396, World Bank, Washington, D.C.

Bessant, J. (1983), 'The Diffusion of Microelectronics', in Jacobsson and Sigurdson (1983).

Bhalla, A.S. (1990), 'Computerisation in Chinese Industry', *Science and Public Policy*, Vol. 17, No. 5.

Bifani, P. (1984), 'New Technologies and the Lagos Plan of Action', OAU/ECA/UNCSTD Expert Group Meeting on the Implications of New Technologies for the Implementation of the Lagos Plan of Action, Mbabane, Swaziland, 22–26 October.

Bogod, J. (1979), *The Role of Computing in Developing Countries*, The British Computer Society, Lecture Series No. 2, Thanet Press, Margate.

Boon, G.K. (1985), *Information Technology: A Brief Assessment in a North-South Perspective*, The Technology Scientific Foundation, Noordwijk, The Netherlands.

Boyer, R. and Coriat, B. (1986), 'Technical Flexibility and Macro Stabilisation', Paper presented at a conference of Innovation Diffusion, Venice, March.

Branson, W.H. (1981), 'Innovation, Economic Growth, and Employment — Summary and Appraisal', in H. Giersch (ed.), *Emerging Technologies: Consequences for Economic Growth, Structural Change and Employment*, Institut für Weltwirtschaft an der Universität Kiel.

Braun, E. (1982), 'Electronics and Industrial Development', *IDS Bulletin*, Vol. 13, No. 2, March.

Brooks, H. (1981), 'Towards an Efficient Technology Policy: Criteria and Evidence', in H. Giersch (ed.), *Emerging Technologies: Consequences for Economic Growth, Structural Change and Employment*, Institut für Weltwirtschaft an der Universität Kiel.

Brundenius, C. (1984), 'Swedish Technology Transfer in the Telecommunications Industry — A Case Study of Ericsson do Brazil', Discussion Paper No. 163. Research Policy Institute, University of Lund, Lund, Sweden.

Brundenius, C. and Göransson, B. (1986), 'Technology Policies in Developing Countries, the Case of Telecommunications in Brazil and India', Special Issue of *Vierteljahresberichte: Problems of International Cooperation*, No. 103, Friedrich-Ebert Foundation, Bonn.

Bruton, H. (1976), 'Employment, Productivity and Income Distribution', in A. Cairncross and M. Puri (eds), *Employment, Income Distribution and Development Strategy, Problems of the Developing Countries*, Holmes and Meier, London.

Buckley, P.J. and Casson, M. (1976), *Future of the Multinational Enterprise*, Macmillan Press Ltd., London.

Callarotti, R.C. (1984), 'State-of-the-Art Series on Microelectronics: No. 1 *Venezuela*, Report No. UNIDO/IS.489, United Nations Industrial Development Organization, Vienna.

Chesnais, F. (1988), 'Multinational Enterprises and the International Diffusion of Technology', in Dosi et al. (1988).

Chon, K. (1984), 'State-of-the-Art Series on Microelectronics: No. 3 *Republic of Korea*', Report No. UNIDO/IS.490, United Nations Industrial Development Organization, Vienna.

Chopra, R. and Morehouse, W. (1981), 'Frontier Technologies, Developing Countries, and the United Nations System after Vienna; Analysis of the Impact of Technological Trends in Developed Countries on Developing Countries', The UNCSTD Programme of Action and United Nations Science and Technology Policies, Science and Technology Working Paper Series, No. 12, UNITAR, New York.

Cohen, D.L. (1984), 'Locational Patterns in the US Electronics Industry: A Survey', Social Science History Workshop, Department of Economics, Stanford University, Fall.

Cooper C.M. and Clark, J. (1982), *Employment, Economics and Technology: The Impact of Technical Change on the Labour Market*, Wheatsheaf Books Ltd., Brighton.

Cooper, C. and Kaplinsky, R. (eds) (1989), 'Technology and Development in the Third Industrial Revolution: Introduction', *European Journal of Development Research*, Vol. 1, No. 1.

Coopers & Lybrand (1985), *Cost Analysis of a Typical Electronics/Electro-mechanical Assembly Plant in the Caribbean*, Coopers & Lybrand, Inc., Washington, D.C.

Coopers & Lybrand (1985), *Cost Profile of a Typical Electronics Assembly Plant in Sri Lanka*, Coopers & Lybrand, Washington, D.C.

Country Report (1986), 'Electronics in Pakistan Prominent in Five Year Plan', *Journal of Asia Electronics Union*, March.

Development Project Management Centre, U.S. Department of Agriculture (undated), *Evaluating the Appropriateness of Microcomputers for Management Applications in Developing Countries*, U.S. Department of Agriculture, Washington, D.C.

Dosi, G., Freeman, C. Nelson, R.R. Silverberg, G. and Soete, L. (eds) (1988), *Technical Change and Economic Theory*, Pinter, London.

Dray, J. and Memosky, J. (1983), 'Computers and a New World Order', *Technology Review*, No. 13, May/June.

Dunning, J. (1979), 'Explaining Changing Patterns of International Production, in Defence of Eclectic Theory', *Oxford Bulletin of Economics and Statistics*, Vol. 41, No. 4, November.

Edquist, C. and Jacobsson, S. (1984), 'Trends in the Diffusion of Electronics Technology in the Capital Goods Sector, Discussion Paper No. 161. Research Policy Institute, University of Lund, Lund, Sweden.

Eliasson, G. (1981), 'Electronics, Economic Growth and Employment — Revolution or Evolution?', in H. Giersch (ed.), *Emerging Technologies: Consequences for Economic Growth, Structural Change and Employment*, Institut für Weltwirtschaft an der Universität Kiel, Kiel.

Ernst, D. (1980), *The New International Division of Labour, Technology and Underdevelopment — Consequences for the Third World*, Campus, Frankfurt a.M. and New York.

Ernst, D. (ed.) (1981), *Industrial Development and International Transfer of Technology: Trends and Policy Issues'*, Special Issue of *Vierteljahresberichte: Probleme der Entwicklungsländer*, No. 83, Friedrich-Ebert Foundation, Bonn.

Ernst, D. (1981), 'Technology Policy for Self-Reliance: Some Major Issues', *International Social Science Journal*, Vol. XXXIII, No. 3.

Ernst, D. (1981), 'Restructuring World Industry in a Period of Crisis — The Role of Innovation: An Analysis of Recent Development in the Semiconductor Industry', Report No. UNIDO, IS.285, December, United Nations Industrial Development Organization, Vienna.

Ernst, D. (1985), 'Automation and the Worldwide Restructuring of the Electronics Industry: Strategic Implications for Developing Countries', *World Development*, Vol. 13, No. 3, March.

Ernst, D. (1986), *Automating the World Electronics Industry — Actors, Strategies and the International Division of Labour and Capital*, Sage Publications, London.

Filipello, O. and Sagarzazu, R. (1982), 'The Development of Microelectronics in Argentina', Report No. UNIDO ID/WG.372/12, United Nations Industrial Development Organization, Vienna.

Fleury, A. (1988), 'The Impacts of Microelectronics on Employment and Income in the Brazilian Metal-Engineering Industry', ILO Technology and Employment Programme, Working Paper, No. 188, International Labour Organization, Geneva.

Friedrichs, G. and Schaff, A. (eds) (1982), *Microelectronics and Society: For Better or Worse*, Report to the Club of Rome, Pergamon, New York.

Gahan, E. (1990), 'The Software Industry: Developing Countries and the World Market', *Industry and Development*, No. 28.

Galli, E. (1982), 'Microelectronics and Telecommunications in Latin America', Report No. UNIDO ID/WG.372/4, United Nations Industrial Development Organization, Vienna.

Galli, E., Welsch, M. and Herrera, R. (1982), 'Telecommunications and Micro-electronics: Some Observations', Report No. UNIDO ID/WG.372/11, United Nations Industrial Development Organization, Vienna.

Garriott, G.L. (1985), 'Microcomputers and the District Focus for Rural Development in Kenya', Report No. UNIDO ID/WG.437/5, United Nations Industrial Development Organization, Vienna.

Garza, G.F. de la (1985), Research and Development in Microelectronics in Argentina, Brazil, Mexico and Venezuela', Report No. UNIDO ID/WG.440.5, United Nations Industrial Development Organization, Vienna.

Gigch, J.P. van (1984), 'High Technology Transfer and Computer Education: Lessons Drawn from the Case of a Developing Country', *Journal of Technology Transfer*, Vol. 8, No. 2.

Gilpin, R. (1981), 'Trade, Investment, and Technology Policy', in H. Giersch (ed.), *Emerging Technologies: Consequences for Economic Growth, Structural Change and Employment*, Institut für Weltwirtschaft an der Universität Kiel, Kiel.

Girdner, E.J. (1986), 'The Political Economy of Technology Transfer — The Silicon Chip Revolution in India', Paper prepared for the 1986 Annual Meeting of the Association for Asian Studies, Chicago.

Government of India (1985), *National Electronics Policy*, Lok Sabha Secretariat, New Delhi.

Grunwald, J. and Flamm, K. (1985), *The Global Factory: Foreign Assembly in International Trade*, Brookings Institute, Cambridge, Massachusetts.

Haq, K. (ed.) (1988), *Informatics for Development*, North—South Roundtable.

Herrera, R. (1982), 'Microelectronics in Peru', Country Monograph, Report No. UNIDO ID/WG.372/16, United Nations Industrial Development Organization, Vienna.

Hobday, M. (1984), *The Brazilian Telecommunications Industry: Accumulation of Microelectronics Technology in the Manufacturing and Service Sectors*, Technology Division, United Nations Industrial Development Organization, Vienna.

Hobday, M. (1984), 'The Impact of Microelectronics on Developing Countries', *Development and Change*, Vol. 16, No. 2.

Hobday, M. (1985), 'Telecommunications and Information Technology in Latin America: Prospects and Possibilities for Managing the Technology Gap', Report No. UNIDO ID/WG.440/2, United Nations Industrial Development Organization, Vienna.

Hobday, M. (1986), 'Telecommunications — A "leading edge" in the accumulation of digital technology? Evidence from the case of Brazil', Special Issue of *Vierteljahresberichte: Problems of International Cooperation*, No. 103, Friedrich-Ebert Foundation, Bonn.

Hobday, M. (1987), 'The International Telecommunications Industry: The Impact of Microelectronics', *Technology and Implications for Developing Countries*, UNIDO Technology Trends Series, No. 4, United Nations Industrial Development Organization, Vienna.

Hobday, M. (1990), *Telecommunications in Developing Countries: The Challenge from Brazil*, Routledge, London.

Hoffman, K. (1985), 'Clothing, Chips and Comparative Advantage: The Impact of Microelectronics on Trade and Production in the Garment Industry', *World Development*, Vol. 13, No. 3.

Hoffman, K. and Rush, H. (1980), 'Microelectronics, Industry and the Third World', *Futures*, August.

Hoffman, K. and Rush, H. (1982), 'Microelectronics and the Garment Industry: Not Yet a Perfect Fit', *IDS Bulletin*, Vol. 13, No. 2.

Hoffman, K. and Rush, H. (1983), 'From Needles and Pins to Microelectronics — The Impact of Technical Change in the Garment Industry', in Jacobsson and Sigurdson (1983).

House, R.W. and da Silveira e Silva, W. (1983), 'On Transferring Microelectronics Technology Internationally: Brazil's Case', in P. Fleissner (ed.), *Systems Approach to Appropriate Technology Transfer*, International Federation of Automatic Control, Vienna.

Hussain, T. (1984), 'State-of-the-Art Series on Microelectronics: No. 5 *Bangladesh*', Report No. UNIDO/IS.497, United Nations Industrial Development Organization, Vienna.

ILO (1985), *The Socio-economic Impact of New Technologies*, Advisory Committee on Technology, International Labour Organization, Geneva.

ITU/OECD (1983), *Telecommunications for Development*, Organization for Economic Cooperation and Development, Paris.

Jacobsson, S. (1982), 'Electronics and the Technology Gap: The Case of Numerically Controlled Machine Tools', *IDS Bulletin*, Vol. 13, No. 2.

Jacobsson, S. (1983), 'Numerically Controlled Machine Tools — Implications for Newly Industrialised Countries', in Jacobsson and Sigurdson (1983).

Jacobsson, S. (1985), 'Technical Change and Industrial Policy: The Case of Computer Numerically Controlled Lathes in Argentina, Korea and Taiwan', *World Development*, Vol. 13, No. 3.

Jacobsson, S. and Ljung, T. (1983), 'Electronics, Automation and Global Comparative Advantage in the Engineering Industry', in Jacobsson and Sigurdson (1983).

James, J. (1985), 'Bureaucratic Engineering and Economic Men: Decision-making for Technology in Tanzania's State-owned Enterprises', in S. Lall and F. Stewart (eds), *Theory and Reality in Development*, Macmillan, London.

James, J. (1989), *Improving Traditional Rural Technologies*, Macmillan, London.

Jamison, A. (1983), 'Monitoring the Monitors: A Critique of a Conclusion', in Jacobsson and Sigurdson (1983).

Jequier, N. (1983), 'The Indirect Employment-Generating Effects of Investments in Telecommunications', Paper presented at the World Communications Year Seminar, organized by the International Telecommunication Union and the Government of Costa Rica, San José, Costa Rica, August.

Jiangsu Province (1984), 'The Case of Changzhou City', in *The Electronics Age Comes to China*, Ostasien Institute V., Bonn.

Jones, D. and Womack, J. (1985), 'Developing Countries and the Future of the Automobile Industry', *World Development*, Vol. 13, No. 3.

Jussawalla, M. and Lamberton, D.M. (1982a), 'Communication Economics and Development: An Economics of Information Perspective', in Jussawalla and Lamberton (1982b).

Jussawalla, M. and Lamberton, D.M. (eds) (1982b), *Communication Economics and Development*, Pergamon, New York.

Kaplinsky, R. (1983), 'Computer Aided Design — Electronics and the Technological Gap between DCs and LDCs', in Jacobsson and Sigurdson (1983).

Kaplinsky, R. (ed.) (1984), *Third World Industrialisation in the 1980s*, Frank Cass, London.

Kaplinsky, R. (1986), 'The Electronics Industry in Developing Countries', Special Issue of *Vierteljahresberichte: Problems of International Cooperation*, No. 103, Friedrich-Ebert Foundation, Bonn.

Katz, J.M. (1984), 'Domestic Technological Innovations and Dynamic Comparative Advantage', *Journal of Development Economics*, Vol. 16.

King, A. (1982), 'Microelectronics and World Interdependence', in Friedrichs and Schaff (eds) (1982).

Kopetz, H. (1984), 'Guidelines for Software Production in Developing Countries', Report No. UNIDO/IS.440, United Nations Industrial Development Organization, Vienna.

Kopetz, H. (1985), 'The Prospects for Software Production in Developing Countries', Report No. UNIDO ID/WG.437/4, United Nations Industrial Development Organization, Vienna.

Kreye, O., Heinrichs, J. and Frobel, F. (1987), 'Export Processing Zones in Developing Countries: Results of a New Survey', ILO Multinational Enterprises Programme, Working Paper No. 43, International Labour Organization, Geneva.

Lalor, S.E. (1984), 'Overview of the Microelectronics Industry in Selected Developing Countries', Report No. UNIDO/IS.500, United Nations Industrial Development Organization, Vienna.

Lalor, S.E. (1985), 'The Use of Public Purchasing as a Tool to Develop Technological Competence in Microelectronics', Report No. UNIDO ID/WG.440/1, United Nations Industrial Development Organization, Vienna.

Lalor, S.E. (1986), 'Overview of the Micro-electronics Industry in Selected Developing Countries', *Industry and Development*, No. 16.

Lamberton, D. (1982), 'Telecommunications in the Development Process', in M. Srinivasan (ed.), *Technology Assessment and Development*, Praeger, New York.

Leamer, E. (1984), *Sources of International Comparative Advantage*, MIT Press, Cambridge, Massachusetts.

Leppan, E.D. (1983), 'A Literature Survey and Partially Annotated Bibliography on the Impact of Microelectronics on the "Third World"', Paper prepared for a meeting on the Impact of Microelectronics, Jointly sponsored by Ministry of Industry, Government of Mexico, and IDRC, Canada, Mexico City.

Levy, B. (1989), 'Public Enterprises and the Transfer of Technology in the Ammonia Industry', in J. James (ed.) *The Technology Behaviour of Public Enerprises Developing Countries*, Routledge, London.

Lund, R.T. (1982), 'Microprocessor Applications and Industrial Development', Report No. UNIDO ID/WG.372/14, United Nations Industrial Development Organization, Vienna.

Lund, R.T. (1982), 'Microprocessors and Productivity: Cashing in Our Chips', Report No. UNIDO ID/WG.372/3, United Nations Industrial Development Organization, Vienna.

Lydall, H. (1980), 'Technological Change and Economic Growth', in *Technological Change in Australia*, Report of the Committee of Enquiry into Technological Change in Australia, Vol. 4.

Mageni, O.S. (1985), 'Development of Electronics in Tanzania', Report No. UNIDO ID/WG.437/1, United Nations Industrial Development Organization, Vienna.

Mammana, C.I.Z. (1982), 'Cultural Aspects of Microelectronics', Report No. UNIDO ID/WG.372/13, United Nations Industrial Development Organization, Vienna.

Mehta, S.C. and Varadan, G.S. (1984), 'State-of-the-Art Series on Microelectronics: No. 2, *India*', Report No. UNIDO/IS.492, United Nations Industrial Development Organization, Vienna.

Mody, A. (1986), 'A Comparative Study of Electronics in South Korea and India', Unpublished Manuscript, Boston University, March.

Morawetz, D. (1974), 'Employment Implications of Industrialisation in Developing Countries: A Survey', *The Economic Journal*, Vol. 84, September.

Neary, J. (1981), 'On the Short-run Effects of Technological Progress', *Oxford Economic Papers*, Vol. 33, No. 2.

OECD (1981), *Microelectronics, Productivity and Employment*, ICCP, No. 5, Organization for Economic Cooperation and Development, Paris.

Oliphant, J. (1982), 'Microprocessor Applications for Developing Countries', Report No. UNIDO/IS.351, United Nations Industrial Development Organization, Vienna.

Oliphant, J. (1982), 'Potential Applications Suitable for Microprocessor Implementations: Some Illustrative Possibilities', Report No. UNIDO ID/WG.372/6, United Nations Industrial Development Organization, Vienna.

Olle, W. (1986), 'New Technologies and the International Division of Labour: Retransfer of Foreign Production from Developing Countries?', Special Issue of *Vierteljahresberichte: Problems of International Cooperation*, No. 103, Friedrich-Ebert Foundation, Bonn.

Pack, H. and Westphal, L. (1986), 'Industrial Strategy and Technological Change: Theory vs. Reality', *Journal of Development Economics*, Vol. 22.

Palmer, L., Edquist, C. and Jacobsson, S. (1984), 'Perspectives on Technical Change and Employment', Discussion Paper No. 167. Research Policy Institute, University of Lund, Lund, Sweden.

Patil, S.M. (1985), 'Technological Perspectives in Machine Tool Industry with Special Reference to Microelectronics Applications', Report No. UNIDO/IS.230, United Nations Industrial Development Organization, Vienna.

Paul, C.K. (1981), 'Remote Sensing in Development', *Science*, Vol. 214, October.

Perez, C. and Soete, L. (1988), 'Catching up in Technology: Entry Barriers and Windows of Opportunity', in Dosi et al. (1988).

Pierce, W. and Jequier, N. (1983), *Telecommunications for Development*, International Telecommunications Union, Geneva.

Rada, J. (1982), 'Microelectronics: Its Impacts and Policy Implications', Report No. UNIDO ID/WG.372/5, May, and Corr. 1, United Nations Industrial Development Organization, Vienna.

Rada, J. (1982), *The Impact of Microelectronics and Information Technology: Case-Studies in Latin America*, United Nations Educational Scientific and Cultural Organization, Paris.

Rada, J. (1985), 'Information Technology and the Third World', in T. Forester (ed.), *The Information Technology Revolution*, Blackwell, Oxford.

Rada, J. (1986), 'Information Technology and Services', ILO World Employment Programme Research, Working Paper No. 163, International Labour Organization, Geneva.

Radnor, M. (1982), 'Prospects of Microelectronics Application in Process and Product Development in Developing Countries', Report No. UNIDO ID/WG.372/1, United Nations Industrial Development Organization, Vienna.

Reserve Bank of India (1984), *Report of the Committee on Mechanisation in Banking Industry*, Reserve Bank of India, Bombay.

Rosenberg, N. (1986), 'On Technology Blending', ILO World Employment Programme Research, Working Paper No. 159, International Labour Organization, Geneva.

Sahal, D. (1981), *Patterns of Technological Innovation*, Addison-Wesley, London.

Sande, T. (1984), 'Microcomputers and the Third World', Working Paper. Development Research and Action Programme, Christian Michelsen Institute, Norway.

Saunders, R.J. (1982), 'Telecommunications in Developing Countries: Constraints on Development', in Jussawalla and Lamberton (1982b).

Saunders, R., Warford, J. and Wellenius, B. (1983), *Telecommunications and Economic Development*, Johns Hopkins University Press, Baltimore.

Scheuten, W.K. (1981), 'The Impact of New Electronics', in H. Giersch (ed.), *Emerging Technologies: Consequences for Economic Growth, Structural Change and Employment*, Institut für Weltwirtschaft an der Universität Kiel.

Schmitz, H. (1984), *Technology and Employment Practices: Industrial Labour Processes in Developing Countries*, Croom Helm, London.

Schmitz, H. (1986), 'Microelectronics Based Automation and Labour Utilisation in Developing Countries', Special Issue of *Vierteljahresberichte: Problems of International Cooperation*, No. 103, Friedrich-Ebert Foundation, Bonn.

Schütte, H. (1984), 'Micro-electronics versus Cheap Labour: Questionmarks behind Asia's Export Successes', *Euro-Asia Business Review*, Vol. 3, No. 3.

Scitovsky, T. (1976), *The Joyless Economy*, Oxford University Press, Oxford.

Sek-Hong, N. (1986), 'Training Implications of Technological Change in Manufacturing in New Industrial Countries: The Hong Kong Case', ILO, Training Policies Programme, Discussion Paper No. 12, International Labour Organization, Geneva.

Sheya, M.S. (1985), 'Computer Awareness and Computer Literacy in Africa', *Telematica and Informatics*, Vol. 2, No. 3.

Sigurdson, J. (1986), 'Technological Trends in Selected Aspects of Microelectronic Technology and Applications — Custom and Semi-custom Integrated Circuits and NC Machine Tools', Report No. UNIDO/IS.631, United Nations Industrial Development Organization, Vienna.

Sinclair, P. (1981), 'When Will Technical Progress Destroy Jobs?', *Oxford Economic Papers*, Vol. 33.

Squire, L. (1982), *Employment Policy in Developing Countries*, Oxford University Press, Oxford.

Stewart, F. (1979), 'International Technology Transfer — Issues and Policy Options', *World Bank Staff Working Paper*, No. 344.

Tauile, J. (1987), 'Microelectronics and the Internationalisation of the Brazilian Automobile Industry', in Watanabe (1987).

Taylor, L. (1979), *Macro Models for Developing Countries'*, Mcgraw-Hill, New York.

Teitel, S. and Westphal, L.E. (1984), 'Editor's Introduction', *Journal of Development Economics*, Vol. 16.

Tigre, P. (1985), 'The Mexican Professional Electronics Industry and Technology', UNIDO/IS, United Nations Industrial Development Organization, Vienna.

Tottle, G. (1982), 'Computing for the Needs of Development in the Smallholder Sector', *ICL Technical Journal*, November.

Tsao, Y. (1985), 'Growth without Productivity — Singapore Manufacturing in the 1970s', *Journal of Development Economics*, Vol. 18, pp. 25-38.

Turski, W. (1984), 'Software Engineering: A Survey', Report No. UNIDO/IS.446, United Nations Industrial Development Organization, Vienna.

UN Centre for Science and Technology for Development (1985), 'Microelectronics-based Automation Technologies and Development', *ATAS Bulletin*, Issue 2, United Nations Centre for Science and Technology for Development, New York.

UNCTAD (1982), 'The Impact of Electronics Technology on the Capital Goods and Industrial Machinery Sector: Implications for Developing Countries', Report No. TD/B/C.6/AC.7/3, 4 May, United Nations Conference on Trade and Development, Geneva.

UNCTAD (1987), *Transnational Corporations and the Electronics Industries of ASEAN Economies*, United Nations Conference on Trade and Development, New York.

UNIDO (1982), 'The Impact of Microelectronics on the International Economic Setting: The Case of Computer-Aided Design, Report No. IS. 297, United Nations Industrial Development Organization, Vienna.

UNIDO (1988), 'UNIDO Guide for Industrial Investment and Project Identification and Promotion in the Electronics Sector in Developing Countries', Report No. IPCT. 78, United Nations Industrial Development Organization, Vienna.

UNIDO Secretariat (1981), 'Implications of Micro-electronics for Developing Countries: A Preliminary Overview of Issues', Report No. UNIDO/IS.246 and Corr. 1, United Nations Industrial Development Organization, Vienna.

UNIDO Secretariat (1981), 'Report on Exchange of Views with Experts on the Implications of Technological Advances in Micro-electronics for Developing Countries', Report No. UNIDO/IS.242. Rev. 1 and Corr. 1, United Nations Industrial Development Organization, Vienna.

UNIDO Secretariat (1983), 'Problems of Software Development in Developing Countries', Report No. UNIDO/IS.383, United Nations Industrial Development Organization, Vienna.

UNIDO Secretariat (1984), 'A Silicon Foundry to Service Developing Countries' Needs: A Preliminary Approach,' Report No. UNIDO/ IS.444, United Nations Industrial Development Organization, Vienna.

UNIDO Secretariat (1985), 'Microelectronics and Informatics Policy for Development in Kenya', Report No. UNIDO ID/WG.437/3, United Nations Industrial Development Organization, Vienna.

UNIDO Secretariat (1985), 'Some Considerations on the Content and Modalities of a Programme of Work for REMLAC', Report No. UNIDO ID/WG.440/4, United Nations Industrial Development Organization, Vienna.

U.S. Department of Commerce (1983), 'Telecommunications Policies in Seventeen Countries: Prospects for Future Competitive Access', NTIA-CR 83-24, Contractor Reports.

Unger, K. (1988), 'Industrial Structure, Technical Change and Microeconomic Behaviour in LDCs', in Dosi et al. (1988).

Valaskakis, K. (1982), 'Leapfrog Strategy in the Information Age', in H. Didsbury (ed.), *Communications and The Future*, World Future Society, Bethesda Maryland.

Vernon, R. (1979), 'The Product Cycle Hypothesis in a New International Environment', *Oxford Bulletin of Economics and Statistics*, Vol. 41, No. 4, November.

Vernon, R. (1981), 'Technology's Effects on International Trade: A Look Ahead', in H. Giersch (ed.), *Emerging Technologies: Consequences for Economic Growth, Structural Change and Employment*, Institut für Weltwirtschaft an der Universität Kiel, Kiel.

Vernon, R. and Davidson, W.H. (1979). 'Foreign Production of Technology-Intensive Products by U.S.-Based Multinational Enterprises', Working Paper. Graduate School of Business Administration, Harvard University, U.S.A.

Wajnberg, S. (1985), 'The Brazilian Microelectronics Industry and its Relationship with the Communications Industry, Report No. UNIDO/IS.546, United Nations Industrial Development Organization, Vienna.

Watanabe, S. (1986), 'Implications of New Technologies for Employment and Income in the Third World', Paper presented at the National Seminar on the Effects of Technological Advances on Development, Barbados, 26—27 March.

Watanabe, S. (ed.) (1987), *Microelectronics, Automation and Employment in the Automobile Industry*, Wiley, Chichester.

Weizsäcker, E.U. von, Swaminathan, M.S. and Lemma, A. (eds) (1983), *New Frontiers in Technology Application — Integration of Emerging and Traditional Technologies*, Tycooly Publications, Dublin.

Williams, B. (1986), 'Technical Change and Employment', in Hall (1986).

Williamson, J.G. (1971), 'Capital Accumulation, Labor Saving and Labor Absorption Once More', *Quarterly Journal of Economics*, Vol. LXXXV, No. 1.

Willis, R. (1983), *Software Policies for the Developing World*, International Development Research Council, Ottawa.

Wilshire, W.W. (1984), *Implications of New Technologies for Caribbean Development*, United Nations Centre for Science and Technology for Development, New York.

Index

oligopoly, 11
  in biotechnology, 64, 67
Onn, F. C., 169, 174, 188
open economies, 17, 23, 25–6
Organization for Economic Cooperation and Development
  (OECD), 11–12, 77, 82, 153
output, effects of microelectronics
  on, 173–7, 184–5
Oviatt, V. R., 141
Oxford University, 75

Pack, H., 1
palm oil, 99–100
partial equilibrium analysis, 97–8
patents and intellectual property
  rights, 9, 67–8
  in biotechnology, 45, 50, 55–6,
    69, 75–6, 81–6, 104
Pavitt, K., 10, 16
Perez, C., 124, 204
perfect competition, 10
Perpich, J. G., 141
pharmaceuticals *see* medical science
Philippines, 99
  microelectronics in, 158, 162
Pisano, G. P., 80
plant propagation, 94, 120
Plant Variety Protection Act (US,
  1970), 82–5
Plesch, P., 152, 161–2
Prebisch, R., 22
Preobrazhensky, E., 21–2
process technology, 61–2, 80
  in biotechnology, 47, 48, 57, 106,
    120–21
  innovations in, 47, 62
  in microelectronics, 168
product characteristics in microelectronics, 168, 188
production (manufacturing) system
  in biotechnology, 70, 79, 80, 112
  in microelectronics, 183–4, 191–5
  see also output; process technol-
    ogy

profitability in microelectronics,
  166–71
protein engineering, 47, 57, 94, 127
Protein Engineering Research Institute, 87
public goods, 67, 150–51
public sector *see* government; universities
Pyo, H. K., 169

quasi-monopoly, 6

recombinant DNA technology, 45,
  55, 56–7, 70, 78
research 'clubs', 88
Reuber, G. L., 158
reverse engineering, 68
Riazuddin, S., 111, 140
Ricardo, David, 2, 3
rice, 99
Robinson, Joan, 1, 10
Robson, M., 10
Rockefeller University, 75
Rogers, E., 166, 172
Rosenberg, Nathan, 7, 52, 54, 56,
  59, 60, 198
Rosenstein-Rodan, E., 22
Rothman, H., 112
Rudd, M., 88
Ruivenkamp, G., 59, 90, 105
Rush, H., 168, 186
Ruttan, V., 179, 200

Sabel, C. F., 204
Sakaguchi, K., 141
Sankyo, 79
Sanyo, 66
Sargeant, K., 141
Sasson, A., 91, 123
scale economies, 8, 22
  in biotechnology, 62–5, 107
  in microelectronics, 156, 205
Schmitz, H., 169, 176, 177, 204
Schneider, Nelson, 106
Schneiderman, Howard A., 71–2